The Psychobiology of Childhood

A Profile of Current Issues

Edited by
Laurence L. Greenhill, M.D.
Assistant Professor of Psychiatry
Columbia University
College of Physicians and Surgeons
New York, New York

Baron Shopsin, M.D.
Associate Clinical Professor of Psychiatry
New York University School of Medicine
New York, New York

SP MEDICAL & SCIENTIFIC BOOKS
a division of Spectrum Publications, Inc.
New York

SPECTRUM PUBLICATIONS, INC.
175-20 Wexford Terrace
Jamaica, NY 11432

Library of Congress Cataloging in Publication Data
Main entry under title:

The Psychobiology of childhood.

Bibliography: p.
Includes index.
Contents: Biopsychosocial aspects of the hyperactive child syndrome / Gabrielle Weiss — Ethical considerations in psychobiological research in children / D.H. Langer...[et al.] — Medical model / Dennis P. Cantwell — [etc.]
1. Child psychopathology — Physiological aspects — Addresses, essays, lectures. 2. Hyperactive child syndrome — Addresses, essays, lectures. I. Greenhill, Laurence. II. Shopsin, Baron. [DNLM: 1. Hyperkinetic syndrome. 2. Mental disorders — In infancy and childhood. WS 350 P974]
RJ499.P765 1984   618.92'89   82-25041
ISBN 0-89335-192-X

Printed in the United States of America

Contributors

Michael G. Aman, Ph.D. • MRC Senior Research Fellow, Department of Psychiatry, University of Auckland, New Zealand

George M. Anderson, Ph.D. • Assistant Professor of Laboratory Medicine, Yale University School of Medicine, New Haven, Connecticut

Gerald L. Brown, M.D. • Staff Psychiatrist, Biological Psychiatry Branch, National Institute of Mental Health, Bethesda, Maryland

Dennis P. Cantwell, M.D. • Joseph-Campbell Professor of Child Psychiatry and Director of Residency Training in Child Psychiatry, University of California School of Medicine, Neuropsychiatric Institute, Los Angeles, California

Donald J. Cohen, M.D. • Professor of Pediatrics and Psychiatry, Yale University, New Haven, Connecticut

Michael H. Ebert, M.D. • Chief, Section on Experimental Therapeutics, Laboratory of Clinical Science, National Institute of Mental Health, Bethesda, Maryland

John C. Fletcher, Ph.D. • Assistant for Bioethics, Office of the Director, Clinical Center, National Institutes of Health, Bethesda, Maryland

Rachel Gittelman, Ph.D. • Director of Clinical Psychology, Psychiatric Institute, New York City; Professor of Clinical Psychology, Columbia College of Physicians and Surgeons, New York, New York

Laurence L. Greenhill, M.D. • Assistant Professor of Psychiatry, Columbia College of Physicians and Surgeons, New York, New York

C.R. Lake, M.D., Ph.D. • Professor of Psychiatry and Pharmacology, United Health Service, Bethesda, Maryland

Dennis H. Langer, M.D., L.L.B. • Clinical Associate, Unit on Childhood Mental Illness, Biological Psychiatry Branch, National Institute of Mental Health, Bethesda, Maryland

Morton Levitt, Ph.D. • Research Scientist, Columbia College of Physicians and Surgeons, New York, New York

Jeffrey A. Mattes, M.D. • Research and Staff Psychiatrist, Carrier Foundation, Belle Mead, New Jersey; Assistant Clinical Professor of Psychiatry, UMD-Rutgers Medical School, Piscataway, New Jersey

Linda E. Nee, M.S.W. • Clinical Research Social Worker, Laboratory of Clinical Science, National Institute of Mental Health, Bethesda, Maryland

Judith L. Rapoport, M.D. • Chief, Section on Child Psychiatry, Laboratory of Clinical Science, National Institute of Mental Health, Bethesda, Maryland

Bennett A. Shaywitz, M.D. • Director and Associate Professor, Department of Pediatric Neurology, Yale University School of Medicine, New Haven, Connecticut

Jovan Simeon, M.D. • Professor and Director, Child Psychiatry Research, Royal Ottawa Hospital, Ottawa, Ontario, Canada

David A. Smith, M.D. • Resident, Department of Psychiatry, University of North Carolina School of Medicine, Chapel Hill, North Carolina

Herbert Weingartner, Ph.D. • Chief, Unit on Cognitive Studies, National Institute of Mental Health, Bethesda, Maryland

Gabrielle Weiss, M.D. • Professor of Psychiatry, McGill University, Montreal Children's Hospital, Montreal, Quebec, Canada

John S. Werry, M.D. • Professor of Psychiatry, University of Auckland, New Zealand

J. Gerald Young, M.D. • Professor and Director of Child Psychiatry, Mt. Sinai Hospital, New York, New York

Preface

This volume was inspired by an annual meeting of the American College of Neuropsychopharmacology held in Maui, Hawaii. A panel on psychobiological issues of childhood was held, with presentations devoted to antidepressant drug levels in depressed prepubertal children, responses of normal and hyperactive children to stimulant medication, and the vulnerability of the adolescent offspring of manic-depressive parents to affective illnesses. The session drew a large crowd, and it seemed appropriate to develop these topics in a book. Many of the authors in this volume attended that conference, and the book reflects the fact that psychobiological research in children has moved even further along than was envisioned at Maui.

In keeping with developments in the field, this volume surveys key topics of interest, including nosological issues surrounding the attention deficit disorder of childhood, the ontology of neurotransmitter systems in the human brain, and the relation between child psychiatric disorders and sleep patterns. Other studies link the clinical effects of drugs with plasma DBH activity or with attentional measures. The side effects of drugs on growth are examined, as well as the ethical issues involved in doing research on children. These areas continue to be of vital interest.

The first chapter in this book examines the concept of the hyperactive syndrome, or the Attention Deficit Disorder of Childhood. Gabrielle Weiss is critical of the medical model of the disorder, feeling that it fails to include vital social-interactive effects of this syndrome, in particular, its prevalence, multiple etiologies, treatment responses, or outcome in adolescence or adult life. Dr. Weiss's perspective is unique, based on her classic follow-up studies of hyperactive children into adulthood. She advocates a broader biopsychosocial perspective.

Dennis Cantwell further examines this theme in chapter 3, where he defends the medical model as an ideal tool for research in child psychiatry. He subdivides this approach into six phases, including clinical description, physical and neurological factors, laboratory studies, family studies, longitudinal natural history studies, and treatment studies. He then outlines an ideal study whose goal is the identification of diagnostically homogeneous subgroups within the broader definition of the Attention Deficit Disorder of Childhood. In so doing, Cantwell provides an excellent review and update of this field. He shows the reader how the six stages of medical model interact, as for example the drug responsiveness of a particular group seems to be linked to a particular type of visual evoked response pattern, suggesting a neurodevelopmental etiology for this subgroup. Such conceptualization provides valuable cross-pollination for the development of new understandings in the field.

Langer and his colleagues examine ethical issues in child research in chapter 2. Complexities arise in this area that researchers have not encountered previously. At what age can a child give assent to a procedure, and when should his signature be obtained on a consent form as well as his parent's? Langer advocates research with child subjects, but only after a careful weighing of benefits against risk and the approval of a group of peer investigators on an institutional review board (IRB). The five recommendations of the American Academy of Pediatrics Committee on Drugs are reviewed in detail, including methods for determining benefits and risk, proper selection of subject groups and representative individuals for research, the methods for obtaining informed consent (here Langer suggests thirteen is the proper age for getting signed informed consent), the rules for payment for participation in research, withdrawal from the study, and the use of proper monitoring and follow-up studies. This approach should provide an invaluable reference on ethics and the proper protection of human subjects for the investigator starting out in research in Pediatric Psychiatry.

Gerald Young and associates take up a number of basic developmental issues in chapter 4, which concerns itself with a thorough review of the ontogeny of human central nervous system neurotransmitter systems. Patterns of increasing and decreasing neurotransmitter activity characterize the human brain throughout life, with serum DBH and NE increasing and DA decreasing. Receptor function and hormonal modulation of the central nervous system throughout life is also outlined. In addition, certain psychopathological states such as pervasive developmental disorder (autism) are examined to determine deviations in neurotransmitter ontogeny. The reader is also provided with a brief review of neurotransmitter studies related to sex differences and to the response to psychotropic medication. All in all, Dr. Young's chapter, with its 8 pages of references, will be a valuable resource for the student and experienced researcher alike.

Chapter 5 introduces a new research tool in child psychiatry, the polysomnographic recording of sleep stages and behaviors. Simeon provides a brief but comprehensive overview of the developmental phases of human sleep, from infancy through senescence, with an emphasis on childhood. Sleep patterns in children with associated psychological and neurological disorders are also reviewed. Parasomnias, both those considered developmental and those pathological, are examined. The chapter ends with an overview of his extensive work with child population, including parental surveys of disturbed sleep in child clinical populations, including hyperkinetic males, and in childhood psychosis. The effect of various psychotropic agents on sleep patterns is described in words and graphs.

Herbert Weingartner provides a theoretical chapter which discusses psychobiological methods to assess altered cognitive processes in children. There is an excellent section on cognitive models, which emphasizes methods to assess speed and accuracy of information processing in children by testing efficiency of retrieval of information from memory. Cognitive tracking has become a major feature of many pediatric research projects, particularly in pediatric psychopharmacology, where various drugs (both stimulants and neuroleptics) may impair certain aspects of classroom learning through modulation of cognitive processes in children.

Another side effect of long-term stimulant medication, growth inhibition, is reviewed by this author in chapter 7. The complex methodology necessary to reliably collect and analyze growth data is examined, both in the chapter and a 5 page table that summarizes many of the studies in the field. An attempt is made to generate cross-study comparisons via a new index term, % expected velocity, to show the variable effects on growth determined by dosage and specific drug types. Etiological theories on the mechanism behind the stimulant-related growth inhibition are reviewed and the somatomedin hypothesis is suggested as the cause of the disorder.

The remainder of the book is devoted to three pediatric psychopharmacology studies which test basic hypotheses. Chapter 8, written by Mattes, Gittelman and Levitt, describes an attempted replication of an early Rapoport study which suggested a strong correlation of minor physical anomalies, high serum DBH levels, history of hyperactivity in the father, and an increased rate of obstetrical complications. This would be an important theoretical finding, since it would strongly implicate a problem in early development that could be linked to a genetic etiology. The disorder's phenotypic expression produces high DBH levels, thereby lowering brain norepinephrine, resulting in hyperactivity. Mattes and his colleagues compared a group of hyperactive males to a group with reading disorders, on and off methylphenidate, in a controlled, double-blind design. Although the hyperactive children had significantly lower serum DBH than did their siblings, none of the associations suggested by the earlier Rapoport paper could be replicated.

Werry and Aman tackle another thorny issue in the psychobiological field, namely the concept that hyperactive children show a diagnostically specific, "paradoxical" calming response to stimulants, while other types of children show arousal. A double-blind, counterbalanced study of methylphenidate was carried out in hyperactive males and a control group consisting of eneuretic males free of psychiatric disorder. These investigators were able to measure the direction of response, and their analytic methods allowed for interactive effects between group and drug to be quantitatively assessed. The paradoxical hypothesis would predict differing directions of response. The results showed both groups responded in identical directions on behavioral, clinical, and cognitive measures, although the hyperactive group responded in a greater manner to the same dose of stimulants than did the eneuretics. The authors conclude that the concept of paradoxical response to stimulants could not be supported by their data. The exaggerated response of the hyperactive group may be due to the law of initial values or to a new principle, that of rate-dependency in response to pharmacological agents.

The book ends with an important theoretical chapter by Judith Rapoport's research team at the NIMH clinical center in Bethesda, Maryland. Basically, the authors tested the hypothesis that attention deficit disorders may be related to deficiencies in central noradrenergic systems. Mianserin hydrochloride, a drug that increases norepinephrine turnover in the central nervous system by inhibiting presynaptic alpha-adrenergic receptors, was given to a group of 5 hyperactive males, in a double-blind, parallel design, with a group of 5 other hyperactives treated with placebo. Dependent measures included teacher's reports, motor activity, sustained attention, memory and learning tasks, blood pressure and pulse, urinary MHPG and VMA concentrations and plasma NE levels. The children on Mianserin experienced a number of moderate to severe side effects, including oversedation and hypotension with minimal changes on other measures. The authors concluded that Mianserin's effects were not evident in changes in behavior or cognition. This drug produces very slow changes in NE concentrations in the synaptic cleft, and another agent, that produced immediate increases in NE, might be more successful in ameliorating the attention deficit disorder of childhood.

These research topics reflect the recent upsurge in interest in biological aspects of child mental disorders. The benefits of stimulants in ADDH, of clonodine in Tourette's syndrome, and of imipramine in prepubertal depressions have been the result of psychobiological research in childhood. This growing field represents a powerful new course for those interested in child development, child psychopathology, and basic neuroscience.

February, 1984   Laurence L. Greenhill, M.D.
N.Y., N.Y.

Contents

The
Psychobiology
of
Childhood

$$\boxed{1}$$

Biophysical Aspects of the Hyperactive Child Syndrome

GABRIELLE WEISS

The hyperactive child has received a great deal of attention in the past two decades. For example, it was estimated that more than 2,000 articles had been written on the subject by 1975 (Vinchell, 1975) and several books on the subject were published (Cantwell, 1975; Safer and Allen, 1975; Ross and Ross, 1976). Others have been written for parents of hyperactive children. Excellent review articles are now available on almost every aspect of this syndrome. Reasons for submitting yet another chapter are the author's clinical experience with hyperactive children, involvement with the research on the syndrome, and the wish to review the main body of research related to the hyperactive child to develop a certain model for conceptualizing this puzzling syndrome.

Some time ago, the author was engaged in writing a chapter on conceptual problems regarding the diagnosis of minimal brain dysfunction (Weiss, 1980. A colleague, reading the manuscript, suggested that the author "get off the fence" with respect to an organic or a psychological etiology of this condition. By then, the author had reviewed a great deal of work on this syndrome and the process of trying to decide between an organic or a psychological etiology turned out to be a useful exercise. The author decided that the fence on which she sat was exactly where she wanted to be. The author realized that, with respect to the hyperactive child syndrome, the classical medical model prevalent today — the biomolecular model — was not useful for conceptualizing any aspect of the hyperactive syndrome. The biomolecular model conceptualizes "disease" as being fully accounted for by deviations in biochemical or physiological variables and leaves no room within its framework for psychological or social issues, for the concept of multicausality, or the possibility that etiology is determined by various antecedent variables expressed through a final common pathway.

George Engel has been one of the main critics of the biomolecular model of medicine. In an aricle entitled "The need for a new medical model: A challenge for biomedicine" (Engel, 1977), he wrote:

> The biomolecular model not only requires that disease be dealt with as an entity independent of social behavior, it also demands that behavioral aberrations be explained on the basis of disordered somatic processes. Thus the biochemical model embraces both reductionism, the philosophic view that complex phenomena are ultimately derived from a single primary principle, and dualism, the doctrine that separates the mental from the somatic.

In this model, the body is seen as a machine to be repaired by the doctor, and the proponents of this model argue that we must separate "true disease" from human unhappiness. Engel has argued cogently for a broader medical model which he calls the biopsychosocial model of disease. His view is not merely the obvious fact that psychological and social issues must be taken into account in understanding disease, but rather that these factors interact at all times and must be viewed in terms of this interaction if any disease is to be fully understood.

This approach has been invaluable to the author in understanding the hyperactive child syndrome. For this condition of childhood, whether we are considering the terminology and diagnosis, the prevalence, etiologies, treatment, or outcome, the classical medical model becomes inadequate. This syndrome is best understood by the model that biological, social, and psychological factors interact in children labelled hyperactive to produce a final common pathway which we call by various names, and for the purpose of this chapter "the hyperactive child syndrome."

The author's aim is to conceptualize according to this broader medical model such aspects of the syndrome as terminology and diagnosis, prevalence, etiologies, and outcome. In no way can this chapter serve as a review of the literature on the syndrome in all these areas; rather, these different aspects of the syndrome are shown as examples to highlight interactions between biological, psychological, and social issues. In trying to highlight these interactions, one runs into immediate semantic difficulties of trying to describe interacting variables without separating them. Engel dealt with these difficulties by using general systems theory in which he theorized isomorphies existing across different levels of organization, from molecules to cells to organs to organisms to the person, the family, and society. From these isomorphics fundamental laws can be developed which operate at all levels of organization, compared to those which operate for any one level of organization. Systems theory implies that all levels of organization are linked to one another in a relationship in which there could be no change in any one level which did not effect changes in other levels.

Selected findings related to terminology, diagnosis, prevalence, etiologies, and outcomes of this syndrome will be reviewed to emphasize the role at all these levels of various interacting biopsychosocial aspects.

TERMINOLOGY

The many names given to this syndrome reflect confusion about etiology, and particularly a dichotomy of thought regarding structural damage in the brain, aberrations of physiology, developmental lags, or environmental problems. When Strauss coined the term "minimal brain damage syndrome" he postulated that if retarded children with known brain damage (as detected in his studies by a neurological examination and a history suggestive of brain damage) showed specific behavior and cognitive problems, then other children exhibiting the same behavioral and cognitive problems but without any evidence of brain damage probably suffered from brain damage; however, the latter could not be diagnosed because the "neurological examination is known not to be infallible" (Strauss and Kephart, 1955). Strauss was aware of the circularity of this reasoning, but felt justified in the assumption. The idea of multiple causalities producing a final common pathway of behavioral and cognitive expression was not considered at that time. Strauss' work led to the formation of special classes for children with minimal brain damage syndrome, namely children who showed hyperactivity, distractability, and difficulties in perception, language, and emotion. Recently, Clemmens and Kenny (1972) pointed out that, in some school systems in the United States, it is the practice to require a neurological examination and an electroencephatograph (EEG) prior to placement of children with learning disabilities and hyperactivity into special classes, even though abnormal neurological findings such as the presence of "soft signs" (in the absence of serious neurological disorders such as brain tumors or frank epilepsy) would make no difference whatever to the psychological and educational rehabilitation of the children.

Clements and Peters (1962) were the first to use the term "minimal brain dysfunction" (MBD). They broadened the term minimal brain damage to include constitutional factors and temperament. These authors wrote:

> It is necessary to affirm again that psychiatry must take into account the full spectrum of causality from the unique genetic combination that each individual is, to his gestation and birth experiences, to his interaction with significant persons, and finally to the stresses and emotional traumata of later life after his basic reaction patterns have been laid down.

This view of multiple causality of the syndrome was a conceptual advance from Strauss' structrual damage model. It is, however, of historical interst that Clements and Peters felt the need to coin this new syndrome of MBD, which expands the minimal brain damage syndrome, largely as a reaction to reductionism of thought in the child guidance clinics at that time regarding etiology of behavior problems. Parents were being blamed for all problems of their children and all child psychopathology was considered to be caused by environment alone.

The terminology of developmental hyperactivity (Werry, 1968) emphasizes the concept of delayed development and the fact that children will grow out of the problems as they grow older. This concept has recently been challenged (Weiss et al., 1979; Borland and Heckman, 1976).

Other terms, such as "hyperkinetic child," "hyperkinetic impulse disorder," or "hyperactive child syndrome," are purely descriptive and do not imply any specific etiology. Recently, in the third edition of the American Psychiatric Associations Diagnostic and Statistical Manual (DSM III) (American Psychiatric Association, 1979), the diagnosis of this disorder was changed to "attention deficit disorder with hyperactivity," to emphasize that the attentional disorder may be a more primary deficit than the other symptoms of the disorder.

In spite of the diverse terminology, there is a remarkable similarity in the literature of the clinical description of the syndrome.

DIAGNOSIS

The diagnosis of a hyperactive child is never made on the basis of a single symptom. A number of symptoms clustered together in one child form the syndrome. This syndrome is present from early life and is not a temporary reaction to a particular environmental trauma. Hyperactivity and related symptoms may also occur concomitantly with psychosis, autism, cerebral palsy, and mental retardation. However, most studies of hyperactive children exclude children with the above primary diagnoses.

The following operational criteria for diagnosis are listed in DSM III:

1. Excessive general hyperactivity or motor restlessness for the child's age. In preschool and early school years, there may be incessant haphazard activity, impulsive running, climbing, or crawling. During middle childhood or adolescence, marked inability to sit still, up-and-down activity, and fidgeting are characteristic. The activity differs from the norm for age both in quality and quantity.

2. Difficulty in sustaining attention, such as the inability to complete tasks initiated or a disorganized approach to tasks. The child frequently "forgets" demands made or tasks assigned and shows poor attention in unstructured situations or when demands are made for independent, unsupervised performance.

3. Impulsive behavior as manifested by at least two of the following: (a) sloppy work in spite of reasonable efforts to perform

adequately, (b) frequent speaking out of turn or making inappropriate sounds in class, (c) frequent interruption of, or intrusion into, other children's activities or conversations, (d) difficulty waiting for one's turn in games or in group situations, (e) poor frustration tolerance, and (f) fighting with children in a fashion indicating low frustration tolerance rather than sadistic or mean intention.

4. Duration of at least one year.

In spite of the similarity described in the literature regarding the clinical descriptions of this syndrome, certain interesting variations should be remembered. For example, the syndrome varies considerably as to the presenting complaint at different ages. A description of the syndrome from birth to maturity is not within the scope of this chapter, but was summarized by Weiss and her colleagues (1979). In addition to developmental aspects of the syndrome, some children manifest the behavioral problems in all situations while others manifest them only at school or at home. Some investigators consider some symptoms of hyperactive children to be primary, and other symptoms as secondary to the rejection of the troubled child by his school, peers, and family; symptoms may be related also to his socioeconomic class (Paternite et al., 1976).

A comprehensive assessment of any one child is required before a diagnosis is made because this syndrome extends beyond the presence of single symptoms. The following type of evaluation should be carried out before a diagnosis is made and a rehabilitation program outlined.

1. A careful history of the pregnancy and delivery, and of the child's development from infancy on.

2. Assessment of the child's behavioral aberrations, the specific symptoms present—their severity and frequency, the degree to which individual symptoms are situational, and the duration of the problem.

3. An educational assessment to determine if a specific learning disability is present and, if so, its nature.

4. Assessment of the intrapsychic processes of the child: how he views himself, his family, his peers, and his school, and what his personality strengths are.

5. Assessment of the interaction of the child's family. Cause and effect are irrelevant here because of their constant interaction. Parents should be helped to interact constructively, and their guilt and blame-placing reduced if possible.

6. Assessment of the child's school. Is the child in an environment conducive to learning? Can a specific remedial program be incorporated into his regular school curriculum? How well is the

teacher coping with the child who has these difficulties? The teacher should be brought into the treatment team as an important member for assessment, diagnosis, and management.

7. Assessment of the child's neurological status if a neurological lesion is suspected. Routine neurological evaluations of hyperactive children frequently reveal soft signs such as right-left confusion, clumsy gait, and strabismus. The significance of these soft signs and of EEG abnormalities is not known.

This kind of comprehensive assessment is required because the syndrome is affected in various degrees by biological, psychological (or intrapsychic), and social (family, school, cultural expectations, stability of community) issues.

PREVALENCE

Boys are affected much more commonly than are girls; ratios of 5:1 to 9:1 have been reported. The reasons for this disparity are not known.

Hyperactive children exist all over the world, in industrialized and in developing countries, in rural as well as urban communities. The prevalence data vary greatly; an incidence of 1 in 1000 for 12-year-olds has been reported for the Isle of Wight (Rutter et al., 1970) whereas values of 5 to 6 in 100 have been given for American cities (Miller et al., 1974). There are several possible reasons for this discrepancy. The diagnostic criteria vary from country to country. For example, Stewart (1979) found that 34 percent of children seen in a child psychiatry clinic in Iowa exhibited unsocialized aggressive behavior as well as typical symptoms of the hyperactivity syndrome. In contrast, British workers would be likely to diagnose these children as having "conduct disorder" rather than the hyperactive child syndrome. The discrepancy also reflects differences in procedures for collecting prevalence data. Finally, actual differences in prevalence probably exist between inner-city urban schools and stable rural communities.

Questionnaires concerning children's behaviors were sent to a large random sample of parents in Buffalo, 49 percent of whom reported that their child was overactive (Lapouse and Monk, 1958). When teachers in Urbana, Illinois, were asked to rate a random sample of children by questionnaire, their response indicated that they viewed 48 percent of the children as distractible, 30 percent as hyperactive, and 50 percent as restless and unable to sit still (Werry and Quay, 1971). This indicates that parents' and teachers' expectations of normal children may be unrealistic, and points to the need for an adequate multidisciplinary assessment before a diagnosis is made.

In a comprehensive prevalence study in the East Bay area of San Francisco, Lambert et al. (1978) attempted to reconcile the widely varying estimates of hyperactivity in children. Parents, teachers, and physicians were asked to identify hyperactive children in a random sample of more than 5,000 children encompassing different socioeconomic and ethnic groups. Approximately five percent of children were considered to be hyperactive by at least one defining system (parents, teachers, or physicians), and 1.2 percent were considered to be hyperactive by all three defining systems. Lambert et al. recognized the difficulty of investigating the prevalence of a condition defined by behavior characteristics that are reported subjectively. They suggest that those who report the deviant behaviors (teachers and parents) contribute to the child's environment, and that their attitudes affect both the child's behavior and their perception of it. Robin and Bosco (1976), in their work on estimating prevalence of treatment of hyperactive children, also stressed the importance of recognizing that hyperactive behaviors are defined by the child's social environment.

It seems apparent once again that social factors such as the kind of community a child comes from, which may be a cohesive rural community or an inner-city slum, and the expectations about children of parents and teachers in that community are likely to affect reported prevalence of this condition. In addition to this, the history of medical practice reveals that the diagnosis of a particular condition rises when a "cure" for it is discovered. This was true, for example, for the diagnosis of manic depressive illness when the benefits of lithium became known. The increase of the diagnosis of the "hyperactive child" in North America probably followed the initial hopefulness of stimulant therapy, since the short-term benefits of the latter had been demonstrated beyond reasonable doubt. Culture has a profound influence on what is regarded as normal versus deviant, or healthy versus sick.

ETIOLOGIES

Numerous ideas exist about the etiology of this syndrome, although few have been unequivocally demonstrated; different theories have been in vogue for a period and finally given rise to yet another theory of etiology. The first and earliest theory of the etiology of hyperactivity was probably given by Still (1902), who described children who became hyperactive as a result of head injuries, tumors, epilepsy, and meningitis. Many children were diagnosed to be hyperkinetic following the epidemicc of encephalitis lethargica which followed World War I (Hohman, 1922; Ebaugh, 1923). As already mentioned, Strauss' work on retarded children resulted in confirmation of the "organic" etiology. There is little doubt that any form of damage in the brain can result in hyperactivity in a child who was not previously afflicted; however, the hyperactive syndrome is a rare sequela of brain damage—rare enough that Rutter and coworders (1970), who have done population studies of children with known brain damage, have not found a disproportionate number who became overactive. Rather, it was found that brain-damaged children may manifest any type of psychopathology.

Recently, some studies have been presented which suggest that minimally elevated blood lead levels (for example, those which may be seen in children living in highly polluted areas, or in those who have ingested old paint containing lead) may in some children affect the central nervous system. Oliver David (1976, 1978) has found that those hyperactive children who show elevated levels of lead in their blood respond well to chelating agents such and penicillamine, the response being equal to the response to methylphenidate.

A series of studies (Quinn and Rapoport, 1974; Rosenberg and Weller, 1973; Waldrop and Halverson, 1971; Rapoport and Quinn, 1975) have established an association between the frequency of minor physical anomalies (of hands, feet, ears, face, and mouth) and behavior and/or learning disabilities in early childhood and in children in elementary school. It is thus apparent that there is a subgroup of hyperactive children who clearly have other congenital aberrations besides hyperactivity.

Recently, food additives have received a great deal of attention as a possible cause of hyperactivity following the publication of a book by Ben Feingold entitled "Why Your Child is Hyperactive" (Feingold, 1975) which sold in large numbers and obviously created yet another vogue of theory and cure for this condition. Careful research by different investigators has not confirmed the role of allergy or salicylate sensitivity in hyperactive children (Conners et al., 1976). Conners, after working on the effect of food additives for several years, believes the occasional individual hyperactive child may indeed respond to a diet free of additives. But this is an unusual occurrence and would be hidden in studies which measure response means between groups of hyperactive children.

Although Clements and Peters coined the term "minimal brain dysfunction" in 1962, most hyperactive children show no evidence of structural brain damage. As a result, various investigators have followed the lead of Paul Wender. He suggested that MBD may be caused by abnormalities in monoamine metabolism (Wender, 1973). For example, Shaywitz et al. (1977) presented evidence suggestive of decreased turnover of dopamine in the central nervous system of hyperactive children. They demonstrated the presence of a lower concentration of homovanillic acid in the cerebrospinal fluid of six hyperactive children, compared to normal children, after oral administration of probenecid. Shekim et al. (1977) reported on the possibility of decreased norepinephrine activity in the central nervous system of seven hyperactive children compared to 12 normal children. Urinary excretion of 3-methoxy-4-hydroxyphenyl glycol (MHPG) was lower, and that of normetanephrine (NM) was higher in the hyperactive children. Administration of d-amphetamine for two weeks to the hyperactives depressed the urinary levels of MHPG, NM, and metanephrine. Despite the widespread belief that hyperactive children have a disorder in the catecholamine system, there is no conclusive evidence for it. In addition, it has been demonstrated that the probenecid method used by Shaywitz has severe limitations (Winsberg et al., 1978).

It has been known for some time that genetic factors may play an etiological role. Family studies such as those done by Cantwell (1972) and by Morrison and Stewart (1971) have found less psychiatric disturbance in the adoptive parents of hyperactive children than in natural parents of hyperactive children. The natural parents of hyperactive children showed an unusually high incidence of alcoholism, antisocial personality, and hysteria. However, these workers have not yet compared the parents of other types of emotionally or behaviorally disturbed children to the parents of hyperactive children, so the latter may be a nonspecific finding. In general, the work related to genetic aspects of the syndrome is still far from conclusive, and adequate twin studies have not been carried out.

There have also been several psychological theories and some empirical data regarding a psychogenic etiology. Tizard and Hodges (1978) demonstrated that children who were raised for two years in institutions and later adopted were unpopular in their school years later where they showed restlessness, distractibility, and attention-seeking behavior. Learning theorists, for example O'Leary and O'Leary (1977), have demonstrated that inattention and activity can be reduced or increased by varied forms of teacher attention. Yando and Kagan (1968) have shown that normal children in the first grade would become more reflective or more impulsive over the course of the year, depending on the modelled qualities of their teacher.

In conclusion, having reviewed the various structural, biochemical, congenital, and environmental theories of etiology, it is clear that the hyperactive child syndrome may have many causes and that more than one cause (or antecedent variable) is likely to be at work in any one hyperactive child. Even in those children who indeed have some form of structural or biochemical abnormality in the nervous system, socioeconomic and environmental factors such as poverty, parental types of reinforcements or marital relationship, family and teacher acceptance, and parental and teacher modelling will accentuate or minimize the child's difficulties. Similarly, the expectations of the culture regarding what is considered deviant or normal and the supports a given culture or community can give to the hyperactive child and his family will significantly affect the severity of the condition and the clinical picture as a whole.

OUTCOME

Five-year follow-up studies at the Montreal Children's Hospital indicated that the prognosis for hyperactive children as they mature into adolescence was relatively poor. Despite a decrease of ratings of hyperactivity over a period of five years, as adolescents they continued to be distractible, emotionally immature, and unable to maintain goals, and they had developed poor self-images. The school records of the hyperactive children showed a greater incidence of grades failed and lower ratings on all subjects on report cards compared to matched control children in the same school. They continued to use impulsive rather than reflective approaches to cognitive tasks and over a period of five years showed no improvement on tests of intelligence or visuomotor tasks. There was a decrement of performance on motor skills. About 25 percent of a group of 64 had delinquent behavior, a far higher percentage than that found in matched controls (Minde et al., 1971; Weiss et al., 1971). Similar findings were obtained by Mendelson et al. (1971) .

A comprehensive 10- to 12-year follow-up study on 75 hyperactive students not treated with stimulants and 45 control subjects (Weiss et al., 1979) was completed recently. The hyperactive subjects had a significantly more impulsive lifestyle, as suggested by a higher rate of geographic moves and car and motorcycle accidents, and inferior results on cognitive style tests (Hopkins et al., 1979). Significantly more hyperactive subjects had impulsive and immature personality traits on psychiatric evaluation. The hyperactive subjects were a mean of one year behind the control group in education completed.

No differences were found, however, between the two groups with respect to drug abuse (or use of nonmedical drugs, such as marijuana) and court referrals within the year preceding evaluation. Within five years preceding the evaluation, there was a trend toward more court referrals for hyperactive subjects, but no difference was found between the two groups with regard to drug abuse. Controls used significantly more hallucinogens than did hyperactives within the year before evaluation.

No subjects were psychotic, but two hyperactive subjects were diagnosed as borderline psychotic. The latter difference between groups did not reach statistical significance. Two hyperactive subjects died in motor accidents; no controls were injured or died in car or motorcycle accidents.

Rating scales containing almost identical types of questions regarding behavior and competence were sent to the subjects' high schools and employers. On the teacher's rating scale (for the last year of high school) hyperactive subjects were rated inferior to controls on all seven items, whereas there was no difference between hyperactive and control subjects for any item on the employer's rating scale. This suggested that the setting in which hyperactives are evaluated significantly influences the degree to which they are considered deviant (Weiss et al., 1978).

The use of two different types of self-rating scales produced interesting results. On a self-rating scale of psychopathology, SCL-90 (Derogatis et al., 1973), there was no difference between the hyperactive and the control subjects on any item of psychopathology. On the California Psychological Inventory (Gough, 1957), which was designed to measure "folkloric ideals of social living and interaction," control subjects scored significantly better on a majority of items. This inventory was a most sensitive instrument for distinguishing differences in self concept for hyperactive and control subjects (Weiss et al., 1978).

Between the ages of 6 and 12 years, at initial assessment the EEGs of the hyperactive children showed more slow diffuse dysrhythmias compared to the EEGs of matched normal controls. By young adulthood, at the ten-year follow-up assessment, no significant differences were found between the EEGs of hyperactives and normal controls. Sequential EEGs of hyperactives taken over the ten-year period suggested that many readings had become normal, mainly in adolescence. This supports the hypothesis that many of the EEG abnormalities of hyperactive children represent immature patterns which correct with age (Hechtman et al., 1978).

We have evaluated self-esteem, social skills, and moral development by means of laboratory tasks in 18 matched pairs of hyperactive and control subjects. Hyperactive subjects showed significant impairment of self-esteem and poorer social skills (Hechtman et al., 1980).

The outcome study indicates that while few hyperactive children become grossly disturbed or criminal adults, they continue as young adults to have various symptoms of the hyperactive syndrome—for example, impulsivity, poor social skills, and lower educational achievement. At the same time, unlike the delinquency of the true antisocial child or adult, in our study the majority of hyperactives who as adolescents had committed delinquent acts gained sufficient control of impulsivity by the time they were young adults and did not commit significantly more delinquent acts than control adults.

Loney and her coworkers (1979) have carried out careful predictive studies using multivariate techniques. These findings indicate that socioeconomic class and aggression, which are correlated at referral, contribute to delinquency in the adolescence of hyperactives, whereas treatment variables, achievement, and severity of hyperactivity, which are also correlated at initial assessment, predict achievement in hyperactive adolescents. It is suggested that childhood aggression and hyperactivity have different correlates both at initial assessment and at follow-up. While severity of hyperactivity only predicts achievement, family variables (for example, family relationships, number of children, socioeconomic class, rural or urban residence) predict all aspects of outcome. This work clearly shows the interrelationship of the biological and social aspects of the hyperactive child syndrome on outcome.

CONCLUSIONS

Engel (1977) has challenged the traditional biomolecular model of illness and has suggested that all diseases be viewed not in terms of biochemical aberrations, but in the wider terms outlined by a biopsychosocial model. Nowhere does this wider concept of a medical model apply more aptly than to the hyperactive child. This can be seen from the various studies reviewed here with respect to the prevalence, phenomenology, etiologies, treatment, and outcome of this condition.

For example, the discrepancy between prevalence figures in American cities and the Isle of Wight suggests that qualities of the community may influence the actual incidence of the hyperactive child syndrome, perhaps in part by the degree of tolerance to what is considered deviant. In describing the typical phenomenology of the syndrome, we pointed out that many children were not "typical." They were, for example, symptomatic in some situations and not in others, and some had what were probably various secondary symptoms related to reaction of the family and school to their primary problems.

Various etiologies of an organic nature have been proposed for the syndrome. Whether or not the environment is the primary etiology for some children is not known, but in many hyperactive children it is a highly significant antecedent variable even when not the primary cause.

Treatment of the hyperactive child syndrome was not covered in this chapter. Suffice it to say that while studies of the acute effect of stimulants have all demonstrated marked improvement in hyperactive children at home and at school, long-term stimulant therapy has not demonstrated a significant effect on outcome, at least as measured in adolescence (Weiss et al., 1975). This indicates the complexity of the hyperactive child syndrome and strongly suggests that many of its symptoms are not affected by stimulants, and that these symptoms, such as aggressive behavior, probably have a different origin and are correlated highly with ecological factors.

Finally, as indicated by the questionnaire answered by high school teachers and employers for adult hyperactives, the degree to which hyperactives are viewed as deviant depends on the demands of the environment in which they function.

In conclusion, the hyperactive child syndrome can only be understood in all its complexity when viewed from social, psychological, and biological standpoints; the traditional biomolecular medical model does not fit the various manifestation, etiology, and courses of this disorder of childhood. Multivariate or interactional models, which take into account the complex interaction between the child's environment and his psychological and biolgoical status, are required.

REFERENCES

Borland B, Heckman H: Hyperactive boys and their brothers: A 25-year follow-up study. *Arch General Psychiatry* 33: 669–675, 1976

Cantwell D: Psychiatric illness in the families of hyperactive children. *Arch Gen Psychiatry* 27: 414–417, 1972

Cantwell D (ed): The Hyperactive Child. New York, Spectrum Publications, Inc, 1975

Clements S, Peters J: Minimal brain dysfunctions in the school-age child. *Arch Gen Psychiatry* 6: 185–197, 1962

Clemmens R, Kenny T: Clinical correlates of learning disabilities, minimal brain dysfunction, and hyperactivity. *Clin Pediatr* 11: 311–313, 1972

Connors C, Goyette C, Southwick D, Lees, J, Andrulonis P: Food additives and hyperkinesis: A controlled double-blind experiment. *Pediatrics* 58: 154–156, 1976

David O: Lead and hyperactivity: Behavioral response to chelation: A pilot study. *Am J Psychiatry* 133: 155–156, 1976

David O: Central effects of minimally elevated lead levels. Presented to the National Institute of Mental Health Workshop on the Hyperkinetic Behavior Syndrome, Washington, DC, June 1978

Derogatis L, Lipman R, Covi L: SCL-90: An outpatient psychiatric rating scale: Preliminary report. *Psychopharmacol Bull* 9: 13–28, 1973

Diagnostic and Statistical Manual of Mental Disorders, ed. 3. Washington, DC, American Psychiatric Association, 1979

Ebaugh F: Neuropsychiatric sequelae of acute epidemic encephalitis in children. *Am J Dis Child* 25: 89–97, 1923

Engel G: The need for a new medical model: A challenge for biomedicine. *Science* 196: 129–136, 1977

Feingold B: *Why Your Child is Hyperactive.* New York, Random House, 1975

Gough H: California Psychological Inventory. Palo Alto, Consulting Psychologists Press, Inc., 1957

Hechtman L, Weiss G, Metrakos K: Hyperactive individuals as young adults: Current and longitudinal electroencephalographic evaluation and its relation to outcome. *Can Med Assoc J* 118: 919–923, 1978

Hechtman L, Weiss G, Perlman T: Hyperactives as young adults: Self-esteem and social skills. *Can J Psychiatry* 25: 478–483, 1980

Hohman L: Post-encephalitic behavior disorders in children. *Johns Hopkins Hosp Bull* 33: 372–375, 1922

Hopkins J, Perlman T, Hechtman L, Weiss G: Cognitive style in adults originally diagnosed as hyperactives. *Child Psychol Psychiatry* 20: 209–216, 1979

Lambert N, Sandoval J, Sassone D: Prevalence of hyperactivity in elementary school children as a function of social system definers. *Am J Orthopsychiatry* 48: 446–463, 1978

Lapouse R, Monk M: An epidemiologic study of behavior characteristics in children. *Am J Public Health* 48: 1134–1144, 1958

Loney J, Kramer J, Milich R: The hyperkinetic child grows up: Predictors of symptoms, delinquency, and achievement at follow-up. Presented at the Annual Meeting of the American Association for the Advancement of Science, Houston, Texas, January 1979

Mendelson W, Johnson M, Stewart M: Hyperactive children as teenagers: A follow-up study. *J Nerv Ment Dis* 153: 273–279, 1971

Miller R, Palkes H, Stewart M: Hyperactive children in suburban elementary schools. *Child Psychiatry Hum Dev* 4: 121–127, 1974

Minde K, Lewin D, Weiss G, et al.: The hyperactive child in elementary school: A five-year controlled follow-up. *Except Child* 38: 215–221, 1971

Morrison J, Stewart M: A family study of the hyperactive child syndrome. *Bio Psychiatry* 3: 189–195, 1971

O'Leary K, O'Leary S: *Classroom Management: The Successful Use of Behavior Modification.* Elmsford, New York, Pergamon Press, 1977, pp 63–93

Paternite C, Loney J, Langhorne J: Relationship between symptomatology and SES related factors in hyperkinetic boys. *AM J Orthopsychiatry* 46: 291–301, 1976

Quinn P, Rapoport J: Minor physical anomalies and neurologic status in hyperactive boys. *Pediatrics* 53: 742–747, 1974

Rapoport J, Quinn P: Minor physical anomalies (stigmata) and early developmental deviation: A major biologic subgroup of "hyperactive children." *Int J Ment Health* 4: 29–44, 1975

Robin S, Bosco J: The social context of stimulant drug treatment for hyperkinetic children. *School Review* 85: 141–154, 1976

Rosenberg J, Weller G: Minor physical anomalies and academic performance in young school children. *Dev Med Child Neurol* 15: 131–135, 1973

Ross D, Ross S: *Hyperactivity: Research Theory and Action.* New York, John Wiley & Sons, 1976

Rutter M, Graham P, Yule W: *A Neuropsychiatric Study in Childhood.* London, Heinemann, 1970

Safer D, Allen R: *Hyperactive Children: Diagnosis and Management.* Baltimore, University Park Press, 1976

Shaywitz B, Cohen D, Bowers M: CSF amine metabolites in children with minimal brain dysfunction—evidence for alteration of brain dopamine. *J Pediatr* 90: 67–71, 1977

Shekim W, Dekirmenjian H, Chapel J: Urinary catecholamine metabolites in hyperkinetic boys treated with d-amphetamine. *Am J Psychiatry* 134: 1276–1279, 1977

Stewart M: Personal communication, 1979

Still GF: The Coulstonian lectures on some abnormal physical conditions in children. *Lancet* 1: 1008–1012, 1077–1082, 1163–1168, 1902

Strauss A, Kephart N: *Psychopathology and Education of the Brain Injured Child,* vol. 2. New York, Grune & Stratton, 1955, p 42

Tizard B, Hodges J: The effect of early institutional rearing on the development of eight-year-old children. *J Child Psychol Psychiatry* 19: 99–118, 1978

Waldrop M, Halverson C: Minor physical anomalies and hyperactive behavior in young children, in: Hellmuth J (ed) *The Exceptional Infant.* New York, Brunner-Mazel, 1971, pp 343–381

Weiss G: MBD: Critical diagnostic issues, in: Rie HE, Rie ED (eds) *Handbook of Minimal Brain Dysfunctions: A Critical View.* New York, John Wiley & Sons, 1980, pp 347–361

Weiss G, Hechtman L: The hyperactive child syndrome. *Science* 205: 1348–1354, 1979

Weiss G, Minde K, Werry J, et al.: Studies on the hyperactive child. Part VIII. Five-year follow-up. *Arch Gen Psychiatry* 24: 409–414, 1971

Weiss G, Kruger F, Danielson U, Elman M: Effect of long-term treatment of hyperactive children with methylphenidate. *Can Med Assoc J* 112: 159–165, 1975

Weiss G, Hechtman L, Perlman T: Hyperactives as young adults: School, employer, and self-rating scales obtained during ten-year follow-up evaluation. *Am J Orthopsychiatry* 48: 438–445, 1978

Weiss G, Hechtman L, Perlman T, et al.: Hyperactives as young adults: A controlled prospective ten-year follow-up of 75 children. *Arch Gen Psychiatry* 36: 675–681, 1979

Wender P: Some speculations concerning a possible biochemical basis of minimal brain dysfunction. *Ann NY Acad Sci* 205: 18–28, 1973

Werry J: Developmental hyperactivity. *Pediatr Clin North Am* 15: 581–599, 1968

Werry J, Quay H: The prevalence of behavior syndromes in younger elementary school children. *Am J Orthospychiatry* 41: 136–143, 1971

Winchell C: *The Hyperkinetic Child: A Bibliography of Medical, Educational, and Behavioral Studies.* Westport, Connecticut, Greenwood, 1975.

Winsberg B, Hurwic M, Sverd J, Klutch A: Neurochemistry of withdrawal emergent symptoms in children. *Psychopharmacology (Berlin)* 56: 157–161, 1978

Yando R, Kagan J: The effect of teacher tempo on the child. *Child Dev* 39: 27–34, 1968

$$\boxed{2}$$

Ethical Considerations in Psychobiological Research in Children

DENNIS H. LANGER, JOHN C. FLETCHER,
GERALD L. BROWN, LINDA E. NEE,
and DAVID A. SMITH

Children are afflicted by many illnesses of psychological and biological origin. However, whether children should participate as research subjects is a matter of considerable controversy.

The argument in favor of conducting research involving children involves two important factors: first, the consequences of not conducting research on children, and second, that for some medical and scientific questions, there are no suitable alternative research subjects. The consequences of not conducting research might include the perpetuation of harmful practices, the introduction of untested practices, the failure to ascertain the etiology of illnesses, and the failure to develop new treatments for psychiatric disorders of childhood (National Commission, 1978).

We believe that children should be studied to make rational and scientifically based therapy available to themselves and to other children. This position is, in fact, an imperative shared by many investigators and subjects (American College of Neuropsychopharmacology, 1978). Physicians are obligated to inform patients truthfully about diagnosis, treatment, and prognosis and to preserve the life and well-being of the individual patient. A moral obligation of scientists is to discover why children get ill and to make these findings known to society. The Hippocratic Oath requires that physicians benefit patients, as well as refrain from causing them harm. One major justification of biomedical research is the production of positive benefits for society (Beauchamp and Childress, 1979). We will discuss guidelines for informed consent which not only protect children's right to self-determination, but also allow society to meet its research obligations to children.

Adults and animals could be substituted for children, and are in many instances, but there are limitations to both (National Commission, 1978). No satisfactory animal model has been found for a number of psychiatric disorders that affect children, such as Gilles de la Tourette's syndrome, the attention deficit disorder, and enuresis. Furthermore, animal models are inappropriate and/or inadequate for studying certain processes that are uniquely human, such as development of language and cognitive functions (National Commission, 1978). Adults cannot serve as models for disorders that are unique to childhood, such as infantile autism. Studies of normal development and child-parent interaction, by their very nature, can only be conducted on children (National Commission, 1978). Also, research involving children is important because in sickness and in health, children are not "small adults." Results of studies on adults often cannot be directly extrapolated to children. For example, systematic research of new drugs must be carried out in children because such research is the only method to predict the exact pharmacological effects on children of various ages and states of psychological and biological development.

Volumes of various body fluid spaces, organ development, and metabolic function, among others, change throughout infancy and childhood. The changes do not occur uniformly, nor at constant rates, nor in altogether predictable sequences in relation to each other. These changes, in turn, affect the rate of elimination of the drug, the dosage regimen, and the effectiveness and safety of pharmacologic agents. For example, while amphetamine similarly decreases motor activity and improves attention in children and adults (Rapoport et al., 1980), before puberty children only rarely become euphoric, tolerant, or addicted to stimulants (Goyer et al., 1979), whereas these effects are common in adults.

If children were prohibited from participating in research, efforts to develop and evaluate new treatments for diseases that affect them would be impeded, while research to prevent or treat adult diseases would continue. Even research efforts on adult diseases would be hampered, as many of the most common and serious psychiatric illnesses that affect adults appear to have their origins in childhood. Certainly, this early appearance of "adult" disease in childhood occurs in a number of medical illnesses, including certain movement disorders.

Such a prohibition would also mean that new practices would be introduced without benefit of research or evaluation. The history of misadventures from such untested and nonvalidated innovations argues as strongly for research as does the failure of discovery that would result from restricting research (National Commission, 1978). In our view, for physicians to use untested therapeutic agents on children, outside of a controlled study, would be unethical because of possible harmful, undesired, or unpredicted pharmacological effects. Conclusions cannot be drawn from uncontrolled studies with the degree of confidence that is scientifically acceptable.

Standards for clinical psychobiological research on infants and children should be established with the same humane purpose and scientific objectives as are thought to be necessary for clinical practice.

Recently, there has been increasing interest in and concern for the ethical and moral considerations pertaining to biomedical research in humans, especially children. Before approving a research project, virtually all private or government agencies in the United States that support clinical research now require written assurances from prospective investigators or institutions that the rights and welfare of human subjects will be protected during all phases of the study (Horowitz, 1977).

Research institutions have established permanent or ad hoc committees called Institutional Review Boards (IRBs) to review proposed research on humans. These Boards must be competent to review a proposed study scientifically and to determine its legal, professional, and community acceptability. They should include appropriate scientists and professionals from the institution as well as representatives of the community, such as attorneys, members of the clergy, laymen, and, in some instances, members of specific interest groups (Horowitz, 1977).

Any proposal for clinical investigation should place the interest of the child first. It should satisfy the following basic conditions: (1) the research must be of value to the pediatric population in general and, in many instances, to the child himself; (2) the research design must be appropriate to the stated purpose; (3) the research should be conducted by a scientifically competent investigator who understands the ethical issues involved; and (4) a child and his family must be actively involved in the decision to participate as well as having ongoing involvement with the investigation (Capron, 1973; American Academy of Pediatrics, 1977; Cooke, 1977).

Involving the child and his family in the ongoing investigation is of particular importance in establishing a truly informed consent on their part. Investigators should give the patient as much information as possible about the safety and efficacy of the therapy and the safety and purpose of the procedure being implemented. Investigators should also encourage the child and family to ask questions and provide them with an opportunity to let their attitudes, apprehensions, and feelings be known. In addition, investigators should encourage the family to seek additional information regarding the disease and the benefits and risks of the proposed treatment and/or investigation. It is only through such dialogue between the subject, family, and investigator that consent be truly informed. Thorough planning by the investigator can eliminate or minimize compromises to the scientific design. For example, subjects and parents should know that a study may involve both medication and placebo periods, but they need not know the length or sequence of treatment periods. The investigator, of course, is responsible for monitoring the subject during all periods.

In addition to these basic ethical considerations for human studies, there are also special considerations that apply to children. Because they may be easily influenced, children require guidance and protection against exploitation. They may require protection from their own actions or, in some cases, even parental actions which may be contrary to their self-interest (Annas et al., 1977).

The American Academy of Pediatrics' Committee on Drugs (1977) has described five areas of major concern in clinical pharmacological studies in children: (1) determination of benefits and risks, (2) selection of subject groups and individuals, (3) obtaining informed consent, (4) payment for participation, and (5) option to withdraw from the study.

DETERMINATION OF BENEFITS AND RISKS

Researchers may do studies that are advantageous to the child or other children. The potential benefits should be greater than the potential risks and should be assessed prior to evaluating risks (Capron, 1973; American Academy of Pediatrics, 1977; Annas et al., 1977). Studies that promise no apparent benefits should not be conducted, even if the risks are minimal. Studies that are poorly designed, executed, or analyzed are of no potential benefit to the individual subject or to rational consideration of future studies. Benefits should be construed broadly, and should consider the importance of improving the health care of children in general, the type of child represented by the subject, and, as applicable, the subject himself. Furthermore, the medical evaluation and careful observation the subject receives as a participant in the study have a significant bearing on the ethical nature of the proposal.

Researchers should consider the seriousness of the illness being studied, as well as the current success of standard treatment, in their assessment of a benefit-risk ratio (American College of Neuropsychopharmacology, 1978; American Academy of Pediatrics, 1977). They should also realistically estimate the likelihood of benefit to the individual, the class of patients under study, and children in general. We believe that children should be allowed to participate in carefully monitored studies that promise benefits to society at large or a group of individuals.

The risks of a proposed study should also be broadly evaluated (American Academy of Pediatrics, 1977). These risks include known drug effects which have been demonstrated in vitro and, particularly, in vivo in animals, adults, or children, as well as noncontrolled clinical observations.

Researchers should also consider the potential for psychological damage to children and the possibility that some effects may remain latent for many years (National Commission, 1978; American Academy of Pediatrics, 1977). Studies may pose potential risks for children that are not usually of concern when studying adults. Some of these special risks include pain, fright, and separation from family and familiar surroundings. A stimulus of a given intensity is often considered to have a greater psychological impact on a child than that same stimulus might have on an adult.

Risks and fears can be decreased by limiting the number and type of invasive tests. However, an invasive procedure is no less ethical per se than other procedures and should not be eliminated if the results are central to the study.

A child should not be asked to submit to a venipuncture to obtain blood if fluid from a fingerstick or urine sample would provide sufficient biologic information for an approved investigation. A venipuncture, for example, may be ethically preferable if a higher drug dose would be required to obtain the data from capillary blood or urine specimen (American Academy of Pediatrics, 1977).

SELECTION OF SUBJECT GROUPS AND INDIVIDUALS

Subjects should represent a cross section of society, if possible, when the results are expected to yield information to be applied to a random population. Thus, a study population might contain members recruited from various socioeconomic, racial, and ethnic groups. However, this concern should be balanced against the scientific importance of certain studies which require tightly controlled populations, for example, certain inherited disorders or studies in which the introduction of such population variables would confound the interpretation of results obtained. Ideally, the risks, inconveniences, and benefits of participating in research should be shared equally by all groups in society. If the research is conducted at only one institution, a specific population group may bear undue burdens or will be able to avail itself of undue benefits. If there is an imbalance, the review committee should encourage the participation of other groups from the same community (in the same or separate studies, as is scientifically appropriate), or substitute a multicenter program which could distribute the risks and benefits more evenly without adversely altering particular studies (American Academy of Pediatrics, 1977).

OBTAINING INFORMED CONSENT

No research should be performed on humans without the informed consent of the subject, an individual authorized to act on behalf of the subject, or both (Capron, 1973; Annas et al., 1977; Curran and Beecher, 1969; Curran, 1974).

A patient has the right to give or withhold consent on an informed basis. This ethical and legal right has been incorporated in the Nurenberg Code, the guidelines of the American Medical Association, the Declaration of Helsinki of the World Medical Association, and various government regulations (American College of Neuropsychopharmacology, 1978; Capron, 1973; American Academy of Pediatrics, 1977; Annas et al., 1977).

Informed consent requires that physicians "disclose and explain to the patient as simply as necessary the nature of the ailment, the nature of the proposed treatment, the probability of success or of alternatives, and perhaps the risks of unfortunate results and unforeseen conditions" (*Natanson vs Kline,* 1960). Informed consent is no less applicable in those investigations in which no specific therapeutic intent is involved. This guideline is in keeping with a fundamental tenet of our society: belief in the concept of individual self-determination regarding any interference with one's bodily integrity. Although the ideal consent situation—fully voluntary participation by well-informed subjects who undertake the risks of a drug trial as partners with the clinical investigators—is not possible in pediatric pharmacology (Capron, 1973), the following guidelines reduce the scope of the problem.

Written consent for research on children must always be obtained from someone legally qualified to act on behalf of the child (usually a parent or guardian) (Capron, 1973; American Academy of Pediatrics, 1977; Annas et al., 1977). This may not always be the case for "emancipated minors," who are legally qualified to give consent for themselves without the consent of another individual. In general, written consent should be obtained from both the child, when he is at least 13 years old, and an adult acting on the child's behalf (National Commission, 1978; American College of Neuropsychopharmacology, 1978). Researchers should seek assent—agreement to participate— from any child who is at least seven years old if a legally responsible adult acting in his behalf has previously given written consent (National Commission, 1978; American Academy of Pediatrics, 1977).

Consent should not be based on coercion, inducement, or reward. The consenting individual needs to be informed about the nature of the study, its goals, risks, and benefits, compensation for any unintended effects, and the provisions made to protect the child (Capron, 1973; Annas et al., 1977).

Information provided to the subjects and/or the individuals acting on their behalf must be written in a clear and easily understandable style. "Total" or "full" disclosure of the study's specific design or risk-benefit equation is not needed and may render the results meaningless (such as disclosure of which days a subject will receive a specific medication during a controlled, clinical drug trial). If subjects make demands that would invalidate a research study, the participation of that particular individual in the study, or the study itself, should be reassessed. All significant and reasonably expected consequences should be enumerated and explained, and the consentor must be directed to and have full access to individuals who can knowledgeably and responsibly respond to all questions.

The IRB supervises the process by which the prospective consentor is informed (American Academy of Pediatrics, 1977; Horowitz, 1977). It should specify the minimum amount of information required in a proposed study for valid "informed" consent to be obtained. The investigator and the IRB should decide the amount of information to be given to subjects, though subjects should have access to all information, should they desire, except for specific information that would invalidate the scientific purpose of the study. In the latter case, the facts to be presented to the subject or those acting on the subject's behalf will be determined by the study's nature and the type of research proposed. In no instance should investigators withhold information from the potential consentor unless they have prior approval to do so (American Academy of Pediatrics, 1977).

Potential child subjects are entitled to several sources of protection, including that of the investigator. A researcher conducting studies on children should be concerned with protection of the rights of children involved in scientific investigations. The child's parents or guardian (or someone else acting on the child's behalf), as well as other professionals, should also protect the child during the study's planning and organizational review stages.

Children at certain ages are entitled to participate in determining what is in their best interest. Without desiring to be arbitrary about a specific age, we believe that when subjects are 13 years of age or older, they can be treated as young adults in terms of the requirements for informed consent and should be informed and give their informed consent when enrolling in research studies. This consent can be overridden if the review committee has clear evidence, such as mental retardation, that the subject is not competent to give informed consent. Children of this age do not have the the right to refuse necessary therapy or research that is reasonably expected to result in therapeutic benefit, only the right to refuse to participate in the nontherapeutic research aspects of any protocol. They should be provided with all relevant information before consent, at a level of sophistication appropriate to their age.

Minors should not be asked to consent before consent has been obtained from a parent or guardian (American Academy of Pediatrics, 1977). The IRB and the investigator may sometimes feel that the age at which consent is required for certain studies should be higher than 13 years old. The IRB may then decide that the child's best interest would not be served if his consent were sought. The type of disorder, the state of the child's awareness, and the psychological impact of certain information on children should be considered when allowing investigators to study children older than age 13 without their consent (American Academy of Pediatrics, 1977).

Assent is defined as the agreement to participate in a research study (or to have specimens collected) by a minor not cognitively capable of giving consent (which implies both understanding and agreement), but who has reached the intellectual age of seven years. When the intellectual age is unknown, a chronologic age of seven would be appropriate (National Commission, 1978). Assent should be obtained from such children before they are enrolled in the study. Children older than seven may thus refuse to participate in research studies or procedures (National Commission, 1978; American Academy of Pediatrics, 1977).

Sometimes, when a child is asked to be involved in a research study, questions about the reasons for participation might arise which would cause the child excessive stress. Obtaining the child's assent could thus be detrimental, or at least not in his best interest. The IRB should have the authority to make the final decision, or to establish a process for deciding whether the research may proceed (American Academy of Pediatrics, 1977).

PAYMENT FOR PARTICIPATION

Society traditionally rewards people who participate and cooperate in achieving society's goals. However, serious ethical questions arise when payment is offered to adults for allowing minors to be research subjects (American Academy of Pediatrics, 1977). Although there are altruistic and other incentives inherent in being a research subject, incentives or payments should not be so large as to induce adults to give consent for dependents to participate in a study or to subject dependents to painful or invasive procedures. This principle places major burdens on the investigator and the IRB.

If payment is offered, it should not be of a nature to become the sole inducement (American Academy of Pediatrics, 1977). The waiver of medical costs associated with treatment under a research study may sometimes be allowed. The IRB should examine any proposed remuneration for its fairness and to lessen the possiblity of unreasonable inducement or coercion. The child or his family may be reimbursed for cost incurred because of the child's participation in the study. The question of who receives payment and whether there should be any control of its disposition sometimes presents difficulties.

There are standard protections against negligence by professionals or health care institutions engaged in research. However, there should be an additional mechanism to indemnify subjects and their families on a "no fault" basis for any unintended effects of the study (Capron, 1973; American Academy of Pediatrics, 1977). Thus, it is incumbent upon institutions carrying out investigations to ensure that some form of compensation is provided and that the child's parents or guardians are aware of this coverage. We believe that if a child is injured or becomes ill during a study, the institution and its investigators should provide directly or indirectly the free medical care required to treat the condition. Likewise, if unexpected medical symptoms arise during the course of the investigation, the institution should attempt to diagnose the etiology of the condition.

WITHDRAWAL FROM STUDY

The child and the adult consenting for him should know that the subject can withdraw from the study at any time and that withdrawal will not jeopardize the subject's medical care (American College of Neuropsychopharmacology, 1978; American Academy of Pediatrics, 1977; Horowitz, 1977). Investigators should not coerce or unreasonably induce the subject with incentives when the consentor decides to withdraw the child from a study. IRBs and investigators should be especially alert to departures from ethical practice concerning when a child may be withdrawn from a study.

NEED FOR FOLLOW-UP STUDIES

Follow-up studies are an essential part of many scientifically and ethically valid research studies (Robins, 1977). Information concerning the long-term benefits and risks of interventions is helpful in determining the value and hazards of various treatments in children. Information regarding the benefits and risks of participation in research is likewise essential.

The authors conducted a follow-up study of the reaction of children and their families to participation in clinical drug trials and/or other scientific investigations for hyperactive children at the Clinical Center of the National Institute of Mental Health (NIMH). The purpose of the follow-up study was to ascertain the families' emotional reactions to having their children involved in a research project.

Questionnaires were sent to the first 45 families who entered the National Institute of Mental Health (NIMH) Hyperactive Child Program. Responses were received for 29 of the children who participated, representing 64 percent of the total population. These children were in the program between April 1975 and July 1976. Questionnaires were mailed to families in September 1976, with a second reminder in October 1976. The two-page questionnaire involved 15 questions. Responses do not total 100 percent because families did not answer all questions, indicating uncertainty, or selected more than one answer. It was of interest that 14 families "expected more" than they received from their NIMH experience, yet all but four of the families rated their overall care and communication as adequate to excellent.

SUMMARY

Children are afflicted by numerous illnesses of psychological and biological origin. A moral obligation of physicians and other investigators is to discover the best available treatments and reliable information regarding diagnosis and prognosis for childhood illness. We believe that children should be allowed to participate as research subjects in carefully monitored studies when the potential benefits exceed the potential risks and there is no other way of making rational and scientifically based therapy available to themselves and other children. However, any proposal for clinical investigation must place the interest of the child first. We have described ethical considerations pertaining to biomedical research in children. We have suggested guidelines for clinical psychobiological research in children which we believe not only protect children's right to self-determination, but also allow society to meet its research obligation.

REFERENCES

American Academy of Pediatrics Committee on Drugs: Guidelines for the ethical conduct of studies to evaluate drugs in pediatric populations. *Pediatrics* 66: 91–101, 1977

American College of Neuropsychopharmacology: A statement of the principles of ethical conduct for neuropsychopharmacologic research in human subjects, in Gallant DM, Force R (eds.): *Legal and Ethical Issues in Human Research and Treatment: Psychopharmacologic Considerations.* New York, Spectrum Publications, 1978, pp 1–17

Annas GJ, Glantz LH, Katz BF: *Informed Consent to Human Experimentation.* Cambridge, Massachusetts, Ballinger, 1977, pp 63–101

Beauchamp TL, Childress JF: *Principles of Biomedical Ethics.* New York, Oxford University Press, 1979, p 136

Capron AM: Legal considerations affecting clinical pharmacological studies in children. *Clin Res* 21: 141–150, 1973

Cooke RE: An ethical and procedural basis for research on children, editor's column. *J Pediatr* 90: 681–682, 1977

Curran WJ: Ethical and legal considerations in high risk studies of schizophrenia. *Schizophr Bull* 10: 74–92, 1974

Curran WJ, Beecher HK: Experimentation in children. *JAMA* 210: 77–81, 1969

Goyer PF, Davis GC, Rapoport JL: Abuse in prescribed stimulant medication by a 13-year-old hyperactive boy. *J Am Acad Child Psychiatry* 18: 170–175, 1979

Horowitz HS: Ethical considerations in human experimentation. *J Dent Res* (special issue) C 56: 154–159, 1977

Natanson vs Kline, 186 Kan 383,410 350 P Zd 1093,1106 (1960), *modified,* 187 Kan 186, 354 P Zd 670 (1960)

National Commission for the Protection of Human Subjects of Biomedical and Behavioral Research: Protection of human subjects: Report and recommendations. *Fed Register* 43: 2084–2114, January 13, 1978

Rapoport JL, Buchsbaum MS, Weingartner H, et al.: Dextroamphetamine: Cognitive and behavioral effects in normal and hyperactive children and normal adults. *Arch Gen Psychiatry* 37: 933–943, 1980

Robins LN: Problems in follow-up studies. *Am J Psychiatry* 134: 904–907, 1977

$$\boxed{3}$$

The Medical Model: Is It Useful in Child Psychiatry?

DENNIS P. CANTWELL

There has been a continuing controversy over the value of the medical model in psychiatry (Szasz, 1974; Torrey, 1974). It is the purpose of this chapter to review some basic concepts about the meaning of the medical model and the utility of this model as a framework for understanding the psychiatric disorders of childhood.

Blaney (1975) notes that the term "medical model" is often used as if it stands for *one* framework, while he feels there are *four* separate medical models. Three of these are relevant to our present discussion: the "organic," "symptomatic," and "classification" medical models. Each of these in turn has had another model arise in opposition to it.

In the organic medical model, psychiatric disorders are viewed as organically based disease entities. The opposing psychological model in its simplest form states that not all psychiatric disorders are organically based disease entities.

In the symptomatic model the manifestations of a psychiatric disorder are considered symptoms of some underlying condition which need not be organically based. In opposition to the symptomatic model a social learning theory model has arisen which takes the view that symptoms are not manifestations of any underlying problem and can thus be treated directly.

It should be noted that psychoanalysts and learning theorists would be united in opposition to the organic medical model but would be on opposite sides of the fence with regard to the symptomatic model.

Finally, the classificatory medical model states that psychiatry will progress only when recognizable disease clusters are carefully delineated and described. All fevers were once treated with quinine and only some responded until Sydenham delineated different causes of fever. Proponents of the classificatory model construe the present state of psychiatric treatment as similar to the pre-Sydenham era in medicine. A disease or a disorder in this classificatory model is simply a cluster of symptoms or signs which has a reasonably predictable natural history (Guze, 1972). An antilabeling school has risen in opposition to the classificatory model. It is the opinion of this school that no useful purpose is served by placing a patient in a diagnostic category. Rather, they feel that giving a patient such a diagnosis applies a perjorative label and leads to significant problems in and of itself. Moreover, proponents of this viewpoint argue that emotional disorders cannot be classified in this manner and that any attempt to do so is necessarily arbitrary and not useful for treatment purposes (Szureck, 1956).

Siegler and Osmond (1974) describe three medical models: a "clinical," a "public health," and a "scientific." In each of these medical models the doctor-patient relationship is somewhat different. In the clinical medical model the doctor-patient relationship is a dyad of healer to patient. In the public health model the patient is replaced by population and the doctor becomes a public health official or officials. In the scientific medical model, the patient becomes an experimental subject and the doctor is a scientific investigator.

This chapter will focus on the clinical and the scientific medical models as they relate to the psychiatric disorders of childhood. Some comments will also be made about the organic, symptomatic, and classificatory medical models.

The basic question is: Does the medical model have value to the practicing clinician and to the scientific investigator? Is it a useful framework for organizing clinical and research data about the psychiatric disorders of childhood?

A MEDICAL MODEL FOR CLINICAL AND INVESTIGATIVE WORK WITH THE PSYCHIATRIC DISORDERS OF CHILDHOOD

The medical model described below has been developed by the author for clinical and research work with the psychiatric disorders of childhood. The model was found to be clinically useful as a framework for integrating the data obtained from various parts of the evaluation of a child referred for psychiatric evaluation, as well as for integrating research data. The model has six stages; in its use an investigator begins with an index population of children and carries out studies that can be grouped under the other five stages. The six stages of the model are as follows.

1. Clinical Description

A careful clinical description of the behavior problem the child presents with is the starting point for investigative work in this model. Obtaining this requires detailed, systematic, yet flexible questioning of the parents; obtaining reliable information from the school; and performing a reliable and valid dianostic interview with the child. It also requires taking into account age appropriateness of behaviors, sex of the child, race, social class, and other factors that may affect the clinical picture.

2. Physical and Neurologic Factors

A systematic physical and pediatric neurologic examination is performed and the results recorded in a standardized fashion. Special attention is given to the evaluation of neurodevelopmental abnormalities. Events in the history suggesting possible Central Nervous System (CNS) involvement are systematically investigated.

3. Laboratory Studies

Included here are the results of all types of laboratory investigations: measurements of blood, urine, and spinal fluid; electroencephalograms (EEGs); and neurophysiological studies. Valid, reliable psychometric studies are considered as laboratory investigations in this context.

4. Family Studies

Included in this stage are two different types of investigations: (a) studies of the prevalence and types of psychiatric disorders in the close relatives of a clinically defined index group of child patients, and (b) studies of the relationships and interactions occurring between the members of a family.

5. Longitudinal Natural History Studies

Prospective and retrospective follow-up studies trace the course and outcome of the disorder and can be used to select homogeneous diagnostic groups. These studies also provide a standard against which the effectiveness of various forms of treatment are judged.

6. Treatment Studies

At our present level of knowledge, marked differenes in response to adequate trials of the same treatment, such as between complete recovery and marked deterioration, can be considered as evidence that the original group of children did not form a homogeneous group. Thus, differential treatment response is used to subdivide the original index population of patients.

APPLICATION OF THE MEDICAL MODEL TO THE SYNDROME OF ATTENTION DEFICIT DISORDER

The use of this model in clinical and investigative work will be demonstrated by applying it to a common behavior disorder of childhood: attention deficit disorder with hyperactivity (ADDH)—the hyperkinetic syndrome.

Specific questions that we will attempt to answer by the use of this model are: How can children with the syndrome be divided into meaningful subgroups whose conditions differ in etiology, prognosis, and response to treatment? Which children with the syndrome will respond positively to stimulant drug treatment and why do they do so?

Treatment

A complete discussion of treatment of the hyperkinetic syndrome is beyond the scope of this chapter. The points to be made in this discussion will be limited to stimulant drug treatment of the syndrome.

A critical review of the literature indicates that a significant percentage of behaviorally defined hyperkinetic children do have a positive, short-term response to central nervous system stimulant drugs such as the amphetamines and methylphenidate. However, in all studies a significant minority of children either do not respond to stimulant medication or experience worse symptoms (Barkley, 1977). Following the medical model, these treatment data would lead to two testable hypotheses:

1. These two groups of children, the responders and nonresponders to central nervous system stimulant medication, have conditions which appear similar, but have different etiologic factors.

2. The responders and nonresponders have the same condition etiologically, but either (a) there are mitigating factors which facilitate the response to central nervous system stimulants in the responders, or (b) there are factors present in nonresponders which mitigate against response to the medication. Both of these propositions will be examined below by use of this six-state medical model.

1. Clinical Description

The cardinal symptoms of the ADDH syndrome seem to be attentional problems, hyperactivity, and impulsivity (Cantwell, 1975a). Other symptoms such as learning disabilities, depression and low self-esteem, and conduct disorder are frequently, but not always, found in ADDH children. One of the major drawbacks in the study of this disorder, as in all child psychiatric disorders, has been a lack of precise operational criteria for making the diagnosis. Thus, in selecting a population of children who chronically manifest the core symptom pattern in both the home and school settings, an investigator or a clinician surely would begin with a heterogeneous group of children. Some attempts can be made to obtain a more homogeneous population by adding specific *inclusion* criteria such as those proposed for DSM III (APA, 1980). This diagnostic system requires an onset before age seven and a duration of at least six months. The symptom pattern can be characterized by: (a) two of five DSM III-specified symptoms of hyperactivity, (b) three of five DSM III-specified symptoms of attention, (c) three of six DSM III-specified symptoms of impulsivity. Specifying more inclusion criteria, including male sex, a specific age range, normal IQ, and tested normal vision and hearing, and adding *exclusion* criteria, such as any form of definite organic brain damage, would also restrict the population. However, the population remaining after application of these inclusion and exclusion criteria will still be a rather heterogeneous one. If this is so, subgroups of the original population should be formed when studies in the other five stages of the model are carried out with this index population.

2. Physical and Neurologic Factors

If one excluded ADDH children with demonstrable organic brain damage from the index patient population, the physical examination is usually completely normal. One group of investigators (Waldrop and Halverson, 1971) has reported a high incidence of minor physical anomalies in ADDH children, including epicanthal folds, widely spaced eyes, inwardly curved fifth fingers, adherent ear lobes, etc. Their findings were more consistent for boys than girls with the syndrome. These authors have suggested that the same factors operating in the first week of pregnancy led to both the congenital anomalies and the hyperkinetic behavior.

In a study of 76 boys, Rapoport et al. (1974) confirmed this increased incidence of physical anomalies. If an index population of ADDH children are divided into those with minor physical anomalies and those without minor physical anomalies, do these two subgroups differ in other stages of this model? The evidence indicates that those children with the minor physical anomalies are also characterized by differences in *clinical description picture* —earlier onset of the disorder, greater severity of hyperactivity, and more aggressive behavior. Children with minor physical anomalies also show a greater incidence of obstetrical difficulties in the mother and history of hyperactivity in the family (Rapoport et al., 1974; Quinn and Rapoport, 1974).

Moreover, those fathers of the children with minor physical anomalies who were themselves hyperactive in childhood also had a higher plasma dopamine betahydroxylase activity. Finally, it is notable that within the group with minor physical anomalies there is little overlap between those with a history of hyperactivity in the father and those with a history of obstetrical difficulties in the mother. This suggests that there may be two distinct subgroups of ADDH children with minor physical anomalies—one determined genetically and one determined by adverse events occurring early in pregnancy. If so, comparing the genetic with the obstetrical group should result in finding differences between the two groups in clinical picture, laboratory findings, natural history, or response to treatment. The finding that the fathers who were hyperkinetic as children also had high plasma dopamine betahydroxylase levels would support the idea of a genetic subgroup. To date, no relationship has been demonstrated between the presence of these minor physical anomalies and response to stimulants.

Again, if one excludes children from the index population with demonstrable organic brain disease, "hard" neurological signs are likely to be absent. There is a general consensus that certain "soft" neurological signs are more frequent among behaviorally defined ADDH children (Werry et al., 1972); however, the results are not conclusive. Moreover, most studies have methodological deficiencies such as absence of proper control groups and failure to use a reliable, standardized neurological examination (Werry et al., 1972; Schain, 1972). While there has been a tendency to infer brain pathology from these soft signs (Kennard, 1962; Laufer and Denhoff, 1957), the evidence for doing so is lacking (Werry, 1972; Rutter et al., 1970). It appears that only one study has compared carefully matched ADDH, neurotic, and normal control groups of children using a standardized neurological examination of demonstrated reliability (Werry et al., 1972). The ADDH children did have an excess of minor neurological abnormalities indicative of sensory motor incoordination. However, they did not have an excess of major neurological abnormalities, EEG abnormalities, or histories suggestive of trauma to the brain.

The relevant question then is *not:* Do ADDH children have an excess of soft neurological signs compared to normal children or compared to children with other deviant behavior? *The more important question is:* Do those ADDH children with soft neurological signs differ from those hyperkinetic children without soft neurological signs?

Evidence on this is limited. However, there is some data indicating that those ADDH children with soft neurological signs can be distinguished from those with no such neurological signs by a greater likelihood of response to simulant drug treatment (Satterfield, 1973a; Millichap, 1973), suggesting that they may form a meaningful subgroup.

3. *Laboratory Studies*

Laboratory findings are generally more reliable, more precise, and more reproducible than are clinical descriptions. If some laboratory measure could be found that was uniquely and consistently associated with ADDH syndrome, it would make diagnosis easier and would permit possible subgrouping of the syndrome. No such laboratory study exists at the present time. However, it is possible that there are some relevant laboratory findings which might be used to predict which children are most likely to respond to stimulant treatment.

a. EEG Studies. Hasting and Barkley's excellent review of psychophysiologic research (1978) with ADDH children suggests that between 15 and 40 percent of ADDH children have been reported to have clinical abnormalities in their EEG. This included both borderline and frankly abnormal readings, with an excess of slow wave activity being the most common finding. In a minority of cases, spiking, spike and wave activity, or decreased amount of power in the 8 Hz spectrum have been reported.

Again, in the context of this model, the question we are interested in is: Do ADDH children with an abnormal EEG differ in their likelihood of response to stimulant drug treatment than those ADDH children with a normal EEG?

In an early study, Shetty (1971) gave either d-amphetamine or methylphenidate intravenously to 28 ADDH children. The EEG was measured for 15 minutes before and after medication was given. Of the 15 children who were shown to be clinically good responders to oral medication, nine showed an increased amount of power in the 8–12 Hz range of the EEG when they were given the intravenous stimulant medication. Six of the nine poor responders to oral stimulants showed this kind of change. Satterfield and his colleagues (Satterfield et al., 1972; Satterfield, 1973a, 1973b) have reported a series of studies relating EEG changes and readings to the likelihood of response to stimulant medication, in this case, methylphenidate. In one study of 31 ADDH boys, good responders had a greater proportion of slow wave EEG before being given medication, and the amount of slow wave increased very little after medication. Those who were poor responders to medication did show an increase in slow wave percentage after being given medication. Before treatment, the best responders to methylphenidate had higher power in the 0–8 Hz band than the normal control group, while the five worst responders had lower power. After medication, the worst responders increased the amount of power in the 0–8 Hz spectrum while the good responders did not.

In a study of 57 ADDH children who were given both EEGs and clinical neurological examinations (Satterfield, 1973a), it was found that those who had both abnormal EEGs and an abnormal neurological exam (defined as three or more soft signs) were the ones most likely to respond to stimulant medication, while those who had normal EEGs and a normal neurological exam (no soft signs) were found to be the ones most likely not to respond to stimulant medication. Those who had either an abnormal EEG but a normal neurological exam, or an abnormal neurological exam but a normal EEG, were intermediate in their likelihood of response to stimulant medication.

However, ther are two other studies which do not support the view that abnormal EEGs are indicative of a likelihood to response to central nervous system stimulant medication. Schain and Reynard (1975) found that in the 98 ADDH children they studied, those who had an EEG abnormality were the ones most likely not to respond to stimulant medication after a 14-week trial. Rapoport et al. (1974), in a study of 74 ADDH boys, found that the presence of either EEG abnormalities of soft signs in the neurological exam was not correlated with the likelihood of response to either methylphenidate or imipramine. Thus, while a minority of ADDH children may have clinical abnormalities on the EEG, these do not seem to be useful predictors of the likelihood of response to CNS stimulant medication in an individual case.

b. Neurophysiologic Studies. A review of psychophysiologic research with ADDH children (Hastings and Barkley, 1978) suggests that these children do not seem to differ from normal children in resting level or basal levels of either heart rate or electrodermal measures. However, the same is not true with phasic cardiac measures and phasic electrodermal measures. Most studies indicate that, on these measures, ADDH children respond more slowly to stimulation and, when they do respond, produce smaller responses and habituate faster to the stimuli than normal children do. On these autonomic measures, it seems that ADDH children *on resting levels* are *not* either over-aroused or under-arroused, but with *response to stimulation,* they may be *under-responsive* or *under-aroused* compared to normal children.

Studies with auditory evoked response and visual response are not clearly interpretable as supporting this under-arousable hypothesis; however, it is consistent with findings in many studies. Moreover, these types of measures have not been found to be consistent in predicting poor or good responders to stimulant medication.

There are a number of studies that have used auditory evoked cortical responses and visual evoked cortical responses as measures of response to medication, and have used electrodermal measures such as skin conductive levels and nonspecific and specific galvanic skin responses. Satterfield and his associates, in a series of four studies, have suggested that ADDH children can be divided into two subgroups based on neurophysiologic measures: those with evidence of low central nervous system arousal, and those with normal or high nervous system arousal. They found that ADDH children had lower skin conductive levels, larger amplitude, and slower recovery of evoked cortical responses than normal children. All of these measures, together with high amplitude EEG and higher energy in the 0–8 Hz band in the resting EEG, distinguished those ADDH children who responded best to stimulant drug treatment from those who obtained poor response. In all, the Satterfield group found eight laboratory measures associated with a positive response to methylphenidate; all of these were consistent with the hypothesis that there is a subgroup of ADDH children who have lower levels of basal resting physiological activation.

There are several studies (reviewed in Hastings and Barkley, 1978) that have used evoked response and auditory evoked response measures as parameters of response to stimulant medication. The general effect on the auditory evoked response of ADDH children was an increase under stimulant medication in those indices thought to reflect attention or arousal mechanisms. With visual evoked response measures, findings were the same.

However, these are only a few studies that have attempted to look at these measures as predictors of response. Webber and Sulzbacher (1975) divided their ADDH children into good and poor responders to amphetamine or methylphenidate based on teacher ratings and classroom behavior. Five good responders, before treatment, had lower auditory evoked response thresholds (the threshold being the stimulus intensity required to evoke a cortical response) than the seven poor responders.

Buchsbaum and Wender (1973) divided good and poor responder ADDH children on the basis of response on a visual evoked response measure. The good responders were found to be "reducers" and the poor responders were found to be "augmenters." That is, good responders showed longer latencies at lower stimulus intensities, and their slope in the amplitude latency curve was diminished. Poor responders had the opposite effect.

Halliday et al. (1976) found that good responders showed less variability on a task requiring inattention on the visual evoked response measure than they did in one which required attention. Again, poor responders showed the reverse effect. One particular component of visual evoked response, the N140-P190 component, increased in the good responder group when stimulant medication was given; in the poor responder group it decreased.

c. Biochemical Studies. The positive response of many ADDH children to CNS medications such as amphetamines and tricyclic antidepressants, both of which affect the biogenic amines, offers indirect evidence that a disorder in monoamine metabolism is an etiologic factor in some children with the syndrome. There are several other lines of evidence to support this hypothesis. Dextroamphetamine was thought to be ten times as potent as its isomer, levoamphetamine, in inhibiting norepinephrine uptake by presynaptic norephinephrine terminals in the brain. The two isomers were thought to be of approximately equal potency in inhibiting dopamine uptake by dopaminergic presynaptic terminals (Snyder et al., 1970). Actual clinical trials showed the two isomers to be equipotent. There is a suggestion that the two isomers of amphetamine may have a differential affect on the aggressive and hyperactive behaviors of ADDH children (Arnold et al., 1973), with L-amphetamine offering more potency for control of aggression and d-amphetamine for hyperactivity. These data offer indirect evidence that some symptoms of ADDH children may be medicated by dopaminergic systems and others by norepinephrinergic systems.

More direct studies of a possible metabolic abnormality and the use of biochemical measures as predictors of response to stimulants have been limited.

In a group of ADDH boys, Rapoport et al. (1970) found an inverse relationship between the degree of hyperactive behavior and urinary norepinephrine excretion. In addition, there was an inverse relationship in response of the hyperactivity to dextroamphetamine and urinary norepinephrine levels.

Shekim and his colleagues at the University of Missouri (Shekim et al., 1979), in a series of studies, have been examining urinary 3-methoxy-4-hydroxyphenylglycol (MHPG) levels before and after treatment with fixed doses of amphetamine in children with the ADDH syndrome. They have found that urinary MHPG levels were significantly lower in ADDH children than they were in normal controls. Moreover, the MHPG excretion decreased when d-amphetamine was given to the drug responders but not to the nonresponders. However, pretreatment MHPG levels did not significantly differentiate responders from nonresponders, although the responders did tend to have higher levels. Post-treatment MHPG levels, however, did significantly differentiate the d-amphetamine good responders from the poor responders.

In addition, the drug responders had more neurological soft signs than the poor responders. There was no relationship between the presence of neurological soft signs and pretreatment MHPG levels.

Thus, there does seem to be an emergent body of evidence that at least in some ADDH children there may be an abnormality of monoamine metabolism. Moreover, laboratory studies in this area may pick out children with somewhat different clinical pictures with regard to hyperactivity and aggression. Urinary norephinephrine excretion may be related both to the degree of hyperactivity and to response to stimulant medication.

Thus, children selected by biochemical laboratory studies in one stage of this model may pick out ADDH children who differ somewhat in two other areas of the model: clinical picture and response to stimulant medication.

4. Family Studies

Two studies of biologic parents of biologic parents of ADDH children revealed increased prevalence rates for alcoholism, sociopathy, and hysteria (Morrison and Stewart, 1971; Cantwell, 1972). One of these studies also reported a high prevalence rate for these same psychiatric disorders in the biologic second-degree relatives of ADDH children (Cantwell, 1972). In both studies it was noted that the syndrome also occurred more often in the biologic first- and second-degree relatives of ADDH children than in the relatives of control children. Two further studies of the nonbiologic relatives of adopted ADDH children revealed no increased prevalence rates for psychiatric illness or the ADDH syndrome (Morrison and Stewart, 1973; Cantwell, 1975b). These data suggest that genetic factors may be important in the etiology of the syndrome. They also suggest that these children may be at risk, for both genetic and environmental reasons, for the development of significant pathology in adulthood (Cantwell, 1976).

Do these familial factors play any role in affecting response to stimulants among ADDH children? Few studies have attempted to look at family variables in any systematic way. Conrad and Insel (1967) found that children whose parents were rated as "grossly deviant" or "socially incompetent" were less likely to respond positively to stimulant medication even in the face of other factors which tended to predict a good outcome. Their criteria for grossly deviant and socially incompetent indicate that most of these parents were either alcoholic or sociopathic.

Studies of family interaction in relation to drug response have been limited and inconsistent. The Montreal group (Weiss et al., 1968; Werry et al., 1966) found that the mother-child relationship and the quality of the home were unrelated to drug therapy, but in a later study (Weiss et al., 1971) there was a positive association between response to stimulants and the quality of the mother-child relationship. Other authors (Knobel, 1962; Kraft, 1968) have noted that the attitude of the family to the child taking medication is likely to affect treatment response.

It is apparent from the above review that the six stages of the model interact. New findings in one stage may lead to changes in one or more of the other stages. For example, beginning with a population of children with the clinical picture of the ADDH syndrome, we find that one group shows a positive response to stimulant medication while another group shows a negative response. When we compare these two groups, the responders and the nonresponders, we find they differ in a number of other parameters. The responders show laboratory evidence of low CNS arousal, more abnormal EEGs, and a greater number of abnormalities in neurological examinations. Thus, this group begins to look as if they have their disorder on a neurodevelopmental basis. One might then go back and take a closer look at the clinical picture of the two groups, using techniques such as cluster analysis, to see if differences can be found in the behavioral picture. Little has been done in this area, but Barcai (1971) found that responders to stimulant medication were discovered at clinical interview to have excess body movements, poor language ability, lack of ability to abstract and to use imagination constructively, lack of adjustment to the values of society, and lack of planning ability. Satterfield (1973b) found that a better response to stimulants was seen in older children and children who had more behavioral abnormalities reported by the teacher. Finally, some investigators (Katz et al., 1975) have felt that markedly antisocial children are less likely to respond to psychopharmacologic management.

Thus, the continued application of this medical model to the same index population of children leads to increasingly refined diagnostic criteria and ultimately to more homogeneous subgroups of the original index patient population. These homogeneous patient populations provide the best starting point for studies of etiology and treatment. The role of dynamic factors, family relationships, sociological factors, genetic factors, etc, in the etiology of any psychiatric disorder of childhood is more easily elucidated when the patient population under study is as diagnostically "pure" as possible. Likewise, response to any treatment, be it psychotherapy, pharmacotherapy, behavior therapy, or some other modality, is best evaluated in a homogeneous patient population.

DISCUSSION

Siegler and Osmond (1974) have pointed out that there are many models by which one can conceptualize psychiatric disorder. Aside from the medical model these include the moral model, an impairment model, the psychoanalytic model, the social model, the psychedelic model, a conspiratorial model, and a family interaction model. Each of these carries with it certain assumptions about etiology, diagnosis, explanation of psychopathology, and treatment. None of these models exist in the "real world." And, as such, they are neither right nor wrong by themselves. Any model is simply a way or organizing the data, of forming judgements, and of testing theories (Ludwig, 1976).

Why then, among these models, has the medical model evoked such criticism? It is the author's opinion that the major criticisms concerning it are based upon misconceptions. Outlined below are five common misconceptions.

1. "The medical model implies that psychiatric disorders are organically based disease entities." This misconception arises from the false belief that the organic medical model described by Blaney (1975) is the *only* medical model. While it is true that certain psychiatric disorders of both children and adults are organically based (for example, organic brain syndromes), there is abundant evidence indicating that social, familial, and environmental factors play a large role in shaping both the appearance and nature of a psychiatric disorder even in those children with organic brain damage (Rutter et al., 1970; Seidel et al., 1974).

The medical model does not assume that all psychiatric disorders of childhood are organically based disease entities. It only assumes that a child who presents with one type of disorder may have a different condition from a child who presents with another disorder. Furthermore, if the two disorders are truly different then the two conditions should be able to be characterized and differentiated from each other as outlined in this six stage model.

2. "The medical model implies that organic modes of treatment are preferential for the psychiatric disorders of childhood." This misconception follows from the first misconception outlined above. For if one assumes that a disorder is organically based, it might follow that organic modes of treatment are preferred. However, again there is abundant evidence that even in those psychiatric disorders in which organic factors play a role, nonorganic modes of treatment may be the primary mode of treatment involved. With treatment modalities, as with etiology, the medical model is not an organic one, but is best described as an "agnostic" one (Woodruff et al., 1974). Without evidence, proponents of the medical model do not necessarily assume that pills are better than play therapy, or that play therapy is better than pills. The question is which treatment modality or combination is best suited for which child with what disorder. This question can easily be investigated in the context of this six stage model.

3. "The process of diagnosis is merely a form of labeling the child and is a meaningless exercise for clinical purposes." Making a diagnosis does not result in applying a label to a *child;* it does result in applying a label to a *psychiatric disorder* the child presents with. Just as a child may have measles at one age, pneumonia at another age, and be perfectly well at a third age, he may present with one psychiatric disorder at one time, with another psychiatric disorder at a second time, and be perfectly well at a third time. For clinical purposes no one would state that it is a meaningless exercise to distinguish between measles and pneumonia. Therefore, it is difficult to fathom why it should be a meaningless exercise to similarly distinguish between two psychiatric disorders.

For research purposes, a valid diagnostic classification scheme is a vital necessity (Rutter, 1965; Cantwell, 1975b). If findings from various centers are to be compared, investigators with different theoretical backgrounds must have a "common language" with which they can communicate. A proper classification system will serve this purpose.

One of the reasons for this third misconception is a confusion between the role of a diagnostic classification system and a dynamic formulation. It should be recognized that a diagnostic classification system emphasizes what a particular patient had in common with other patients, while a dynamic formulation emphasizes what a particular patient has that is different from other patients. Both are necessary and one cannot do the work of the other.

4. "The focus on the patient's disorder minimizes the importance of

the patient as an individual." The medical model does imply that the focus of scientific inquiry is the *disorder* the patient presents with rather than the *patient*. The model provides a framework for answering important questions: What factors do cases of disorder A have in common? What factors do cases of disorder B have in common? What factors are present in disorder A that are not present in disorder B and vice versa? However, this focus of inquiry cannot be construed as diminishing the importance of the patient as an individual. Every patient is a unique human being and this uniqueness must be taken into account in any doctor-patient relationship. This is part of the art of medicine. Nevertheless, excess emphasis on the unique aspects of each child patient and lack of recognition of the common factors shared by children who present with a particular disorder will impede scientific study. For if children with psychiatric disorders share no common factors, then training and experience are without value and dealing with each new patient becomes a research project in itself (Guze, 1972).

5. "A disease or disorder oriented approach is incompatible with a humanitarian approach." A tough-minded scientific approach in the study of psychiatric disorders is far from being incompatible with a warm, compassionate humanitarian approach in therapeutic work. For those involved in clinical research, the techniques learned in investigative work may well make them better clinicians. Moreover, it is difficult to see how more knowledge about a patient's disorder makes one less effective in dealing with a patient as an individual. For, as it has been pointed out (Guze, 1972), the effective use of knowledge about a child's psychiatric disorder to relieve the suffering to the child and his family caused by that disorder is humanitarian in the highest sense of the word. The psychiatrist who uses this knowledge can do so in a warm, compassionate way or in a cold, unsympathetic way, quite independently of the model he uses as a conceptual framework (Guze, 1972).

In his discussion of the medical model, Shagass (1975) emphasizes the pluralistic nature of medicine's theoretical structure, its acceptance of multiple causation about pathogenesis, and its pragmatic basis. Because of this, he argues that there is a greater chance of relevant information being discovered and applied in psychiatry in the context of the medical model than in any of the other possible models for two reasons: (1) that the medical model adheres to a value system which is centered around the benefit to the individual patient; (2) that tradition in medicine of pragmatic relevance means that new information will be adopted even if it means discarding hallowed theoretical assumptions.

This chapter has not attempted to argue that the medical model is the only framework or the best framework for viewing psychiatric disorders of childhood. Rather, it has attempted to show that the model does have relevance and value as a framework for organizing data on individual patients in a clinical setting and for organizing research data in the study of psychiatric problems in children. It remains for proponents of other models to demonstrate their utility in the same way.

REFERENCES

Arnold L, Kiriluck V, Corson S, Corson E: Levoamphetamine and dextroamphetamine: Differential effect on aggression and hyperkinesis in children and dogs. Am J Psychiatry 130:165-170, 1973

Barcai A: Predicting the response of children with learning disabilities and behavior problems to dextroamphetamine sulfate: The clinical interview and the finger twitch test. Pediatrics 47:73-80, 1971

Barkley RA: A review of stimulant drug research with hyperactive children. J Child Psychol Psychiatry 18:137-165, 1977

Blaney PH: Implications of the medical model and its alternatives. Am J Psychiatry 132:911-914, 1975

Buchsbaum M, Wender P: Average evoked responses in normal and minimally brain dysfunctioned children treated with amphetamine. Arch Gen Psychiatry 29:764-770, 1973

Cantwell DP: Genetic factors in the hyperkinetic syndrome. J Am Acad Child Psychiatry 15:214-223, 1976

Cantwell DP: The Hyperactive Child: Diagnosis, Management and Current Research. New York, Spectrum Publications, 1975a, p 195

Cantwell DP: A model for the investigation of psychiatric disorders of childhood: Its application in genetic studies of hyperkinetic children, in Anthony EJ (ed): Explorations in Child Psychiatry. New York, Plenum Publishers, 1975b, pp 57-59

Cantwell DP: Psychiatric illness in families of hyperactive children. Arch Gen Psychiatry 27:414-417, 1972

Conrad W, Insel J: Anticipating the response to amphetamine therapy in the treatment of hyperkinetic children. Pediatrics 40:96-99, 1967

Diagnostic and Statistical Manual of Mental Disorders (DSM-III). Washington, DC, American Psychiatric Association 1968, pp 41-45

Guze S: Psychiatric disorders and the medical model. Biol Psychiatry 3:221-224, 1972

Halliday R, Rosenthal JH, Naylor H, Callaway E: Averaged evoked potential predictors of clinical improvement in hyperactive children treated with methylphenidate: An initial study and replication. *Psychophysiology* 13:429-439, 1976

Hastings JE, Barkley RA: A review of psychophysiological research with hyperkinetic children. *J Abnorm Child Psychol* 6:413-447, 1978

Katz S, Saraf K, Gittelman-Klein R, Klein D: Clinical pharmacological management of hyperkinetic children. *Int J Ment Health* 4:157-181, 1975

Kennard M: Value of equivocal signs in neurologic diagnosis. *Neurology* 10:753-764, 1960

Knobel M: Psychopharmacology for the hyperkinetic child: Dynamic considerations. *Arch Gen Psychiatry* 6:198-202, 1962

Kraft I: The use of psychoactive drugs in the outpatient treatment of psychiatric disorders of children. *Am J Psychiatry* 124:1401-1407, 1968

Laufer MW, Denhoff E: Hyperkinetic behavior syndrome in children. *J Pediatr* 50:463-474, 1957

Ludwig A: The proper domain of psychiatry. *Psychiatr Digest* 37:15-24, 1976

Millichap J: Drugs in management of minimal brain dysfunction. *Ann NY Acad Sci* 205:321-334, 1973

Morrison Jr, Stewart MA: A family study of the hyperactive child syndrome. *Bio Psychiatry* 3:189-195, 1971

Morrison JR, Stewart MA: The psychiatric status of the legal families of adopted hyperactive children. *Arch Gen Psychiatry* 28:888-891, 1973

Quinn P, Rapoport J: Minor physical anomalies and neurologic status in hyperactive boys. *Pediatrics* 53:742-747, 1974

Rapoport J, Lott Il, Alexander D, Abramson A: Urinary noradrenaline and playroom behavior in hyperactive boys. *Lancet* 2:1141, 1970

Rapoport J, Lott I, Alexander D, Abramson A: Urinary noreadrenaline and dopamine-beta-hydroxylase activity in hyperactive boys. *Am J Psychiatry* 131:386-390, 1974

Rutter M: Classification and categorization in child psychiatry. *J Child Psychol Psychiatry* 6:71-83, 1965

Rutter M, Graham P, Yule W: *A Neuropsychiatric Study in Childhood.* Philadelphia, Lippincott, 1970

Satterfield JH: EEG issues in children with minimal brain dysfunction. *Semin Psychiatry* 4:35-46, 1973a

Satterfield JH: Personal communication, 1973b

Satterfield JH, Cantwell DP, lesser LI, Podosin RL: Physiological studies of the hyperkinetic child: I. *Am J Psychiatry* 128:1418-1424, 1972

Schain R: *Neurology of Childhood Learning Disorders.* Baltimore Williams & Wilkins, 1972

Schain RJ, Reynard CL: Observations on effects of a central stimulant drug (methylphenidate) in children with hyperactive behavior. *Pediatrics* 55:709-716, 1975

Seidel UP, Chadwick OFD, Rutter M: Psychological disorders in crippled children with and without brain damage. *Dev Med Child Neurol* 17:563-573, 1975

Shagass CL: The medical model in psychiatry. *Compr Psychiatry* 16:405-413, 1975

Shekim WO, Dekirmenjian H, Chapel JL: Urinary MHPG excretion in minimal brain dysfunction and its modification by d-amphetamine. *Am J Psychiatry* 136:667-671, 1979

Shelly E, Riester A: Syndrome of minimal brain damage in young adults. *Dis Nerv Syst* 33:335-338, 1972

Shetty T: Alpha rhythms in the hyperkinetic child. *Nature* 234:476, 1971

Siegler M, Osmond H: *Models of Madness, Models of Medicine.* New York, Macmillan, 1974

Snyder S, Taylor K, Coyle J, Meyerhoff J: The role of brain dopamine in behavioral regulation and the actions of psychotropic drugs. *Am J Psychiatry* 127:199-207, 1970

Szasz TS: *The Myth of Mental Illness.* New York, Harper & Row: 1974

Szureck SA: Psychotic episodes and psychotic maldevelopment. *Am J Orthopsychiatry* 26:519-543, 1956

Torrey EF: *The Death of Psychiatry.* Radnor, Pennsylvania, Chilton Book Co. 1974

Weber BA, Sulzbacher SI: Use of CNS stimulant medication in averaged electroencephalic audiometry with children with MDB. *J Learn Disability* 8:300-313, 1975

Weiss G, Minde K, Werry JS, Douglas V, Nemeth E: Studies on the hyperactive child. VIII. Five-year follow-up. *Arch Gen Psychiatry* 24:409-414, 1971

Weiss G, Werry J, Minde K, Douglas V, Sykes D: Studies on the hyperactive child. V. The effects of dextroamphetamine and chlorpromazine on behavior and intellectual functioning. *J Child Psychol Psychiatry* 9:145-156, 1968

Werry JS: Organic factors in childhood psychopathology, in Quay H, Werry, J (eds): *Psychopathological Disorders in Childhood.* New York, John Wiley & Sons, 1972 pp 81-121

Werry J, Minde K, Guzman A, Weiss G, Dogan K, Hoy E: Studies on the hyperactive child. VII. Neurological status compared with neurotic and normal children. *Am J Orthopsychiatry* $42:441-450, 1972

Werry JS, Weiss G, Douglas V, Martin J. Studies on the hyperactive child. III. The effect of chlorpromazine upon behavior and learning ability. *J Am Acad Child Psychiatry* 5:292-312, 1966

Woodruff R, Goddwin D, Guze S: Psychiatric Diagnosis. New York, Oxford University Press, 1974

$$\boxed{4}$$

Neurotransmitter Ontogeny as a Perspective for Studies of Child Development and Pathology

x

J. GERALD YOUNG,
DONALD J. COHEN,
GEORGE M. ANDERSON,
and BENNETT A. SHAYWITZ

Clinical studies of child development can now be extended to include the biochemical investigation of neuronal maturation. Determination of normal and impaired patterns of molecular development will aid in understanding biochemical findings in childhood neuropsychiatric disorders and the natural history of adult illnesses.

The clinical investigation of neurochemical development can be organized according to molecular interactions affecting neuro-transmission (Young and Cohen, 1979). The developmental patterns of monoamine neurotransmitter systems in animals, during fetal and postnatal periods, will be used as models for studies of these systems in humans.

ANIMAL STUDIES: NEUROTRANSMITTER ONTOGENY

The development of monoamine-containing nerve cells of the rat brainstem has been investigated by fluorescence histochemistry, autoradiography, and enzymology (Coyle, 1974; Mabry and Campbell, 1977) (Table 1). Monoamines can be demonstrated in these cells by the 13th day of fetal life (F 13) (Golden, 1973; Lauder and Bloom, 1974). Division of these cells occurs up to days F 12–F 14, but once this period is completed, neuronal maturation becomes a process of cellular differentiation without further multiplication of cells. Axons gradually move toward the areas they will ultimately innervate. By the end of the fetal period, some dopamine (DA) terminals are present in the relatively circumscribed terminal fields of dopamine axons, while few norepinephrine (NE) terminals, which will eventually spread throughout the neuraxis, are yet present. On the other hand, serotonin (5-HT) terminals are distributed throughout the brain. In a parallel way, the enzymes required for the synthesis of monoamines appear in the brainstem nuclei by F 13–F 14: tyrosine hydroxylase (TOH) (Coyle and Axelrod, 1972b) and aromatic amino acid decarboxylase (AAAD) (Lamprecht and Coyle, 1972) for both DA and NE neurons; dopamine-beta-hydroxylase (DBH) (Coyle and Axelrod, 1972a) for NE neurons; and tryptophan hydroxylase (Schmidt and Sanders-Busche, 1971; Deguchi and Barchas, 1972) and AAAD (Lamprecht and Coyle, 1972) for 5-HT neurons. Differential centrifugation is used to determine the location of enzymes within a cell, since the enzymes remain with specific cellular components separated according to weight. During gestation, monoamine-synthesizing enzymes are found in the supernatant fluid following centrifugation, indicating that they are active in the cytosol (Coyle, 1974; Coyle and Axelrod, 1972b). This is additional evidence that the principal neurotransmitter-related activity is located in the neuronal cell bodies during fetal life, rather than the nerve endings. The amino acid precursors of the monoamine

TABLE 1. Development of Monoamine Neuronal Systems in Rat Brain
During Fetal and Postnatal Periods

	Gestation	*Postnatal*
Cell body	Transmitters present by F 13–F 14. Cell division until F 12–F 14; limited to differentiation after this period.	Increase in cell size. Increase in fluorescent intensity, followed by decline.
Axon terminals	DA terminals present. Few NE terminals. 5-HT terminals throughout brain.	Terminal growth is primarily NE terminals complete by PN 40. DA terminals complete by PN 60.
Membrane uptake	Appears during fetal life.	Affinity remains same. Uptake capacity (V max) increases over 100-fold. More NE in synaptosomal fraction.
Precursors	Tyrosine is 200% adult level. Tryptophan is 300% adult level.	Tyrosine and tryptophan gradually decrease to adult level.
Enzymes (TOH, AAAD, DBH, TRPOH)	Appear by F 13–F 14. Mostly in medulla-pons. Soluble enzymes in cytosol.	500-fold increase during development. Shift to more rostral brain regions. Enzymes mostly in synaptosomal fraction.

Glossary
F 13 = fetal day 13
PN 13 = postnatal day 13
DA = dopamine
NE = norepinephrine
5-HT = serotonin
TOH = tyrosine hydroxylase
AAAD = aromatic amino acid decarboxylase
DBH = dopamine-beta-hydroxylase
TRPOH = tryptophan hydroxylase

transmitters—tyrosine (for DA and NE) and tryptophan (for 5-HT)—are present in abundance during gestation. Tyrosine reaches twice, and tryptophan three times, the eventual adult level in the brainstem nuclei (Tyce et al., 1964).

The specific active uptake process at the membrane of the presynaptic neuron, a critical regulatory system controlling the amount of transmitter active in the synaptic space, appears during fetal life; for example, a high affinity system for NE is present by day F 18 (Coyle and Axelrod, 1971). Monoamine oxidase (MAO), an essential monoamine-degrading enzyme in the nervous system, is detectable at the same time that synthesizing enzymes appear, days F 13–F 14 (Shimizu and Morikawa, 1959). These studies of biochemical development point to the presence of essential molecular mechanisms in the rat brain during fetal life; pharmacological studies elicit effects similar to the those in the adult animal, indicating that monoamine neuronal systems are functionally active during gestation. This implies that monoamine transmitters are released before differentiation has been completed (Mabry and Campbell, 1977).

Although there is no further cell division after birth, there is an increase in cell size. A temporary increase in fluorescent intensity of cell bodies in histochemical studies indicates progressive synthesis of the transmitter, which eventually declines as the fluorescence spreads peripherally (Loizou and Salt, 1970; Loizou, 1972). This centrifugal migration of monoamine transmitters away from the cell bodies and

TABLE 2. Whole Brain Monoamine Concentrations in Rat Brain
During Postnatal Period
(Expressed as Percent of Eventual Adult Concentration)

Postnatal Age	NE	DA	5-HT
Birth	20%	30%	50%
10 days	30%	30%	60%
20 days	50%	40%	75%
30 days	70%	50%	95%
40 days	Adult level	75%	Adult level
50 days	Adult level	90%	Adult level
60 days	Adult level	Adult level	Adult level

Glossary
NE = norepinephrine
DA = dopamine
5-HT = 5 hydroxytryptamine (serotonin)

toward the fields they will innervate is typical of postnatal brain maturation. The growth of nerve cell terminals is primarily a postnatal process, although serotonin terminals have spread widely in the brain before birth. The distribution of noradrenergic terminals through the brain is completed around the 40th postnatal day (PN 40), while dopaminergic terminals reach their final pattern of innervation at about the 60th postnatal day (Loizou and Salt, 1970; Loizou, 1972). The concentrations of these amines, as measured in whole brain homogenates, reach adult levels during the same period (Agrawal et al., 1966; Agrawal and Himwich, 1970; Coyle and Henry, 1973; Karki et al., 1962; Bennett and Giarman, 1965) (Table 2).

A pronounced increase in the activities of monoamine-synthesizing enzymes (up to 500-fold through development) continues in the postnatal period (Coyle and Axelrod, 1972a, 1972b; Lamprecht and Coyle, 1972; Schmidt and Sanders-Busche, 1971; Deguchi and Barchas, 1972; Porcher and Heller, 1972) (Table 3). Maximal enzyme activity shifts toward the forebrain, with relatively less enzyme activity in the region of monoamine cell bodies (Lamprecht and Coyle, 1972; Coyle and Axelrod, 1972a; N Robinson, 1967; N Robinson, 1968).

TABLE 3. Activities of Monoamine-Synthesizing Enzymes in Whole Rat Brain
During Fetal and Postnatal Periods
(Expressed as Percent of Eventual Adult Activity)

Age	TRPOH	TOH	AAAD	DBH
F 13	Present	Present	Present	Present
F 15	10%	10%	15%	10%
F 17–F 18	15%	30%	35%	15%
Birth (21 days)	25%	40%	40%	30%
PN 7	25%	45%	45%	45%
PN 14	55%	75%	50%	55%
PN 28– PN 30	Adult activity	Adult activity	70%	70%
PN 45+	Adult activity	Adult activity	Adult activity	Adult activity

Glossary
F 13 = fetal day 13
PN 13 = postnatal day 13
TRPOH = tryptophan hydroxylase
TOH = tyrosine hydroxylase
AAAD = aromatic amino acid decarboxylase
DBH = dopamine-beta-hydroxylase

This implies the presence of active synthetic enzymes in nerve terminals, as has also been shown by the fact that enzymes are no longer located primarily in the soluble fraction (cytosol) following differential centrifugation, but sediment out with the synaptosomal fraction (Coyle, 1974; Coyle and Axelrod, 1972b).

Amino acid precursors, formerly at high levels in the cell bodies during gestation, decline to levels characteristic of maturity (Tyce et al., 1964; Hoff et al., 1974). The affinity of the membrane reuptake mechanism for specific transmitters does not change, but the overall uptake capacity (V max) continues to gradually increase following birth, ultimately achieving a 100-fold increase during the course of development. The functional impact of this change is evident in the predominant localization, for example, of NE in the synaptosomal fraction of the postnatal brain — a 300-fold increase between F 18 and adulthood (Coyle, 1974; Coyle and Axelrod, 1971). Catabolic enzymes in the rat brain, MAO, and catechol-O-methyltransferase (COMT) are characterized by sharp increases in their activities, reaching adult levels by the 20th postnatal day (Kuzuya and Nagatsu, 1969; Ghosh and Guha, 1972; Baker et al., 1974; Shih and Eiduson, 1971; Baker and Quay, 1969; Halgren and Varon, 1972).

ANIMAL STUDIES: FUNCTIONAL DEVELOPMENT

In order to examine functional effects of molecular development on behavior, drugs are selected according to effects at discrete points of monoamine synthesis, function, and metabolism. When administered, their behavioral effects are assumed to be due to facilitation or inhibition of a particular transmitter's function, an assumption which is too frequently tenuous. Some general results bearing on the behavioral concomitants of developing monoamine systems will be summarized.

Brain catecholamines are critically significant in behavioral activation from the time of birth. Compounds interfering with catecholamine function depress activity from the neonatal period forward, while drugs mimicking catecholamines stimulate behavioral activity (Kellogg and Lundborg, 1972a, 1972b, 1973; Lal and Sourkes, 1973; Breese and Traylor, 1972). In contrast, the inhibitory serotonergic tracts do not immediately exert their influence. This inhibitory function appears at the 15th postnatal day, so that a serotonin synthesis-blocker administered then enhances behavioral arousal (Mabry and Campbell, 1974, 1977). Acetylcholine (ACh) also has a strong inhibitory component to its function, which matures at the 25th postnatal day (Fibiger et al., 1970). Once the serotonergic and cholinergic systems are fully developed, drugs antagonizing ACh and 5-HT function potentiate the stimulating effects of catecholamine agonists (Mabry and Campbell, 1977). The balancing and compensating functions of these neuronal systems are critical underpinnings to healthy adaptation throughout the remainder of the life-cycle.

The development of monoamine neuronal systems in the rat highlights several points to be examined in studies of human development. There is a predictable sequence in molecular development, the sequential events are activated at specific time points, and this developmental profile is related to both anatomical features and physiological function. While there is some room for variation (one source of individual behavioral differences), outside a certain limit this leads to impaired function. During the postnatal period, when nerve terminals are moving toward the fields they will innervate, there is ample opportunity for variation and the influence of environmental features (Rutledge, 1974). Finally, there is a lack of synchronism in the maturation of neuronal systems; that is, the time points for changes in the rate of maturation do not coincide among the transmitter systems. This feature facilitates development in particular ways, and alterations in the pattern will have variable effects depending on the time at which they occur.

ENVIRONMENTAL EFFECTS ON BRAIN STRUCTURE AND CHEMISTRY

Studies of human neurotransmitter ontogeny examine a much longer developmental period and use body fluids instead of brain tissue, which is generally unobtainable. Maturational processes which lead to full function in the animal over a period of weeks or months are expanded dramatically in the human (Solnit, 1979), so that changes are difficult to detect. In addition, the relative behavioral immaturity of the human infant at birth makes the infant more sensitive to environmental factors (Solnit, 1978), which affect both behavior and the biochemical development of neuronal systems. Profound environmental molding takes place when surroundings do not "fit" the encoded genetic program for maturation of an organism; less dramatic biochemical changes can aid the organism in adapting to prevailing conditions. The following animal studies are examples of the influence of environment on neuronal development.

Mice allowed to exercise in the late postnatal period have structural changes in cerebellar Purkinje cells, when compared to litter mates with restricted physical activity. Larger dendritic trees and more numerous spines on Purkinje cells reflect more physical activity during this period (Pysh and Weiss, 1979). Monkeys reared in a colony have larger cell bodies and more extensive spiny branchlets on Purkinje cells than monkeys reared in isolation, apparently corresponding to the greater amount of physical activity in these monkeys (Floeter and Greenough, 1979).

Monoamine oxidase activity fluctuates markedly in several brain areas in mice exposed to aggression and defeat by trained fighters (Eleftheriou and Boehlke, 1967). Social isolation causes a decrease in rat adrenal tyrosine hydroxylase (TOH) and phenylethanolamine-N-methyl transferase (PNMT), while social stimulation has the opposite effect (Axelrod et al., 1970). During the period of "protest" following separation of an infant monkey from its mother, its behavioral response is similar to that of a human infant and is accompanied by increased activity of NE-related enzymes in the adrenal gland and sympathetic nervous system (Breese et al., 1973).

Environmental effects on developing neurotransmitter systems can be observed even in the presence of a known brain lesion; pathological behavior caused by the lesion can be aggravated or ameliorated by environmental changes. Rat pups with brains depleted of dopamine by administration of 6-hydroxydomaine (6-OHDA) are characterized by hyperactivity and learning deficits early in development, and are used as an experimental model for hyperactivity and learning deficits in children (B Shaywitz et al., 1976). Administration of stimulant medication leads to a reduction in activity levels and improved learning, the same effects observed in hyperactive children (B Shaywitz et al., 1978). Nevertheless, 6-OHDA–treated animals reared with normal litter mates (nondepleted) are improved when compared to 6-OHDA–treated animals reared only with other dopamine-depleted animals. The degree of improvement is comparable to that achieved with methylphenidate, indicating that environmental manipulation is an alternative to medication (Pearson et al., 1980; Satterfield et al., 1979).

STUDIES OF NEUROTRANSMITTER ONTOGENY IN HUMANS

These examples demonstrate multiple ways that environment can alter neurotransmitter ontogeny and are a background for later consideration of the development of neuronal systems in disease states. They also suggest a congruence between the results of animal experimentation and clinical developmental theories. Yet few conclusions can be drawn about neurochemical correlates of human development because of the inaccessibility of brain tissue for study. The best indirect technique for assessing brain chemistry is the assay of compounds in cerebrospinal fluid (CSF), where there is good reason to believe that the substances measured reflect brain metabolic activity (Cohen et al., 1980a; Garelis et al., 1974; B Shaywitz et al., 1980a). More typically, a peripheral tissue (such as skin fibroblasts) or a peripheral fluid (such as blood or urine) must be utilized, and interpretation of results is accompanied by assumptions and inferences (Cohen and Young, 1977). Nevertheless, the use of peripheral specimens does have value if findings are assessed with restraint. An economical feature of development is that the same functional mechanism is often utilized in multiple systems for the solution of apparently different problems of adaptation. A phenomenon initially observed in peripheral tissues or fluids can be applied in clinical investigation because the mechanism at the two sites is, if not always identical, at least analogous. The importance of mapping developmental sequences for human monoamine systems is a rationale for accepting methodological limitations and moving ahead with the examination of central and peripheral fluids; generalization to brain neuronal systems must be cautious.

NORADRENERGIC SYSTEM

The noradrenergic system is involved in the control of movement, behavioral activation and arousal, modulation of anxiety, reward functions, pain, affect, brain plasticity, memory, and learning. These functions include processes critically affected by the pathology of childhood neuropsychiatric disorders.

Norepinephrine

Plasma norepinephrine has a half-life of two minutes and is acutely responsive to a variety of external influences (eg, posture, stress, exercise, temperature, etc.); this requires special conditions while obtaining samples. In order to study plasma NE across the life-cycle (age 10 to 65 years), measures were obtained separately in the supine, resting position; after assuming an upright posture; and following isometric exercise with a hand dynamomter. In each of these situations there was an association between age and plasma NE level, with a correlation coefficient of about +0.50. There was no sex difference in levels. There was an age-related increase in the response of plasma NE to exercise stress in absolute units, but older subjects had higher baseline levels, so there was no actual increase in the percent increment over baseline levels (Ziegler et al., 1976). These findings imply increasing noradrenergic function as a person grows older; nevertheless, studies of NE levels in human brain tissue obtained at autopsy indicate declining brain NE concentrations during adulthood (D Robinson, 1975; D Robinson et al., 1977; D Robinson and Nies, 1980).

NE Precursors and Synthesizing Enzymes

Developmental changes in levels of NE precursors (tyrosine, dopa, or dopamine) in body fluids have not yet been identified. Tyrosine hydroxylase (TH) and aromatic amino acid decarboxylase (AAAD), the synthetic enzymes in the catecholamine pathway, are located intracellularly and are not measurable in human body fluids. Human brain TH activity has been assayed, in autopsy tissue, and decreased (McGeer et al., 1971; McGeer and McGeer, 1973) or was not associated with age during adulthood (Robinson et al., 1977). Dopamine-beta-hydroxylase (DBH), although it functions intracellularly, is released proportionally with NE from vesicles during exocytosis, so that it can be measured in serum. Serum DBH activity increases with age, particularly over the first few years of life; levels during the neonatal period approach the lower sensitivity limits of the assay (Freedman et al., 1972). The normal activity of serum DBH varies up to over 100-fold in a normal population, largely on a genetic basis, so that changes with age are difficult to demonstrate.

While subsequent studies replicated the reported increase in serum DBH activity over childhood and adolescence, the magnitude of the developmental effect was not as great (Weinshilboum et al., 1973; J Young et al., 1980f). Nevertheless, developmental changes in plasma NE and serum DBH activity appear to be consistent in indicating an increment in noradrenergic function.

NE Metabolism

Phenylethanolamine-N-methyltransferase (PNMT) converts NE to epinephrine (E), and might contribute to the regulation of developmental changes in NE levels. PNMT is an intracellular enzyme, so no age-related studies in peripheral fluids can be done. Similarly, no studies of developmental changes in plasma or urinary E levels have been completed.

Norepinephrine clearance from the synaptic space is accomplished by active reuptake and enzymatic catabolism. While age-related changes in the reuptake process have been demonstrated early in life in animal studies, it is not known if a similar developmental trend occurs at human neuronal membranes. Two enzymes degrade norepinephrine — catechol-O-methyltransferase (COMT) and monoamine oxidase (MAO). Clinical studies of monoamine oxidase (MAO) measure the activity present in blood platelets, although it is also accessible in human skin fibroblasts (Giller et al., 1980) and jejunal mucosa. In a study of children and adolescents with psychiatric disorders, and control subjects ranging from childhood through adulthood, there was a decrease in platelet MAO activity during childhood and adolescence. Although platelet MAO activity is greater in females, both sexes showed this age-related decrease in MAO activity (J Young et al., 1980b). Platelet and plasma MAO activities increase during the adult years (D Robinson, 1975; D Robinson et al., 1971, 1972, 1977; D Robinson and Nies, 1980; Belmaker et al., 1976; Mann, 1979), a pattern which holds true for brain autopsy tissue (D Robinson, 1975; D Robinson et al., 1971, 1972, 1977; D Robinson and Nies, 1980; Grote et al., 1974; Gottfries et al., 1974, 1975). A decrease in platelet MAO activity over the first two decades might result in a lower rate of degradation of NE, leading to higher levels of this amine. Obviously, it must be recalled that MAO is only one aspect of a complex control system for norepinephrine levels. In addition,

MAO occurs in two enzyme forms, Type A and Type B. Platelet MAO is Type B, whereas Type A MAO is much more active toward NE. Nevertheless, a decrease in platelet MAO activity agrees with a general trend of related compounds suggesting increasing levels of NE with age.

General patterns for enzyme maturation must be established for individual tissues, because differences occur in the activity of an enzyme across species, across organs within a single species, and among strains within a single species, as well as across development for an individual tissue. For example, COMT activity increases during early development in all tissues examined. (Stanton et al., 1975; Parvez et al., 1977), but there are critical differences with functional implications. The COMT activity in liver and kidney of the Fischer-344 (F-344) strain of rats is half that of the Wistar-Furth (W-F) strain; this difference, inherited in an autosomal recessive fashion, is present in newborn rats. In both strains, the COMT activity in liver and kidney generally is 10 to 100 times greater than that in other tissues (eg, brain, heart, or erythrocytes), and the relative maturational increase in COMT acitivity in liver and kidney is 5 to 10 times that of other tissues (Goldstein et al., 1980). While the developmental profile of enzyme activity in a particular human tissue might suggest a similar course in other tissues, this hypothesis always requires validation in the specific tissue.

The activity of COMT in brain autopsy material declines slightly during adulthood, but the lack of statistical significance suggests there is no relation with age (D Robinson et al., 1977). Clinical studies of the developmental pattern of COMT activity in red blood cells (Weinshilboum and Raymond, 1977) have not yet been reported. Human erythrocyte COMT activity is highly correlated with the activity of the enzyme in lung and kidney (Weinshilboum, 1978). It might be predicted that COMT activity in the erythrocyte will increase during childhood, as it does in the liver over the first six decades (Agathopoulos et al., 1971), as well as in other species.

The degradative enzymes apparently have opposite changes in their activity during childhood and adolescence: MAO decreases while COMT increases. MAO exerts its catabolic effects predominantly intraneuronally, so that a decrease in its activity would presumably have the functional effect of increasing the amount of neurotransmitter substrate available at the nerve terminal for release. On the other hand, there is a predominant extraneuronal locus for COMT activity, and its activity is greatest in metabolic-excretory organs—

liver, kidney, and lung (Goldstein et al., 1980; Weinshilboum, 1978). COMT functions especially in the degradation of catecholamines following release and activation of postsynaptic receptors. This indicates that COMT acts to remove circulating catecholamines present in the extracellular fluids. Its increasing activity parallels the increasing requirement for degradation of NE in body fluids during early development. In contrast to the action of MAO, which degrades intraneuronal NE before it is released into the synaptic space as an active neurotransmitter, COMT degrades NE after its release and exertion of its postsynaptic effect.

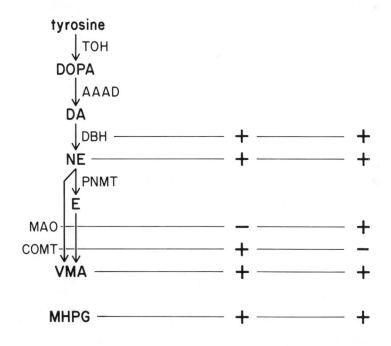

FIG. 1. Preliminary Survey of Known Developmental Changes in Norepinephrine-Related Compounds in Blood, Urine, and Spinal Fluid During Childhood and Adolescence, With Hypothetical Effect on Noradrenergic Activity.

Degradation of NE and E produces two major metabolites, vanillylmandelic acid (VMA) and 3-methoxy-4-hydroxy-phenyl-ethylene glycol (MHPG). There is a sharp increase in urinary VMA levels until puberty, when they appear to stabilize, although urinary VMA levels have not been well-characterized in adolescence (McKendrick and Edwards, 1965). It has been suggested that levels of MHPG in body fluids provide an index of brain noradrenergic activity (Maas et al., 1979, 1982); VMA is principally a metabolic product of peripheral sympathetic activity. A preliminary study of normal and autistic boys between ages 6 and 15 years indicated a strong correlation between urinary MHPG level and age (J Young et al., 1979).

These studies of NE metabolism indicate that two major NE metabolites, VMA and MHPG, increase in concentration in 24-hour urine samples over childhood, while platelet MAO activity decreases; the status of red blood cell COMT is not clear. Increasing levels of metabolite might be more likely to be associated with increasing activity of a catabolic enzyme, so the relation of these findings is not yet clear. Nevertheless, both a reduction in catabolic activity and an increase in metabolites appear to be associated with an increase in the neurotransmitter substrate (NE).

The composite developmental profile constructed for human noradrenergic activity through assessment of NE-related compounds in body fluids is consistent in indicating increasing noradrenergic function with age, particularly through early adulthood (Fig. 1).

DOPAMINERGIC SYSTEM

Assessment of the development of the human dopaminergic system includes a consideration of the conversion of dopamine (DA) to NE. Serum DBH activity and plasma NE increase with age over childhood, suggesting that more DA is converted to NE as the child grows older; this might imply that dopaminergic activity decreases with age, in agreement with the observation that DBH inhibitors increase DA synthesis and DA metabolites (Nyback, 1971; Anden et al., 1973). Developmental studies of plasma dopamine have not been done, but dopamine and 3-methoxytyramine (a DA metabolite) levels in brain tissue examined in autopsy decline during the adult years (D Robinson et al., 1977; Carlsson, 1976). MAO and COMT degrade dopamine, but the effects of developmental changes in COMT activity are not yet

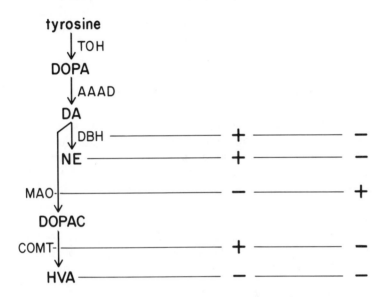

Compound	Change with development in childhood and adolescence	Postulated functional meaning for dopaminergic activity
tyrosine		
DOPA		
DA		
DBH	+	−
NE	+	−
MAO	−	+
DOPAC		
COMT	+	−
HVA	−	−

FIG. 2. Preliminary Survey of Known Developmental Changes in Dopamine-Related Compounds in Blood, Urine, and Spinal Fluid during Childhood and Adolescence, With Hypothetical Effect on Dopaminergic Activity.

clear. The gradual decline in platelet MAO activity during childhood and adolescence increases dopamine levels, hypothetically balancing the reduction in levels secondary to increasing DBH activity. The major metabolites of dopamine are 3,4-dihydroxyphenylacetic acid (DOPAC) and homovanillic acid (HVA). Levels of DOPAC in body fluids during childhood have not yet been determined, but spinal fluid HVA has been examined from 2 to 67 years of age (Bowers and Gerbode, 1968; Leckman et al., 1980). The negative relation between age and CSF HVA level implies a reduction in dopaminergic activity over the life-cycle (Leckman et al., 1980). Probenecid blocks the egress of acid metabolites from CSF, so that measurement of HVA in spinal fluid represents the accumulation of metabolite over the 12–18 hour period following probenecid administration. The direct relation of CSF to brain metabolism gives more assurance that the developmental profile of this metabolite reflects the changing activity of a brain neuronal system, rather than the potential intervening factors which may affect peripheral fluid findings. In summary, the developmental profile constructed by assessing serum DBH activity, platelet MAO activity, plasma NE levels, CSF HVA levels, and dopamine concentrations in autopsied brain tissue indicates decreasing dopaminergic activity as an individual grows older (Fig. 2).

SEROTONERGIC SYSTEM

Development of the serotonergic system is illustrative of effects of altering the balance between neuronal systems. Developmental profiles for precursor levels (tryptophan and 5-hydroxytryptophan) and synthesizing enzyme activities (tryptophan hydroxylase and AAAD) in body fluids and tissues have not yet been determined. Whole blood serotonin levels decrease over childhood and adolescence (Ritvo et al., 1971; J. Young et al., 1980a), while platelet MAO activity also decreases; a reduction in MAO activity might counterbalance decreasing levels of serotonin. However, the relation of platelet serotonin and MAO to each other and to their levels in brain has not been clarified.

Spinal fluid concentrations of 5-hydroxyindoleacetic acid (5-HIAA) are stable throughout the life-cycle (Leckman et al., 1980; S Young et al., 1981); in contrast to decreasing blood 5-HT levels, this indicates that serotonin turnover in the brain is maintained at a constant rate. Blood serotonin and spinal fuid 5-HIAA levels are stable measures in an individual, fluctuating within a relatively narrow range. Although both measures have not been obtained simultane-ously, their stability suggested examination of the relation between blood 5-HT and CSF 5-HIAA levels obtained from the same individuals at different times. In nine individuals there was a moderately strong association between the two. If further developmental studies were to substantiate a consistent relation between the two indices, blood serotonin could be utilized to directly estimate brain serotonin turnover.

Studies of both serotonin and 5-HIAA in human brain autopsy tissue have indicated that there is no relation of either to age

(D Robinson, 1975; Grote et al., 1974; Gottfries et al., 1974, 1975). Nevertheless, brain 5-HIAA was positively correlated with brain MAO activity, while NE and MAO levels were negatively related in brain (D Robinson, 1975). This suggests a functional correspondence among substrates, degradative enzyme, and metabolites with aging.

Whether there is a decrease in functional activity of the serotonergic system with development, or whether it remains constant, its ontogenetic profile is quite different from the increasing levels of NE (Fig. 3). This implies a changing balance between the two systems similar to that described in animals; while other potentially contributing neuronal systems must be considered in assessing overall effects, there might be functional effects secondary to the changing relation between these two neuronal systems. If serotonergic activity in the brain is predominantly inhibitory, then the increase in noradrenergic effects is subject to diminished opposition as an individual grows older.

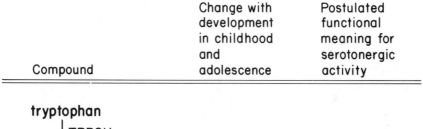

Compound	Change with development in childhood and adolescence	Postulated functional meaning for serotonergic activity
tryptophan		
↓TRPOH		
5-OHTRP		
↓AAAD		
5-HT (serotonin)	−	−
↓MAO	−	+
5-HIAA	no change	no change

FIG. 3. Preliminary Survey of Known Developmental Changes in Serotonin-Related Compounds in Blood, Urine, and Spinal Fluid in Childhood and Adolescence, With Hypothetical Effect on Serotonergic Activity.

DEVELOPMENTAL ALTERATIONS IN RECEPTOR FUNCTION

The development of receptor function consists of a change in the number of receptors (receptor density); the affinity of the receptor for a ligand remains constant. For example, the dissociation constant (K_d) for muscarinic binding in mouse cerebellum fails to change during the period when receptor number increases greatly (East and Dutton, 1980). This corresponds to the way that receptor function changes during senescence: the number of muscarinic receptors in aging mice brain decreases, while muscarinic receptor affinity is unchanged (Freund, 1980).

Developmental patterns for receptors cannot be generalized across neurotransmitters, brain regions, or species. For example, the density of receptors for neurotransmitters in the rat cerebral cortex is usually very low at birth, eg, β-adrenergic (Harden et al., 1977), muscarinic (Coyle and Yamamura, 1976), opiate (Coyle and Pert, 1976), and gabanergic (GABA) receptors (Coyle and Enna, 1976). However, this is not uniformly the case, as there is a relatively high density of benzodiazepine receptors at birth in the cortex, approximately two thirds of adult levels (Braestrup and Nielsen, 1978; Candy and Martin, 1979).

Species differences also occur in the developmental pattern for a specific type of receptor. A maximal level of muscarinic binding sites is achieved at a relatively earlier stage in the rabbit cerebellum than in the mouse cerebellum, where the maximal increase occurs during the second week (East and Dutton, 1980; Yavin and Harel, 1979).

How is receptor ontogeny related to the lines of development of other components of synaptic function? The concentration of β-adrenergic receptors in the rat cerebral cortex is very low at birth and the first week of life. A rapid increase occurs over the 7th to 14th postnatal days, so that adult levels of receptor number are reached by the end of the second week (Harden et al., 1977). There is a corresponding pattern for catecholamine stimulated adenylcyclase at the postsynaptic membrane: it is barely detectable in the first postnatal week, then rapidly increases to adult levels during the second week. This suggests that the development of catecholamines receptors permits activity of the catecholamine-sensitive adenylcyclase (Harden et al., 1977). On the other hand, there is little correlation between the ontogeny of presynaptic nerve terminals and postsynaptic development of β-adrenergic receptors, since, for example, the NE stored in the rat cerebral cortex reaches adult levels at two months after birth. Unlike the lack of relation between β-adrenergic receptor development and synaptogenesis, the development of muscarinic binding in both chick and rat brain is closely associated with the development of profiles for acetylcholine and choline acetyltransferase, implying a relation between increased binding and synaptogenesis (Coyle and Yamamura, 1976; Enna et al., 1976). Development of maximum synaptogenesis and increased muscarinic binding also coincides in the mouse cerebellum (East and Dutton, 1980).

There are possible behavioral correlates to the development of neurotransmitter receptors. When aged rats, with impairments in adaptive coordinated movements, are given agents which increase dopamine receptor stimulation (such as apomorphine or L-dopa) their coordination improves (Marshall and Berrios, 1979). Receptor-stimulating agents might compensate for the decreasing receptor density characteristic of various types of receptors during senescence.

Similarly, the number of β-adrenergic receptors (but not the affinity) decreases with age in the pineal gland of aged rats, leaving the pineal gland less responsive to diurnal changes in lighting conditions (Greenberg and Weiss, 1978).

HORMONAL MODULATION

The developmental course of a neuronal system, and levels of compounds which reflect these maturational changes, are affected by neuromodulators. For example, determination of the maturational sequence for thyroid function is critical for understanding its interaction with other developing systems. Thyroid hormones affect most tissues in the body, including neuronal systems and their neurotransmitters (Grave, 1977).

Developmental profiles have been mapped for rat serum triiodothyronine (T_3) and T_4 (DuBois and Dussault, 1977), the free forms of both hormones (Walker et al., 1980), serum thyroid-stimulating hormone (TSH) (Dussault, 1975), pituitary TSH (Dussault, 1975) hypothalamic TRH (Dussault, 1975), and brain T_3 nuclear receptors (Schwartz and Oppenheimer, 1978) in the late fetal and neonatal periods. During this period, the various thyroid hormones critically and permanently affect nervous tissue structure (Grave, 1977; McEwen, 1976). Activational effects, characteristic of the remainder of the lifespan, are permissive in nature and are reversible (McEwen, 1976); maturational patterns for thyroid function have not been as carefully assessed over the longer period.

A considerable portion of the maturation of the pituitary-thyroid axis in the rat occurs following birth. For example, the simultaneous developmental sequences for free T_3 (FT_3), free T_4 (FT_4), and TSH mirror increasing thyroidal responsiveness and the maturation of the negative feedback mechanism (DuBois and Dussault, 1977; Walker et al., 1980; Dussault, 1975). A preparatory surge in rat brain T_3 nuclear receptor concentration precedes the rise in serum T_3 level (Schwartz and Oppenheimer, 1978); this combined readiness then brings about the organizational effects of thyroid hormone on brain, such as facilitation of brain protein synthesis, enzyme function, and myelinogenesis (Grave, 1977).

Human umbilical cord serum has a low FT_3 concentration compared to euthyroid adults (Erenberg et al., 1974; Larsen et al., 1975). The cord FT_3 concentration is 50 percent of that in maternal serum; FT_4 and T_4 concentrations are similar in maternal and cord serum. Maximum T_3 levels are attained within the first 24 postnatal hours, fall to a nadir at 72 hours, and are mildly elevated at six weeks of age. Serum T_4 rises abruptly for the first two postnatal days, then gradually falls to the levels of cord serum by six weeks of age (Erenberg et al., 1974; Larsen et al., 1975).

When examined over the lifespan (5 to 93 years of age), serum T_3 decreases in both men and women (Rubenstein et al., 1973). This is not accounted for by a decrease in thyroxine-binding globulin (TBG).

Comparison of the abrupt, dramatic changes in thyroid function in the neonatal period and the subtle, gradual course over the rest of the lifespan emphasizes the association of organizational effects with sudden shifts, while activational effects operate through smaller, transient changes in thyroid function. However, the cumulative effect of such change can be profound.

Thyroid-catecholamine interactions occur in several tissues (Spaulding and Noth, 1975). Plasma NE and DBH and spinal fluid homovanillic acid (HVA, the major DA metabolite) have a negative relation with serum thyroxine levels when thyroid function is outside the normal range (Christensen, 1973; Stoffer et al., 1973; Noth and Spaulding, 1974; Nishizawa et al., 1974; Klawans and Shenker, 1972). This suggests a tendency toward a reciprocal, balancing relation between catecholamines and thyroxine, particularly at the extremes of their normal range. Clear relations between thyroxine levels and

platelet MAO activity or serum DBH activity in euthyroid subjects
have not been established (J Young et al., 1980b, 1980c, 1980e, 1980g).
However, there is a consistent relation between serum thyroxine levels
and age. Estimated free thyroxine levels decrease with age in males, in
both normal subjects and psychiatric patients (J Young et al., 1980d).
The simultaneous increase in noradrenergic activity and decrease in
thyroid function might reflect an ontogenetic functional balance
similar to that observed in short-term changes.

DEVELOPMENTAL TRENDS AND TRANSITIONS

Monoaminergic systems are active at the relatively abrupt transition
points of development. Neonatal adjustments to the external environment or pubertal maturation are periods associated with elevated
catecholamine turnover rates. Monoamines regulate the hypothalamic
releasing factors which control pituitary function and influence general
body homeostasis. These systems are particularly active during periods
requiring a major resetting of metabolic patterns and rates.

Assessment of childhood activity levels in relation to development
of dopaminergic function illustrates the relations of neuronal
maturation to slowly evolving developmental lines. Dopamine neurons
contribute to the organization and tempo of motor activity, and greater
dopaminergic activity is associated with increased motor activity and a
higher frequency of abnormal movements. Decreasing dopaminergic
activity during childhood and adolescence predicts what every parent
observes: peak levels of motor activity during early childhood, and
gradual tapering with development. Simultaneously, stable levels of
serotonergic activity assert more strength in their antagonistic
balance with dopaminergic activity, so that the inhibitory serotonergic
effects on motor function are increasingly evident. The noradrenergic
system tends to have an activating effect on motor behavior, and its
behavioral effects are not readily differentiated from the dopaminergic
system. Evidence implicating the noradrenergic system in movement
disorders has been difficult to isolate, and increasing noradrenergic
activity with age appears to not "fit" with decreasing activity levels.
These subtle distinctions between similar effects of two neuronal
systems on a single dimension of behavior crystallize the need to
determine relative contributions of neuronal systems with complementary effects. This will be a question for developmental research in the

next decade, and will be considered in relation to learning, anxiety, and other clinical dimensions.

The impact of neurotransmitter ontogeny on clinical phenomena might be more apparent during abrupt transitional periods, such as puberty or menarche. For example, the interaction of changing NE concentration and MAO activity at puberty could be a critical component of sexual maturation. Utilizing platelet MAO activity for the construction of a developmental curve for the enzyme, the point of greatest inflection is at puberty (J Young et al., 1980b). This decrease in activity of the platelet enzyme is accompanied by a reduction in MAO activity in the brain at puberty. The hypothalamus has the highest concentration of MAO activity in the brain (D Robinson et al., 1977), and hypothalamic NE regulates the output of gonadotropins and growth hormone, which participate in sexual development and growth at puberty. The intersection of decreasing MAO activity and increasing NE concentration in the hypothalamus might play a role in the initiation or elaboration of the phenomena of puberty. Whether they play a major or supporting role, or not part at all, in the onset of sexual changes mediated by pituitary hormones is a question for future research. The study of clinical maturational changes and meticulous sampling of neurotransmitters and related compounds will be a fundamental means for understanding development and pathology during adolescence (Cohen and Frank, 1975).

PATHOLOGY OF NEUROTRANSMITTER ONTOGENY

As profiles of neurotransmitter maturation are established with more assurance, the relation of abnormal developmental sequences at the molecular level to familiar clinical pathology will be clarified. Preliminary work suggests how this perspective might be applied. Studies of autistic and normal boys indicate that autistic children, as a group, excrete less urinary MHPG (J Young et al., 1979) and free catecholamines (J Young et al., 1978) over a 24-hour period. While serum DBH activity (J Young et al., 1980f) and thyroid function (Cohen et al., 1980b) in autistic children appear to be within the normal range, early studies of age-related changes in these measures suggest that their maturation might differ in these children. Serum DBH activity tends to increase with age during childhood and adolescence; yet in a group of autistic children this association did not hold. There appears to be no developmental change in DBH activity in autistic patients. Final conclusions cannot be drawn, since the large variance in serum DBH activity might mask developmental changes, or the autistic children might have been so close in age as to obscure age-related changes (J Young et al., 1980f).

Estimated free thyroxine (EFT) decreases with age in normal males, yet in autistic patients, this age-related change does not occur (J Young et al., 1980d). In contrast, there was a greater than normal age-related decrease in EFT in patients with Tourette's syndrome of chronic multiple tics (J Young et al., 1980d). These preliminary findings suggest the impact of alterations in developmental mechanisms. The negative, compensatory relation between catecholamine and thyroid hormone function was discussed earlier. The apparent reduction in noradrenergic activity in autistic children might induce a compensatory mechanism through which thyroid function is established at a higher level in these children. Conversely, the unusually fast rate of decrease in free thyroxine levels in children with Tourette's syndrome could be a compensatory mechanism; in a child with heightened noradrenergic activity (Cohen et al., 1979a), the overall effect would be to bring noradrenergic function closer to a normal level. The ameliorative effects of clonidine, which reduces noradrenergic activity, on Tourette's symptoms might be mediated through restoration of this balance (Cohen et al., 1979b).

A ratio can be formed to examine the functional linkage between two neuronal systems. When comparable indices are assayed in the same fluid or tissue, this is a productive approach. For example, in epileptic children spinal fluid HVA decreases with age, reflecting low central catecholamine levels characteristic of epilepsy, whereas CSF 5-HIAA levels are not changed. When expressed as a ratio, 5-HIAA/HVA, there is a positive association with age, also observed in other subject groups (B Shaywitz et al., 1980b). Expression in the form of a ratio succinctly describes the functional developmental change observed clinically. For example, there is less excessive, unmodulated motor activity as the individual grows older, reflecting a growing predominance of serotonergic inhibitory mechanisms. A ratio is not as clearly applicable when compounds are not in identical tissues or fluids (eg, platelet MAO activity and serum DBH activity); do not reflect a similar rate of clearance or metabolism in the fluid (eg, plasma NE and spinal fluid MHPG); or are not obtained simultaneously (eg, blood serotonin and urinary 5-HIAA). Investigation in the future may indicate that the use of ratios "across" fluids or time-frames may be permissible and useful in certain restricted instances.

SEX DIFFERENCES IN BIOCHEMICAL DEVELOPMENT

Sex differences in spinal fluid 5-HIAA levels and 5-HIAA/HVA ratios point out diagnostic implications of the developmental course of neurotransmitter systems (Leckman et al., 1980; B Shaywitz et al., 1980b; S Young et al., 1981). The higher 5-HIAA level and 5-HIAA/HVA ratio in girls could explain the greater capacity for modulation of behavior characteristic of girls during childhood, and their relatively reduced activity level when compared to a group of boys. The higher prevalence in boys of neuropsychiatric illnesses involving an excess of motor behavior, whether in quality or quantity, implies that the relative balance between dopamine and serotonergic activity may play a role in the genesis of these disorders (Leckman et al., 1980; B Shaywitz et al., 1980b, 1980c). A reduction in spinal fluid 5-HIAA levels, for example, has been described in autism (Cohen et al., 1977), Tourette's syndrome (Cohen et al., 1978), and attention deficit disorders (ADD) (B Shaywitz et al., 1978). Each of these disorders has a dysfunction of motor regulation as a principal component symptom, and each occurs primarily in males. Sex differences in the activity of an enzyme (eg, MAO may also have critical effects on development and pathology (J Young et al., 1980b).

DEVELOPMENTAL CHANGES IN RESPONSE TO MEDICATION

Developmental changes in neurotransmitter levels influence the response to medication. A familiar example is the "paradoxical" response to stimulants during childhood: rather than eliciting increased activity as in adults, stimulants affect children by organizing behavior so that they are more focused, less distractible, and show either a lower overall level of activity, or a reduction in undirected, adventitious activity. The explanations for this phenomenon at a tissue level have included a possible underarousal of inhibitory systems, a functional deficiency of dopaminergic activity on the basis of maturational lag or more serious pathology, or altered receptor sensitivity (S Shaywitz et al. 1978; B Shaywitz et al., 1980c). An alternative explanation suggests that catecholamine presynaptic autoreceptors are more sensitive to synaptic levels of the transmitter than the postsynaptic receptor (Carlsson, 1977; Bunney and Aghajanian, 1978). Low concentrations of a stimulant medication cause feedback, inhibition of catecholamines through effects at the autoreceptor, reducing overall activity, while the stimulant concentration is too low to affect postsynaptic receptors. The therapeutic effect in children is related to presynaptic inhibition, while in adults it results from postsynaptic activation. Changing levels of the neurotransmitter or a related enzyme would affect this delicate balance and critically influence which children are responders or nonresponders, and which children would experience toxic effects (J Young, 1981). A dose which was satisfactory for a child might not be sufficient two years later, or might be excessive, depending upon the neuronal system targeted. This might be viewed entirely in terms of drug tolerance, while actually it also reflects developmental changes in neurotransmitter levels. At this point, we cannot pinpoint abnormal transmitter interactions in an individual child. Most research findings reflect mean group levels. Relative levels of neurotransmitters and metabolites at a specific period of childhood need to be measured in large groups of children, and individual children followed longitudinally before typical developmental patterns among neuronal systems can be established. An intensive focus on mapping the maturation of specific neuronal systems in children, and correlating this with the development of behavioral dimensions, is required before these concepts can be confidently applied to determination of a dosage for an individual child.

RATE OF DEVELOPMENTAL CHANGE

An interesting finding has been the low 0.25 to 0.35 (positive or negative) correlation between age and the concentration of a particular compound, whether transmitter, metabolite, or enzyme. This low correlation reflects the many other actual or potential influences on levels of a particular compound, from genetic to environmental stress. It is apparent that a low correlation will not always be observed in a study with a small subject number. When the number of subjects reaches well over 100, there is a much better chance of detecting such an association. Until this low rate of development has been identified several times with different substances, it is easily dismissed as too small to be significant and probably the result of random chance. In fact, these might well be the "constitutional" influences on development which gradually will be articulated with developmental patterns established in other disciplines, as we attempt to understand the disorders of childhood (Young and Cohen, 1979).

OVERVIEW

The relatively prolonged development of animal neuronal systems is magnified in the human nervous system. Typical maturational patterns at the molecular level are emerging in studies of human neurotransmitter metabolism; limits of variation are becoming recognizable; and the beginnings of molecular disease are being defined. Different neuronal systems develop sequentially and simultaneously, but the times of specific maturational rate changes do not coincide. The complex time relationship among systems accentuates the potential hazards of developmental variation, since particular points of time might be characterized by a precarious balance among systems. The functional biological advantages of dissimilar developmental profiles for neuromaturational systems in the human nervous system are only beginning to be considered.

While compromised by methodological limitations and the inherent complexity of neuronal systems, the foundations of human developmental neurochemistry are being laid. The flexible structure of a child's emerging development, as well as pathological deviations, can now be examined through technical approaches capable of delineating aspects of biological maturation underlying psychological development.

ACKNOWLEDGMENTS

We would like to express our gratitude to Dr. A.J. Solnit, Director of the Child Study Center, New Haven, Connecticut, who has encouraged and directed our interest in child development. Ms. Janet Holliday, Ms. Mary Ellen Kavanagh, and Ms. Barbara Caparulo assisted at various critical points in these studies, and Ms. Diane Harcherik performed data analysis. Ms. Margrethe Cone and Ms. Sandra Greer prepared the manuscript.

This research was supported by the Irving Brooks Harris Fund, the William T. Grant Foundation, MG-CRC Grant #MH30929, CCRC Grant #RR 00125, NICHD Grant HD-03008, Mr. Leonard Berger, and The Solomon R. & Rebecca D. Baker Foundation, Inc.

REFERENCES

Agathopoulos A, Nicolopoulos D, Matsaniotis N, Papadatos C: Biochemical changes of catechol-O-methyltransferase during development of human liver. *Pediatrics* 47:125–128, 1971

Agrawal HC, Glisson SN, Himwich WA: Changes in monoamines of rat brain during postnatal ontogeny. *Biochi Biphys Acta* 130:511–513, 1966

Agrawal HC, Himwich WA: Amino acids, proteins and monoamines of developing brain, in Smith WA (ed): *Developmental Neurobiology,* 1970

Anden NE, Atack CV, Svensson TH: *Neural Transm* 34:93–000, 1973

Axelrod J, Mueller RA, Henry JP, Stephens PM: Changes in enzymes involved in the biosynthesis and metabolism of noradrenaline and adrenaline after psychosocial stimulation. *Nature* 225:1059–1060, 1970

Baker PC, Hoff KM, Smith MD: The maturation of monoamine oxidase and 5-hydroxyindoleacetic acid in regions of the mouse brain. *Brain Res* 65:255–264, 1974

Baker PC, Quay WB: 5-Hydroxytryptamine metabolism in early embryogenesis, and the development of brain and retinal tissues: A review. *Brain Res* 12:273–295, 1969

Belmaker RH, Ebbesen K, Ebstein R, Rimon R: Platelet monoamine oxidase in schizophrenia and manic-depressive illness. *Br J Psychiatry* 129:227–232, 1976

Bennett DS, Giarman NJ: Schedule of appearance of 5-hydroxytryptamine (serotonin) and associated enzymes in the developing rat brain. *Neurochem* 12:911–918, 1965

Bowers MB, Gerbode FA; Relationship of monoamine metabolites in human cerebrospinal fluid to age. *Nature* 219:1256, 1968

Braestrup C, Nielsen M: Ontogenetic development of benzodiazepine receptors in the rat brain. *Brain Res* 147:170–173, 1978

Breese GR, Traylor TD: Developmental characteristics of brain catecholamines and tyrosine hydroxylase in the rat: Effects of 6-hydroxydopamine. *Br J Pharmacol* 44:219–222, 1972

Breese GR, Smith RD, Mueller RA, et al.: Induction of adrenal catecholamine synthesizing enzymes following mother-infant separation. *Nature* 246:94–96, 1973

Bunney BS, Aghajanian GK: D-amphetamine-induced depression of central dopamine neurons: Evidence for mediation by both autoreceptors and a striato-nigral feedback pathway. *Naunyn Schmiedebergs Arch Pharmacol* 304:255–261, 1978

Candy JM, Martin IL: The postnatal development of the benzodiazepine receptor in the cerebral cortex and cerebellum of the rat. *J Neurochem* 32:655–658, 1979

Carlsson A: Some aspects of dopamine in the basal ganglia, in Yahr MD (ed): *The Basal Ganglia*. New York, Raven Press, 1976, pp. 181–189

Carlsson A: Dopaminergic autoreceptors: Background and implications, in Costa E, Gessa GL (eds): *Advances in Biochemical Psychopharmacology*, vol. 16. New York, Raven Press, 1977, pp 439–441

Christensen NJ: Plasma noradrenaline and adrenaline in patients with thyrotoxicosis and myxoedema. *Clin Sci Molec Med* 45:163–171, 1973

Cohen DJ, Frank R: Preadolescence: A critical phase of biological and psychological development, in Sandar DVS (ed): *Mental Health in Children*, vol. 1. Westbury, New York, PJD Publications Ltd, 1975, pp 129–165

Cohen DJ, Caparulo BK, Shaywitz BA, Bowers MB Jr: Dopamine and serotonin metabolism in neuropsychiatrically disturbed children: CSF homovanillic acid and 5-hydroxyindoleacetic acid. *Arch Gen Psychiatry* 34:545–550, 1977

Cohen DJ, Shaywitz BA, Caparulo B, et al.: Chronic, multiple tics of Gilles de la Tourette's disease. *Arch Gen Psychiatry* 35:245–250, 1978

Cohen DJ, Shaywitz BA, Young JG, et al.: Central biogenic amine metabolism in children with the syndrome of chronic multiple tics of Gilles de la Tourette: Norepinephrine, serotonin, and dopamine. *J Am Acad Child Psychiatry* 18:320–341, 1979a

Cohen DJ, Shaywitz BA, Young JG, Bowers MB Jr: Cerebrospinal fluid monoamine metabolites in neuropsychiatric disorders of childhood, in Wood J (ed): *Neurobiology of Cerebrospinal Fluid*. New York, Plenum Press, 1980a

Cohen DJ, Young JG: Neurochemistry and child psychiatry. *J Am Acad Child Psychiatry* 16:353–411, 1977

Cohen DJ, Young JG, Lowe TL, Harcherik D: Thyroid hormone in autistic children, 1980b

Cohen DJ, Young JG, Nathanson JA, Shaywitz BA: Clonidine in Tourette's syndrome. *Lancet,* September 15, 551–553, 1979b

Coyle JT: Development of central catecholamine neurons, in Schmitt FO, Worden FG (eds): *The Neurosciences: Third Study Program*. New York, Rockefeller University Press, 1974, pp 877–884

Coyle JT, Axelrod J: Development of the uptake and storage of L-(^{3}H) norepinephrine in the rat brain. *J Neurochem* 18:2061-2175, 1971

Coyle JT, Axelrod J: Dopamine-beta-hydroxylase in the rat brain: Developmental characteristics. *J Neurochem* 19:449–459, 1972a

Coyle JT, Axelrod J: Tyrosine hydroxylase in rat brain: Developmental characteristics. *J Neurochem* 19:1117–1123, 1972b

Golden GS: Prenatal development of the biogenic amine systems of the mouse.

Coyle JT, Enna SJ: Neurochemical aspects of the ontogenesis of Gabanergic neurons in the rat brain. *Brain Res* 111:113–119, 1976

Coyle JT, Henry D: Catecholamines in fetal and newborn rat brain. *J Neurochem* 21:61–67, 1973

Coyle JT, Pert CB: Ontogenetic development of (^{3}H)naloxone binding in rat brain. *Neuropharmacology* 15:555–560, 1976

Coyle JT, Yamamura HI: Neurochemical aspects of the ontogenesis of cholinergic neurons in the rat brain. *Brain Res* 118:429–440, 1976

Deguchi T, Barchas J: Regional distribution and developmental change of tryptophan hydroxylase activity in rat brain. *J Neurochem* 19:927–929, 1972

DuBois JD, Dussault JH: Ontogenesis of thyroid function in the neonatal rat: Thyroxine (T_4) and triiodothyronine (T_3) production rates. *Endocrinology* 101:435–441, 1977

Dussault JH: Development of the hypothalamic-pituitary-thyroid axis in the neonatal rat, in Fisher DA, Burrow GN (eds): *Perinatal Thyroid Physiology and Disease.* New York, Raven Press, 1975, pp 73–78

East JM, Dutton GR: Muscarinic binding sites in developing normal and mutant mouse cerebellum. *J Neurochem* 34:657–661, 1980

Eleftheriou BE, Boehlke KW: Brain monoamine oxidase in mice after exposure to aggression and defeat. *Science* 155:1693–1694, 1967

Enna SJ, Yamamura HI, Snyder SH: Development of muscarinic cholinergic and GABA receptor binding in chick embryo brain. *Brain Res* 101:177–183, 1976

Erenberg A, Phelps DL, Lam R, Fisher DA: Total and free thyroid hormone concentrations in the neonatal period. *Pediatrics* 53:211–216, 1974

Fibiger HC, Lytle LD, Campbell BA: Chroninergic modulation of adrenergic arousal in the developing rat. *J Comp Physiol Psychol* 72:384–389, 1970

Floeter MK, Greenough WT: Cerebellar plasticity: Modification of Purkinje cell structure by differential rearing in monkeys. *Science* 206:227–229, 1979

Freedman LS, Ohuchi T, Goldstein M, et al.: Changes in human serum dopamine-beta-hydroxylase activity with age. *Nature* 236:310–311, 1972

Freund G: Cholinergic receptor loss in brains of aging mice. *Life Sci* 26:371–375, 1980

Garelis E, Young SN, Lal S, Sourkes TL: Monoamine metabolites in lumbar CSF: The question of their origin in relation to clinical studies. *Brain Res* 79:1–8, 1974

Ghosh SK, Guha SR: Oxidation of monoamines in developing rat and guinea pig brain. *J Neurochem* 19:229–231, 1972

Giller EL, Young JG, Breaefield XO, et al.: Monoamine oxidase and catechol-O-methyltransferase activities in cultured fibroblasts and blood cells from children with autism and the Gilles de la Tourette syndrome. *Psychiatry Res* 2:187–197, 1980

Dev Biol 33:300–311, 1973

Goldstein DJ, Weinshilboum RM, Dunnette JH, Creveling CR: Developmental patterns of catechol-O-methyltransferase in genetically different rat strains: Enzymatic and immunochemical studies. *J Neurochem* 34:153–162, 1980

Gottfries CG, Oreland L, Wiberg A, Winblad B: Lowered monoamine oxidase activity in brains from alcoholic suicide. *J Neurochem* 25:667–673, 1975

Gottfries CG, Roos BE, Winblad B: Determination of 5-hydroxytryptamine, 5-hydroxyindoleacetic acid and homovanillic acid in brain tissue from an autopsy material. *Acta Psychiatr Scand* 50:496–507, 1974

Grave GD (ed): *Thyroid Hormones and Brain Development.* New York, Raven Press, 1977

Greenberg LH, Weiss B; Beta-adrenergic receptors in aged rat brain: Reduced number and capacity of pineal gland to develop supersensitivity. *Science* 201:61–63, 1978

Grote SS, Moses G, Robins E et al.: A study of selected catecholamine metabolizing enzymes: A comparison of depressive suicides and alcoholic suicides with controls. *J Neurochem* 23:701–802, 1974

Halegren E, Varon S: Serotonin turnover in cultured raphe nuclei from newborn rat: In vitro development and drug effects. *Brain Res* 48:438–442, 1972

Harden TK, Wolfe BB, Sporn JR, et al.: Ontogeny of beta-adrenergic receptors in rat cerebral cortex. *Brain Res* 125:99–108, 1977

Hoff KM, Baker PC, Buda RD: Free tryptophan levels in regions of the maturing mouse brain. *Brain Res* 73:376–379, 1974

Karki N, Kuntzman R, Brodie BB: Storage, synthesis, and metabolism of monoamines in the developing brain. *J Neurochem* 9:53–58, 1962

Kellogg C, Lundborg P: Inhibition of catecholamine synthesis during ontogenetic development. *Brain Res* 61:321–329, 1973

Kellogg C, Lundborg P: Ontogenetic variations in responses to L-dopa and monoamine receptor-stimulating agents. *Psychopharmacologia* 23:187–200, 1972a

Kellogg C, Lundborg P: Uptake and utilization of (^{3}H) 5-hydroxytryptophan by brain tissue during development. *Neuropharmacology* 11:363–372, 1972b

Klawans HL Jr, Shenker DM: Observations on the dopaminergic nature of hyperthyroid chorea. *J Neural Transm* 33:73–81, 1972

Kuzuya H, Nagatsu T: Flavins and monoamine oxidase activity in the brain, liver, and kidney of the developing rat. *J Neurochem* 16:123–125, 1969

Lal S, Sourkes TL: Ontogeny of stereotyped behavior induced by apomorphine and amphetamine in the rat. *Arch Int Pharmacodyn* 202:171–182, 1973

Lamprecht F, Coyle JT: Dopa decarboxylase in the developing rat brain. *Brain Res* 41:503–506, 1972

Larsen RP, Abuid J: Serum tri-iodothyromine and thyroxine in neonates and in early infancy, in Fisher DA, Burrow GN (eds): *Perinatal Thyroid Physiology and Disease.* New york, Raven Press, 1975, pp 211–220

Lauder JM, Bloom FE: Ontogeny of monoamine neurons in the locus coeruleus, raphe nuclei and substantia nigra of the rat. *J Comp Neurol* 155:469–482, 1974

Leckman JF, Cohen DJ, Shaywitz BA, et al.: CSF monoamine metabolites in child and adult psychiatric patients. *Arch Gen Psychiatry* 37:677–681, 1980

Loizou LA: The postnatal ontogeny of monoamine-containing neurons in the central nervous system of the albino rat. *Brain Res* 40:395–418, 1972

Loizou LA, Salt P: Regional changes in monoamines of the rat brain during postnatal development. *Brain Res* 20:467–470, 1970

Maas JW (ed): *MHPG in Psychopathology.* New York, Academic Press, 1982

Maas JW, Hattox SE, Greene NM, Landis DH: 3-Methoxy-4-hydroxyphenethyl-eneglycol production by human brain in vivo. *Science* 205:1025–1027, 1979

Mabry PD, Campbell BA: Developmental psychopharmacology, in Iversen LL, Iversen SD, Snyder SH (eds): *Handbook of Psychopharmacology,* vol. 7. New York, Plenum Press, 1977, pp 393–444

Mabry PD, Campbell BA: Ontogeny of serotonin inhibition of catecholamine-induced behavioral arousal. *Brain Res* 49:381–391, 1974

Mann J: Altered platelet monoamine oxidase activity in affective disorders. *Psychol Med* 9:727–736, 1979

Marshall JF, Berrios N: Movement disorders of aged rats: Reversal by dopamine receptor stimulation. *Science* 206:477–479, 1979

McEwen BS: Endocrine effects on the brain and their relationship to behavior, in Siegal GJ, Albers RW, Katzman R, Agranoff BW (eds): *Basic Neurochemistry.* Boston, Little, Brown, & Co., 1976, pp 737–764

McGeer EG, McGeer PL: Some characteristics of brain tyrosine hydroxylase, in Mandell AJ (ed): *New Concepts in Neurotransmitter Regulation.* London, Plenum Press, 1973, pp 53–68

McGeer EG, McGeer PL, Wada JA; Distribution of tyrosine hydroxylase in human and animal brain. *J Neurochem* 18:1647–1658, 1971

McKendrick T, Edwards RWH: The excretion of 4-hydroxy-3-methoxy-mandelic acid by children. *Arch Dis Child* 40:418-425, 1965

Nishizawa Y, Hamada N, Fujii S, et al.: Serum dopamine-beta-hydroxylase activity in thyroid disorders. *J Clin Endocrinol Metab* 39:599–601, 1974

Noth RH, Spaulding SW: Decreased serum dopamine-beta-hydroxylase in hyperthyroidism. *J Clin Endocrinol Metab* 39:614–617, 1974

Nyback H: *Acta Pharmacol Toxicol (Copenh)* 30:372

Parvez S, Ishmahan G, Parvez H: Influence of perinatal adrenalectomy and adrenal demedullation upon development of enzyme catechol-O-methyltransferase in peripheral organs of the rat. *Horm Res* 8:159–170, 1977

Pearson DE, Teicher MH, Shaywitz BA, et al.: Environmental influences on body weight and behavior in developing rats after neonatal 6-hydroxydopamine. *Science* 209:715–717, 1980

Porcher W, Heller A: Regional development of catecholamine biosynthesis in rat brain. *J Neurochem* 19:1917–1930, 1972

Pysh JJ, Weiss GM: Exercise during development induces an increase in Purkinje cell dendritic tree size. *Science* 206:230–231, 1979

Ritvo E, Yuwiler A, Geller E, et al.: Maturational changes in blood serotonin levels and platelet counts. *Biochem Med* 5:90–96, 1971

Robinson N: Histochemistry of monoamine oxidase in the developing rat brain. *J Neurochem* 14:1083–1089, 1967

Robinson N: Histochemistry of rat brain stem monoamine oxidase during maturation. *J Neurochem* 15:1151–1158, 1968

Robinson DS: Changes in monoamine oxidase and monoamines with human development and aging. *Fed Proc* 34:103–107, 1975

Robinson DS, Davis JM, Nies A, et al.: Relation of sex and aging to monoamine oxidase activity of human brain, plasma and platelets. *Arch Gen Psychiatry* 24:536–539, 1971

Robinson, DS, Nies A: Demographic, biologic, and other variables affecting monoamine oxidase activity. *Schizophr Bull* 6:298–307, 1980

Robinson DS, Nies A, Davis JN, et al.: Ageing, monoamines, and monoamine-oxidase levels *Lancet,* February 5, 1972, 290–291

Robinson DS, Sourkes TL, Nies A, et al.: Monoamine metabolism in human brain. *Arch Gen Psychiatry* 34:89–92, 1977

Rubenstein HA, Butler VP Jr, Werner SC: Progressive decrease in serum triiodothyronine concentrations with human aging: Radioimmunoassay following extraction of serum. *J Clin Endocrinol Metab* 37: 247–253, 1973

Rutledge CO: Factors influencing the effects of drugs administered during development on adult behavior, in Vernadakis A, Weiner N (eds): *Drugs and the Developing Brain.* New York, Plenum Press, 1974, pp 61–65

Satterfield JH, Cantwell DP, Satterfield BT: Multimodality treatment: A one-year follow-up of 84 hyperactive boys. *Arch Gen Psychiatry* 36:965–974, 1979

Schmidt MJ, Sanders-Busche E: Tryptophan hydroxylase activity in developing rat brain. *J Neurochem* 18:2549–2551, 1971

Schwartz HL, Oppenheimer JH: Ontogenesis of 3,5,3'-triiodothyronine receptors in neonatal rat brain: Dissociation between receptor concentration and stimulation of oxygen consumption by 3,5,5' triiodothyronine. *Endocrinology* 103:943–948, 1978

Shaywitz BA, Cohen DJ, Bowers MB Jr: Cerebrospinal fluid monoamine metabolites in neurological disorders of childhood, in Wood J (ed): *Neurobiology of Cerebrospinal Fluid.* New York, Plenum Press, 1980a, pp 219–236

Shaywitz BA, Cohen DJ, Leckman JF, et al.: Ontogeny of dopamine and serotonin metabolites in the cerebrospinal fluid of children with neurological disorders. *Dev Med Child Neurol* 22:748–754, 1980b

Shaywitz BA, Cohen DJ, Shaywitz SE, Young JG: Biochemical influences in attention deficit disorder (ADD)—results from human and animal investigations, in Wise G, Blaw M, Procopis PG (eds): *Topics in Child Neurology.* New York, Spectrum Publications, in press

Shaywitz BA, Klopper JH, Gordon JW: Methylphenidate in 6-hydroxydopamine treated developing rat pups. Effects on activity and maze performance. *Arch Neurol* 35:463, 1978

Shaywitz BA, Yager RD, Klopper JH: Selective brain dopamine depletion in developing rats: An experimental model of minimal brain dysfunction. *Science* 191(4224):305–308, 1976

Shaywitz SE, Cohen DJ, Shaywitz BA: The biochemical basis of minimal brain dysfunction. *J Pediatr* 92:179–187, 1978

Shih JH, Eiduson S: Multiple forms of monoamine oxidase in developing brain: Tissue and substrate specificities. *J Neurochem* 18:1221–1227, 1971

Shimizu N, Morikawa N: Histochemical study of monoamine oxidase in the developing rat brain. *Nature* 184:650–651, 1959

Solnit AJ: Change and the sense of time, in Anthony EJ, Chiland C (eds): *The Child in His Family in a Changing World.* New York, John Wiley & Sons, 1979, pp 21–37

Solnit AJ: The meaning of change in child development, in Anthony DJ, Chiland C (eds): *The Child in His Family: Children and Their Parents in a Changing World.* New York, John Wiley & Sons, 1978, pp 299–317

Spaulding SW, Noth RH: Thyroid-catecholamine interactions. *Med Clin North Am* 59:1123–1131, 1975

Stanton HC, Cornejo RA, Mersmann HJ, et al.: Ontogenesis of monoamine oxidase and catechol-O-methyltransferase in various tissues of domestic swine. *Arch Int Pharmacodyn Ther* 213:128–144, 1975

Stoffer, SS, Jiang NS, Gorman CA, Pikler GM: Plasma catecholamines in hypothyroidism and hyperthyroidism. *J Clin Endocrinol Metab* 36:587–589, 1973

Tyce G, Flock EV, Owen CA: Tryptophan metabolism in the brain of the developing rat. *Prog Brain Res* 9:198–203, 1964

Walker P, Dubois JD, Dussault JH: Free thyroid hormone concentrations during postnatal development in the rat. *Pediatr Res* 14:247–249, 1980

Weinshilboum R: Human erythrocyte catechol-O-methyltransferase: Correlation with lung and kidney activity. *Life Sci* 22:625–630, 1978

Weinshilboum R, Raymond FA: Inheritance of low erythrocyte catechol-O-methyltransferase activity in man. *Am J Hum Genet* 29:125–135, 1977

Weinshilboum R, Raymond FA, Weidman WH: Serum dopamine-beta-hydroxylase activity: Sibling-sibling correlation. *Science* 181:943–945, 1973

Yavin E, Harel S: Muscarinic binding sites in the developing rabbit brain, regional distribution and ontogenesis in the prenatal and early neonatal cerebellum. *FEBS Lett* 94:151–154, 1979

Young JG: Methylphenidate-induced hallucinosis: Case histories and possible mechanisms of action. *Dev Behav Pediat* 2:35–38, 1981

Young JG, Belendiuk K, Freedman DX, et al.: Blood serotonin in early childhood autism and Gilles de la Tourette's syndrome. Submitted for publication, 1980a

Young JG, Cohen DJ: The molecular biology of development, in Noshpitz J (ed): *Basic Handbook of Child Psychiatry*. New York, Basic Books, Inc, 1979, pp 22–62

Young JG, Cohen DJ, Brown SL, Caparulo BK: Decreased urinary free catecholamines in childhood autism. *J Am Acad Child Psychiatry* 17:671–678, 1978

Young JG, Cohen DJ, Caparulo BK, et al.: Decreased 24-hour urinary MHPG in childhood autism. *Am J Psychiatry* 136:1055–1057, 1979

Young JG, Cohen DJ, Waldo MC, et al.: Platelet monomaine oxidase activity in children and adolescents with psychiatric disorders. *Schizophr Bull* 6:324–333, 1980b

Young JG, Feiz R, Roth JA, et al.: Studies of catecholamine-thyroid hormone interactions. I. Thyroid hormone and platelet monomaine oxidase activity in psychiatrically disturbed children. *J Autism Dev Disord,* in press

Young JG, Holliday J, Lowe TL, Cohen DJ: Developmental changes in serum thyroxine indices. Submitted for publication, 1980d

Young JG, Kyprie RM, Cohen DJ: Studies of catecholamine-thyroid hormone interactions. III. Lack of association between serum dopamine-beta-hydroxylase activity and thyroxine in euthyroid subjects. *J Autism Dev Disord,* in press, 1980c

Young JG, Kyprie RM, Ross NT, Cohen DJ: Serum dopamine-beta-hydroxylase activity. *J Autism Dev Disord* 10:1–14, 1980f

Young JG, Sprague MM, Cohen DJ, et al.: Studies of catecholamine-thyroid hormone interactions. II. Thyroid hormone and platelet monoamine oxidase activity in patients with thyroid disorders. *J Autism Dev Disord,* in press 1980g

Young SN, Gauthier S, Anderson GM, Purdy WC: Tryptophan, 5-hydroxyindoleacetic acid and indoleacetic acid in human cerebrospinal fluid: Interrelationships and the influence of age, sex, epilepsy and anticonvulsant drugs. *J Neurol Neurosurg Psychiatry* 222:112–115, 1981

Ziegler MD, Lake CR, Kopin IJ: Plasma noradrenaline increases with age. *Nature* 261:333–335, 1976

5

Sleep Studies in Children with Psychiatric Disorders

JOVAN SIMEON

Most sleep problems in children are transient and developmental phenomena, and are usually ignored, minimized, or not recognized by their parents. These disorders come to the attention of professionals when they become disturbing to the parent, or when the child's complaints persist, and usually pediatricians and not child psychiatrists are asked for help. Most parents know very little about their child's sleep patterns, preoccupations, and other manifestations associated with sleep. As child psychiatrists evaluate and treat children with psychiatric problems almost exclusively, they tend to form strongly biased opinions that the child's sleep problems are invariably associated with psychopathology, and due to emotional difficulties.

The older literature contains many statements and assumptions about sleep in children apparently derived from clinical observations, anecdotal reports, or theories and speculations that have little factual basis. In the past 20 years a great deal of sleep research in children has been undertaken; advances have been due largely to the remarkable progress in electronics, computer technology, and statistics. Some of the many sophisticated quantitative methods have been reviewed or described by Itil and Shapiro (1968), Dumermuth and Scollo-Lavizzari (1972), Williams et al. (1974), Williams and Karacan (1976), Saletu (1976) and Bowe and Anders (1979). Sleep electroencephalogram (EEG) investigations have facilitated the diagnosis and treatment of many childhood disorders. Significant progress has been made in the understanding of sleep mechanisms of various sleep disorders, such as nightmares, sleepwalking, sleeptalking, and nocturnal enuresis; the development of sleep patterns in the newborn and during childhood; medical disorders such as infant prematurity, brain damage, mental retardation, and epilepsy; and the circadian patterns of hormonal activity.

In spite of the remarkable progress made in the study of sleep, the diagnosis and therapy of sleep disorders in most children are still empirical. Furthermore, in daily practice the frequent sleep pathology associated with many child psychiatric disorders — such as hyperactivity, anxiety, depression, and psychosis — is frequently ignored or minimized. This is partly due to the belief that the sleep pathology will improve if the primary disorder is effectively treated, and partly to the time-consuming and expensive nature of all-night sleep EEG investigations. Most neglected areas of sleep research have been those of pediatric psychopharmacology (especially when compared to the extensive research in adults) and of children with hyperkinetic, aggressive, depressive, and learning disorders.

There are three overlapping areas in the study of sleep in children: (1) the development of sleep patterns, (2) sleep disorders in general, and (3) sleep in psychiatric disorders. This review will focus on the last area, and on relevant data from the first two.

DEVELOPMENT OF SLEEP PATTERNS IN CHILDHOOD

There are marked similarities as well as important individual differences in the development of sleep patterns from infancy to adolescence. Newborns alternate between sleep and awake states in cycles of about 50 to 60 minutes, and usually sleep for about 16 hours a day. There are individual differences, however, possibly indicating lifelong patterns, as some newborns sleep for only 10 hours a day and others sleep for over 20 hours. Maturation of the ability to sustain sleep and wakefulness coincides with the development of sustained visual attention (Parmelee, 1970). A night-day rhythm becomes established by the end of the first month, and the waking periods decrease from about six to two a day in the first year. With age, there are decreases in the length of sleep, REM percent, and Stage 4 sleep. The duration of sleep shortens from about 16 hours a day at birth, to about 8 to 9 hours in 12 to 17-year-old adolescents, to about 7 hours between the ages of 25 and 45. REM duration decreases from about 50 percent of the total sleep time at birth, to 38 percent at the age of 43 weeks, to 25 percent around one to two years of age, to 20 percent at puberty. The duration of Stage 3 and 4 sleep also decreases from about 20 percent to 30 percent in childhood, to about 15 percent to 20 percent by the age of 20, to 10 percent to 15 percent in the young adult; by the age of 60 there is practically no delta sleep. As one grows older sleep becomes lighter and less efficient (Hauri, 1977).

It is becoming increasingly apparent that to properly understand the various physical and psychological manifestations of wakefulness and sleep, normal and abnormal behavior—especially in the developing organism—it is essential to investigate the circadian and ultradian rhythms and mechanisms, rather than phenomena during fixed or limited time periods. During childhood the various physiological systems develop adult circadian rhythms at different ages (Hellbrügge et al., 1964). This staggered acquisition of circadian rhythms suggests more than one "clock" in the brain. An example of the importance of circadian rhythms in relation to sleep-wake cycles, growth, and psychopharmacology is the development and secretion of hormones. The secretion of human growth hormone (HGH), luteinizing hormone during puberty, and prolactin is increased during the first two hours of sleep, when Stages 3 and 4 predominate (Sassin et al., 1969, 1972; Boyar et al, 1972; Broughton, 1974). This relationship of HGH secretion to sleep was not seen in infants, and at about five weeks of age HGH was higher during REM sleep (Anders et al., 1970). Cortisol secretion in the newborn increases in response to arousal and stress and is highest when crying; no ciradian rhythm or correlation with the sleep schedule is apparent (Anders et al., 1970). Children under the age of two show no consistent adult circadian rhythm of cortisol secretion (Tennes and Vernadakis, 1977). It is only at about the age of three that an adult-type circadian rhythm develops with a maximum secretion in the second half of the night when REM sleep predominates (Franks, 1967). Our knowledge of the role of psychoendocrinological factors in child psychiatry disorders is extremely limited. An illustration of the clinical usefulness of quantitative analysis of sleep which allows for the control of therapy is in hypothyroid infants in whom sleep spindles during quiet sleep appear two weeks after thyroid hormone administration (Schultz et al., 1968).

According to Ames (1964), sleep difficulties seen in normal children are characteristic for the various age groups: for example, rocking and head-banging are most frequent during the going-to-sleep period in the first two years of life, bedtime demands in the two year old, bedtime rituals in the 2½ year old, and waking up and getting up in the middle of the night in the three year old. The type of night fears is also characteristic for various age groups: the 2½ year olds are afraid of the dark, the 3½ of bugs, the 5½ of wild animals, the six year old of somebody hiding under the bed, and the seven year old of shadows, ghosts, and robbers. The peak age periods for nightmares are five to seven years and ten to thirteen. In general, during the first eight years sleep problems first appear at bedtime, move to the middle of the night, and then move to the waking period. By eight years of age, sleep problems again occur at bedtime, in the preteen years during the night, and in early teens in the morning. These and other sleep-related problems are real to the child and should be recognized.

In a developmental study of normal children, 21 months to 14 years of age, Macfarlane et al. (1954) investigated the frequency of disturbing dreams and restless sleep, and their correlations with other behavioral and physical factors. They reported that the age peaks for disturbing dreams were at three years for both boys and girls (29 percent), and six years for girls (35 percent), with the highest peak at ten years for both groups (47 percent for girls, 33 percent for boys). Disturbing dreams were highly correlated with restless sleep, temper tantrums, irritability, and poor nutrition in boys, and restless sleep and overdependence in girls. Restless sleep was most frequent for both sexes at 21 months (38 percent for boys, 27 percent for girls), and following a drop at the age of four, it increased at the age of ten to twelve years (27 percent for boys, 17 percent for girls). Restless sleep was highly correlated with disturbing dreams, and in boys with negativism, soiling, speech difficulties, and tempers; with timidity and excessive dependence in girls.

A great deal is as yet unknown about the relationship between healthy or pathological sleep patterns and daytime behavior and learning. From a practical viewpoint, clinicians often see cases where developmental sleep difficulties have become a constant source of conflict between parents and children. Preconceived rigid or overly permissive parental attitudes on bedtime, need for naps, and amounts of sleep can turn a developmental sleep irregularity into a problem.

DAYTIME SLEEPINESS

The quantity and quality of sleep in children has immediate effects on daytime waking behavior and important long-term consequences. Poor and inadequate sleep often results in obvious impairments of behavior the following day. In many cases, however, such impairments and their causes are much less obvious. Professionals and parents often fail to recognize that there are large differences between individual children of the same age with regard to the quantity of sleep needed and that the average norms do not apply to every child. If a child remains sufficiently alert and energetic in all of his daytime activities, it can be assumed that sleep is adequate. If there are periods of sleepiness and tiredness, and increased nighttime sleep does not result in improvement, medical or psychological pathology should be further investigated. Diseases of excessive daytime sleepiness such as narcolepsy and sleep apnea should be suspected. Daytime sleepiness does not appear to be a common problem in the 10 to 13-year-old children, in contrast to adolescents in whom chronic sleep deficits begin to occur, affecting later functioning (Anders et al., 1978). Studies on the chronically sleepy child are practically nonexistent, and teachers, pediatricians, and child psychiatrists often fail to recognize the disorder. Children with excessive daytime sleepiness are often labeled as "lazy," "inattentive," "poor learners," "hyperactive," "mentally retarded," or as having emotional problems (Navelet et al., 1976). These authors studied the histories of 88 adult narcolepsy patients, and showed that about 20 percent were considered "long sleepers" by their families both at the ages of five and ten, and that in 37 percent, diurnal sleepiness and inappropriate napping interfered with learning and social adjustment by the age of 15. In addition, 13 percent were considered hyperactive prior to their later recognition as "sleepy" children or adolescents. Daytime sleepiness, "microsleep" episodes, and the rare syndrome of sleep apnea in children (Guilleminault et al., 1976) result in school failure and abnormal daytime behavior. Sleep apnea has also been related to the infant sudden death syndrome (Weitzman and Graziani, 1974).

A promising development in the understanding and treatment of sleep and arousal disorders is gamma-hydroxybutyrate (GHB), a substance which is a normal constituent of the central nervous system (CNS). It has hypnotic properties but does not inhibit REM or NREM sleep, and does not show the development of tolerance. Successful efforts to treat patients with narcolepsy, cataplexy, and severe insomnia (Cleghorn et al., 1979) by "normalizing" their nocturnal sleep patterns (Broughton and Mamelak, 1979) ought to stimulate studies of GHB in childhood sleep disorders.

SLEEP IN CHILDREN WITH CNS AND ASSOCIATED MENTAL DISORDERS (PREMATURITY, BRAIN DAMAGE, MENTAL RETARDATION, EPILEPSY):

The sleep patterns in infancy develop according to a precise time schedule which allows for a determination of the conceptual age. In premature infants the normally present cyclic rhythm during sleep is absent. Awake and sleep states have a similar morphology and spatial distribution; there is an absence of interhemispheric synergy, and electrical activity is discontinuous, paroxysmal, and with long silences (Dreyfus-Brisac, 1964). At the conceptual age of eight months a differentiation appears between the awake and sleep states, with a continuous electrical activity and some interhemispheric synergy. In neonates there are two distinct sleep stages — active and quiet sleep; a reduction of sleep spindles and a generalized slowing is a possible indication of abnormal brain maturation (Parmelee et al., 1968). From a diagnostic and prognostic view, according to these investigators, it is important to identify the amount of sleep spindles and slow waves at various ages, as they may indicate deviations in the normal sequence of EEG maturation.

In the severely brain-damaged newborn there is a complete lack of sleep cycling. In infants with lesser neurological impairment there are unusually frequent and irregular sleep state shifts (Dreyfus-Brisac, 1975). Abnormalities of quiet sleep organization have been described in mild birth trauma (Prechtl et al., 1969), and in children of diabetic (Schulte et al., 1969), toxemic (Schulte et al., 1972), and heroin-addicted mothers (Schulman, 1969).

In patients with mental retardation of various etiologies, findings have included decreased REM activity, decreased percentages of Stage

1, 2 and 3 sleep accompanied by decreased sleep spindles in subjects under ten years of age, and no significant changes of the percentage of Stage 4 sleep. There is also a dissociation between the electromyogram (EMG) on one hand and the EEG and electro-oculogram (EOG) of REM sleep on the other (Petre-Quadens, 1972). It was not possible to differentiate between the various types of mental retardation on the basis of sleep characteristics. The "normalization," of the sleep stages and EMG at puberty may be due to endocrine influences. REM sleep abnormalities have also been found in children with chromosome abnormalities (Petre-Quadens and Jouvet, 1967) and nonspecific mental retardation (Feinberg, 1968). A positive association has been reported between the amount of REM and intellectual levels in retarded adults (Feinberg, 1968). It has been suggested that during sleep the brain carries out processes required for cognition, and that REM time is increased when active learning processes are going on during waking.

Sleep EEGs are important diagnostic tools in epilepsy. Most of the generalized epileptic discharges appear activated in some form during NREM sleep, and suppressed during REM sleep (Gastaut and Broughton, 1972). In some cases of petit mal and partial seizures, REM sleep may have an activating effect (Passouant and Cadilhac, 1970). Epileptic discharges can also be activated by sleep deprivation (White, 1970). Rarely, epileptic seizures occur only during sleep. In children with occasional episodes of bedwetting, nightmares, and poor sleep, the sleep EEG may clarify the differential diagnosis.

PARASOMNIAS (SOMNAMBULISM, NIGHT TERRORS, SLEEPTALKING, ENURESIS, BRUXISM)

These sleep disorders are rather frequent in children, and research findings have been extensively reported. Children are most difficult to arouse during the first two hours after sleep onset, when sleep Stages 3 and 4 predominate and when most of these sleep disorders occur. Somnambulism, night terrors, and less often enuresis, appear as manifestations of a partial arousal from delta sleep, and have been defined as disorders of arousal (Broughton, 1968). The disorders are usually outgrown by late adolescence. Parasomnias are rarely associated with dreaming, carry no symbolic meaning, and are unlikely to be manifestations of psychopathology, especially in the younger child. Somnambulism can be triggered in most sleepwalkers by lifting the child to his feet during delta sleep (Kales et al., 1966a). Sleepwalking can be associated with other clinical conditions or sleep disorders, such as epilepsy (Jacobsen and Kales, 1967), EEG abnormalities, CNS infection, or trauma (Huber, 1962), enuresis (Bakwin, 1970), sleeptalking (Kales et al., 1966b) and nightmares (Edmonds, 1967). Somnambulism can also be induced by various psychotropic drugs (Huapaya, 1979). Sleepwalkers up to age 16 show more frequent bursts of high voltage delta activity during slow-wave sleep than normal subjects (Kales et al., 1966a).

There has been some confusion in the use of the terms night terrors and nightmares. Night terrors (pavor nocturnus in children) are slow-wave sleep arousal phenomena, while nightmares are bad dreams or dream anxiety attacks which take place during REM sleep (Fisher et al., 1970). There are many similarities between somnambulism and night terrors: in both, onset and termination are sudden, there is no awareness of the environment during the attack, patients are difficult to arouse, and there is no recollection of the event, which occurs during Stage 4 sleep. There is often a family history of either or both disorders (Kales et al., 1977). Night terrors are associated with marked expressions of fear and autonomic discharge; sometimes they can be the first manifestation of temporal lobe epilepsy or sleep apnea. In contrast, the REM sleep nightmare is usually related to psychopathology and psychological conflicts.

Enuresis may occur during any sleep stage during changes from deeper to lighter EEG sleep or wakefulness. Only occasional episodes have been observed during REM (Ritvo et al., 1969). While in some cases of nocturnal enuresis EEGs are reported abnormal or immature (Turton and Spear, 1953), in others EEG abnormalities are either absent or very rare (Poussaint et al., 1967).

Most sleep talking also occurs during NREM sleep, although certain individuals seem to talk almost exclusively during REM sleep (André-Balisaux and Gonsette, 1956). Bruxism occurs during Stage 2 sleep and is also an arousal phenomenon (Satoh and Harada, 1971).

SLEEP IN CHILDREN WITH VARIOUS PSYCHIATRIC DISORDERS

In a study of sleep disturbances in 1,000 children referred to a child psychiatry clinic, Shirley and Kahn (1958) found that parents had 188 complaints about their children's sleep habits. The number of complaints was related to restless sleep (52), talking in sleep (27), nightmares (25), irregular sleep habits (19), night terrors (15), walking in sleep (13), and objections to going to bed (7); other complaints were less frequent.

In a large study of children's behavior syndromes and parental responses by Jenkins et al. (1966), sleep patterns were related to the diagnosis. Unsocialized children with conduct disorder were found to have irregular bedtimes and trouble going to sleep; socialized delinquent children had a significant frequency of sleepwalking; brain-damaged children were early risers; overanxious children were more prone to nightmares; and withdrawn children were more prone to difficulties in going to sleep.

From a sample of 831 emotionally disturbed 12 to 18-year-old adolescents in therapy, Monroe and Marks (1977) compared 53 poor sleepers with 53 good sleepers. They reported that poor sleepers scored high on measures of neuroticism, while good sleepers scored high on measures of pseudonormalcy or psychopathy. Of the 831 patients, 12.5 percent had been referred for treatment because of sleep difficulties and 19.5 percent were judged by their therapists to have difficulties in going to sleep. In contrast to the emotionally disturbed good sleepers, the poor sleepers were referred because they were nervous, anxious, fearful, phobic, sad, depressed, obsessed, shy, overly sensitive, dreamy; had difficulty concentrating and excessive fantasy; and reported excessive fatigue and somatic involvement. As preschool children they were more fearful. Good sleepers had character disorders, were impulsive, aggressive, demanding, resentful, used rationalizations, and acted out.

To determine the type and frequency of sleep patterns, as well as the severity of sleep problems in child psychiatry patients, two studies were undertaken by this author—one retrospective and one prospective. In the retrospective study information on sleep in 120 outpatients was obtained: 106 male and 14 female patients, 5.5 years to 19.7 years of age (mean, 11.1 years). These patients had participated in various diagnostic and treatment programs, none specifically related to sleep or sleep disorders. Routine evaluations on admission had included the Conners' Parent's Questionnaire, which contains six items related to sleep: "restless sleep," "nightmares," "awakens at night," "cannot fall asleep," "bedwetting," and "a very early riser." Parents had rated the presence and severity of these symptoms as either "not at all," "just a little," "pretty much," or "very much." These

TABLE 1. Frequency and Severity of Sleep Problems
in Child Psychiatry Patients (N = 120)

Problem	Absent	Mild	Moderate	Severe
A very early riser	47	26	27	20
Restless sleep	56	26	18	20
Cannot fall asleep	55	32	20	13
Awakens at night	47	45	20	8
Bedwetting	92	12	2	14
Nightmares	72	32	13	3
Total	369	173	100	78

symptoms are presented here as "absent," "mild," "moderate," or "severe." Of the 120 child psychiatry outpatients, 48 were diagnosed as hyperkinetic, 35 as learning disorders, 19 as unsocialized aggressive, 12 as psychotic, and 6 as overanxious reaction. At least one of the six sleep problems was rated by the parents as severe in 50 patients, as moderate in 37, as mild in 20, and in 13 there were no sleep problems. Thus, 72.5 percent of the patients had at least one sleep problem rated as either moderate or severe. These sleep problems were rated on 78 occasions as severe, on 100 as moderate, on 173 as slight, and on 369 as absent (Table 1). The frequency and severity of these problems are shown in Table 1. When the moderate and severe degrees of symptoms are combined, 47 patients (39 percent) were rated as very early risers, 38 (32 percent) as suffering from restless sleep, 33 (27.5 percent) could not fall asleep, 28 (23 percent) awakened at night, and 16 (13 percent) each had enuresis and nightmares.

A comparison of the moderate and severe sleep problems between the 48 hyperkinetic and the 35 learning disabled patients showed that in hyperkinetic children restless sleep was about 2½ times more frequent, very early rising over twice as frequent, and difficulties in falling asleep over 1½ times more frequent (Table 2). These differences are statistically significant ($p \leqslant 0.01$).

The prospective study—still in progress—is an attempt to obtain comprehensive information on sleep in child psychiatry inpatients, day care patients, and outpatients, as well as on their siblings, based on self-ratings, and ratings by parents, child care workers, and teachers. The rating forms include a sleep questionnaire, the Sleep Habits Questionnaire (Anders et al., 1978), the Parent's Questionnaire (Conners, 1970), and the Preliminary School Report (Conners, 1969). The specific questions considered are: (1) whether patients suffer from

TABLE 2. Moderate and Severe Sleep Problems in Children
With Hyperkinetic and Learning Disorders

	A Very Early Riser (%)	Restless Sleep (%)	Cannot Fall Asleep (%)	Awakens At Night (%)	Night- mares (%)	Bed- wetting (%)
Hyperkinesis (N = 48)	47.9	45.8	35.4	25	16.7	16.7
Learning disability (N = 35)	22.8	17.1	22.8	22.8	11.4	8.6

a greater variety and severity of sleep problems than their siblings;
(2) whether there are significant differences between data supplied by
parents, professionals, and patients; and (3) whether there are
significant differences in sleep problems between various diagnostic
groups. Preliminary data on 19 day care and 14 inpatients rated by
their parents indicate that the most frequent sleep problems of moderate
or marked severity are early morning awakening (N=13), inability to
fall asleep (N=8), sleeptalking (N=8), poor or restless sleep (N=7),
awakening at night (N=7), betwetting (N=5), nightmares (N=4), teeth
grinding (N=4), and sleepwalking (N=1) (Table 3). In total, the parents
of the 33 patients rated these sleep problems as marked in severity 30
times, 27 times as moderate, 54 times as slight, and 186 times as
absent. In 20 inpatients, the child care workers evaluated 18 sleep
problems as marked, 4 as moderate, and 35 as slight. According to the

TABLE 3. Number of Sleep Problems, Rated by Parents,
in Day Care (N = 19) and Inpatients (N = 14)

Problem	Absent	Slight	Moderate	Marked
Awakens early in the morning	14	6	6	7
Cannot fall asleep	18	7	2	6
Poor or restless sleep	16	10	3	4
Awakens at night	16	10	4	3
Sleeptalking	20	5	5	3
Nightmares	20	9	3	1
Bedwetting	26	2	1	4
Grinds teeth	25	4	3	1
Sleepwalking	31	1	0	1
Total	186	54	27	30

parents, 93% of the inpatients had at least one sleep problem of a moderate or marked severity, compared to 58 percent of the day patients. According to the child care workers, 10 of the 20 inpatients (50 percent) had at least one sleep problem of a marked severity.

The data presented clearly indicate that there is an association between child psychiatric disorders and sleep disorders. It is more difficult but important, however, to determine their causal relationship. While a number of medical, psychological, family, social, and other environmental factors can cause disturbances of sleep, it is also possible that sleep disorders in themselves can be the cause of a variety of behavioral problems, such as excessive daytime somnolence, poor school performance, mood disorders, aggression, hyperactivity, and poor impulse control. This interaction between psychopathology and sleep disorders may become a vicious cycle, making the cause-and-effect relationships difficult to clarify. While most sleep difficulties in children are developmental, isolated sleep problems can also be an early sign of psychopathology or organic pathology. The persistence of sleep problems in the older child is much more likely to indicate psychopathology. Children are unlikely to have a primary or severe psychiatric disorder if they suffer from somnambulism (Kales et al., 1966b), primary enuresis (Kales and Kales, 1974), night terrors (Gastaut and Broughton, 1965), and narcolepsy (Yoss and Daly, 1960). However, children who suffer from hypersomnia, insomnia, or secondary enuresis (Werry, 1967) are more likely to have other psychiatric or medical disorders (Kales and Kales, 1974). Adults with night terrors frequently have daytime anxiety (Gastaut and Broughton, 1965), while adult somnambulists also suffer from either neurosis, schizophrenia, or schizoid disorders (Sours et al., 1963).

Available knowledge on the sleep EEGs of children with specific psychiatric syndromes is very inadequate. The sleep EEGs of 12 children with depressive symptomatology of varied clinical diagnoses were virtually identical to normative sleep data (Kupfer et al., 1979). Findings on hyperactive and psychotic children are reviewed in further sections of this chapter.

SLEEP IN HYPERKINETIC CHILDREN

Very few studies have compared the sleep EEG patterns of hyperactive children to those of normal children. Small et al. (1971) reported a similarity of sleep patterns in three markedly disturbed hyperactive children with those in seven age-matched controls. The main difference consisted of a high level of muscle artifact in the hyperactive group, presumably indicating sleep restlessness. Haig et al. (1974) reported in six hyperactive children significant increases in latency to both sleep onset and the first REM period in comparison to six normal boys. Nahas and Krynicki (1977) reported in four hyperactive patients increased Stage 2 sleep and sleep stage changes, and decreased Stage 4 sleep and REM sleep, compared to normative data in normal children obtained by Ross et al. (1968). These variable findings cannot be considered as final, as they are based on very small numbers of patients with large individual differences in their sleep patterns. The heterogeneity of the hyperactivity syndrome and its relevance to the study of sleep is illustrated by the finding already mentioned — 13 percent of adult narcoleptic patients were considered "hyperactive" prior to their later recognition as "sleepy" children or adolescents (Navelet et al., 1976). Diurnal microsleep episodes may be one of the factors associated with hyperactive behavior, and 24-hour polygraphic investigations may result in more meaningful data on vigilance, attention, and sleep patterns in hyperactive children.

In many clinical texts it is stated that hyperactive and MBD children suffer from restless sleep and other sleep problems. As already stated, parents' ratings indicated that in hyperactive children treated by this author, restless sleep, very early rising, and difficulties in falling asleep were far more frequent than in nonhyperactive patients. In treatment trials, clinical evaluations indicate that a large number of hyperactive children suffer from various sleep problems. In a study of eight hyperactive children who also had clinical and laboratory evidence of various allergies, significant sleep problems were present in all, and sleep problems, hyperactivity, and allergies improved in most patients following treatment with cromolyn DSG (Simeon et al., 1979). While sleep problems in hyperactive children may be related to a postulated basic disorder of arousal mechanisms, they may be also caused by nonspecific factors. Hyperactive children have different degrees of hypermotility, attentional deficits, impulsivity, excitability, emotional lability, nonlocalized "soft" neurological signs, EEG abnormalities, etc, and "abnormal" sleep patterns may be related to only some of the above features of the disorder. Further studies should determine the relationship between these problems and the various parameters of hyperactivity.

SLEEP STUDIES IN CHILDHOOD PSYCHOSES

Very few investigators have undertaken all-night sleep studies in psychotic children. In general, these studies have failed to show any major differences in the sleep EEG between psychotic and normal children. Onheiber et al. (1965) reported no differences between their sample of schizophrenic children and a sample of normal children investigated by others in relation to Stage 1 sleep and the time of onset of the first REM period. Caldwell et al. (1970) reported an increase of Stage 1 sleep in psychotic children but no group differences for Stage 4 sleep, which is in marked contrast with the decrease of Stage 4 sleep reported in chronic adult schizophrenics. In an extensive series of studies of autistic children undertaken by Ornitz and coworkers (Ornitz et al., 1965, 1968, 1969, 1973; Ornitz, 1972) and reviewed by Ornitz (1978), the REM-NREM sleep cycle patterns were reported as normal, but the REM activity was reduced, implying a delayed development of the differentiation of REM sleep in autistic children. The normal inhibition of the auditory-evoked responses during REM sleep was also markedly overriden in autistic children. According to these investigators, these findings indicate maturational defects and vestibular dysfunction.

About one third of mentally retarded autistic children develop epileptic fits, but very few of those with normal intelligence did so (Rutter et al., 1967). Twenty-eight percent of autistic children who had no evidence of a neurological disorder in early childhood developed epileptic seizures between the ages of 15 and 29 (Rutter, 1970). It is often very difficult to obtain good EEG records in most psychotic children as they are unable to cooperate with routine EEG investigations. When such records are obtained, they are usually contaminated with many artifacts. Resting EEG records even in epileptic children often show no evidence of epileptic activity, and various activating procedures are used to demonstrate a seizure disorder. The usefulness of activating procedures such as hyperventilation and photic and pentylenetetrazol (Metrazol) stimulation is very limited with psychotic children. Sleep by itself maximizes the manifestation of EEG seizure activity, and as no patient cooperation is required to obtain good EEG tracings during sleep in psychotic children, sleep EEGs in our hospitalized patients were obtained as part of the comprehensive diagnostic evaluation. The best diagnostic procedure to determine if psychotic children also suffered from epilepsy was to obtain all-night sleep EEG recordings. It was postulated that such findings would contribute to the choice of drug therapy. Any specific psychotropic drug effects on the sleep pattern could also help determine the optimum type and dosage of medication, and demonstrate possible associations between behavioral pathology and sleep. Sleep recordings were made in seven patients and seven normal subjects matched for age and sex to obtain "sleep EEG prints" (Itil and Shapiro, 1968) on patients and normal children, and compare their sleep patterns. The patients, hospitalized in a research ward, had chronic and severe psychiatric disabilities. Diagnoses were infantile autism in three, and atypical psychosis and severe personality disorders in two each (Table 4). Their age ranged from 7 years 9 months to 13 years 4 months (mean, 11 years). The age of the controls ranged from 7 years 5 months to 13 years 7 months (mean, 11 years 1 month).

Sleep EEG evaluations were done during a drug-free period and were repeated in four patients after six weeks of drug therapy. Findings related to the drug effects on sleep are reported in the section on pediatric psychopharmacology and sleep. To minimize the children's anxiety, the EEG technicians became well acquainted with each patient before the actual sleep investigation, and familiarized them with the laboratory setting. The sleep EEGs were recorded for three nights, of which the first two were adaptation nights. Two of the EEG leads, two EOG leads, and the EMG were recorded on tape for computer analyses. Five different runs of a resting EEG were recorded first, each run was recorded for three minutes. Upon reaching sleep Stage 2, each run was again recorded for three minutes. When sleep Stage 4 was reached, the five clinical runs were again recorded for three minutes each.

The normal controls were screened by a psychiatrist, and the parents completed a behavioral rating scale. Children with evidence of physical or psychiatric disorders were not accepted. After the study was completed it was discovered that one of the normal controls had

TABLE 4. Patient Population

Patient	Diagnosis	Age (Years-Months)
CJ	Autism	8-2
ET	Autism	10-10
MM	Autism	13-4
KM	Psychosis	7-9
BC	Psychosis	12-4
KG	Personality disorder	11-9
SH	Personality disorder	12-10

enuresis, but during the three nights in the sleep laboratory he did not wet the bed. The control group also slept in the EEG laboratory for three nights, of which the first two were adaptation nights. The setting, EEG combinations, and procedures were the same as for the patients. In addition to computerized sleep EEG analysis (sleep print) the records were visually analyzed. A rating scale on the child's behavior before going to sleep, during the night, and after awakening were completed. The study was explained to all the parents and to the normal children, and each parent and control child gave their written consent. The parents of the control children were allowed to spend the night in the EEG laboratory if they so desired, but no parent requested this.

A. Sleep Behavior

Sleep ratings based on behavioral observations showed that the patients had greater difficulties in getting to sleep and difficulties in getting back to sleep, and that their sleep was more restless compared to the controls (Table 5). Once they were asleep both patients and

TABLE 5. Sleep Ratings of Children with Psychiatric Disorders
and Matched Normal Controls
(Mean Scores)

	Patients (N = 7) (Placebo)	Controls (N = 7)
Slept well	2.42	2.29
Difficulty getting to sleep	1.42	0.29
Restless sleep	1.28	0.57
Awakened during sleep	1.14	1.57
Difficulty getting back to sleep	0.85	0.14
Talking in sleep	0.57	—
Slow to awaken	0.42	0.29
Difficulty getting fully alert	0.42	0.57
Nightmares	0.14	—
Up to bathroom	0.14	0.57
Wet the bed	0.14	0.57

Severity
0 = None or absent
1 = Slight or sometimes
2 = Moderate or often
3 = Marked or very often

controls seemed to sleep about equally well. The controls awakened slightly more often than the patients. Sleeptalking was observed in some of the patients but not in the controls. With medication, there were improvements in the patients' difficulties in getting to sleep and getting back to sleep, sleep became less restless, and there was no sleeptalking.

B. Visual Evaluation of Sleep Prints

Visual evaluation of the computerized sleep prints showed that two autistic patients (ET and MM) had long latencies of the onset of Stage 4 sleep (after 85 and 135 minutes, respectively). One patient (BC) showed Stage 4 sleep after 45 minutes and another (SH) after 25 minutes from the start of the recordings. None of the normal controls had delays in the onset of sleep longer than 20 minutes. The psychotic patients had a high variability in their sleep patterns; their sleep fluctuated between awake, light sleep, and moderate sleep from one minute to the next. The patients and the normal controls did not show the well-known sleep profiles of the normal adult, where after the first cycle of deep sleep the next cycles have progressively lesser amounts of deep sleep. Visual evaluations of the EEG records showed that various EEG abnormalities (paroxysmal, epileptiform, or disorganized tracings) were present in four patients (KM, BC, KG, SH) and one control subject.

C. Comparisons of Sleep Stages Between Patients and Controls

The sleep patterns of children with psychiatric disorders compared to those of the matched controls, using a five-stage digital computer classification, showed statistically significant differences for Stages 2 and 4 ($P<0.05$ and <0.01, respectively, based on two sample t tests); the patients had less Stage 4 sleep and more Stage 2 sleep (Fig. 1). A comparison for each of the five sleep stages as a function of recording time showed that over the six hours of sleep, the patients had consistently higher percentages of Stage 2, and consistently lower percentages of Stage 4 sleep (Fig. 2).

While this study was undertaken to develop the application of quantitative sleep EEG analyses in child psychiatry and psychopharmacology, the findings demonstrate significant differences between the sleep process of patients compared to normal children in spite of the small number of subjects. Findings on significant differences between psychotic, high risk for schizophrenia and normal children using resting computerized EEGs and evoked potentials have been previously reported (Simeon and Itil, 1975).

PEDIATRIC PSYCHOPHARMACOLOGY AND SLEEP

Studies of psychotropic drug effects on sleep EEG patterns and sleep disorders in children have been greatly neglected, in contrast to the extensive research in adults. Table 6 summarizes some of the findings in children. In a clinical trial of diazepam in somnambulism, results were positive (Glick et al., 1971). While benzodiazepines suppress

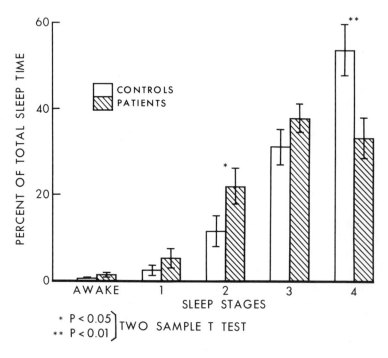

FIG. 1. Comparison of sleep stages in seven unmedicated boys with psychotic (N=5) and personality disorders (N=2), and seven matched for age normal controls. There are statistically significant differences: the patient group had less Stage 4 sleep (p<0.01), and more Stage 2 sleep (p<0.05) than the control group. The computerized sleep EEG analyses are based on a five sleep stage classification.

Stage 3 and 4 sleep, the treatment of somnambulism did not produce clear-cut results (Kales and Scharf, 1973; Kales and Kales, 1974). Imipramine was also reported to be effective in somnambulistic children (Pesikoff and Davis, 1971). In children suffering from night terrors, both diazepam (Glick et al., 1971) and imipramine (Pesikoff and Davis, 1971) were reported clinically effective. In adults suffering

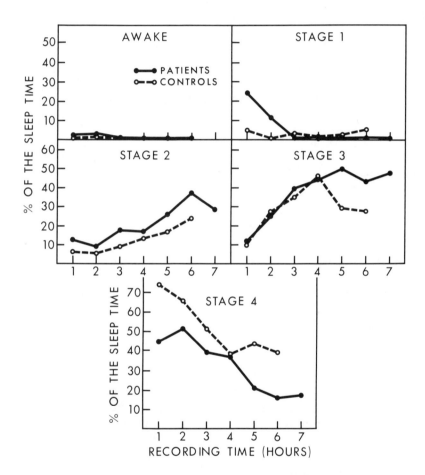

FIG. 2. All-night sleep stages in children with psychiatric disorders (N=7) compared with normal controls (N=7). The group of seven unmedicated boys with psychiatric disorders has consistently higher percentages of Stage 2 sleep and lower percentages of Stage 4 sleep compared to the group of normal controls for the entire six-hour sleep period. The sleep stage classification is based on computerized sleep prints.

TABLE 6. Psychotropic Drug Effects on Sleep Patterns and Disorders in Children

	Stimulants	Imipramine	Diazepam	Diphenhy-dramine	Neuroleptics
Somnambulism		6	12,13		
Night terrors		6	12,14**		
Enuresis		7,8,9,10			
Insomnia			12	15	
Hyperkinesis	1,2,3*,4*,5*				
Psychosis					16
Depression		11			

*No effect
**In adults
[1]Small et al., 1971
[2]Feinberg et al., 1974
[3]Haig et al., 1974
[4]Nahas and Krynicki, 1977
[5]Puig-Antich et al., 1978
[6]Pesikoff and Davis, 1971
[7]Poussaint and Ditman, 1965
[8]Ritvo et al., 1967
[9]Miller et al., 1968
[10]Kales et al., 1971
[11]Kupfer et al., 1979
[12]Glick et al., 1971
[13]Kales and Scharf, 1973; Kales and Kales, 1974
[14]Fisher et al., 1973
[15]Russo et al., 1976
[16]Simeon, this chapter

from night terrors, diazepam therapy resulted in a decrease of both the frequency of the attacks and Stage 4 sleep (Fisher et al., 1973). The clinical efficacy of imipramine in nocturnal enuresis has been demonstrated in many studies (Poussaint and Ditman, 1965; Ritvo et al., 1967; Miller et al., 1968; Kales et al., 1970), and its use in this condition abroad is widespread (Simeon and Itil, 1973). Imipramine decreases REM sleep and increases REM sleep latency (Ritvo et al., 1967), but this does not explain its mode of action in enuresis. Imipramine therapy of depressed children resulted in a decrease of the sleep-efficiency percentage which was related to increases of the number of arousals and in intermittent wakefulness, in the increase of Stage 2 and decrease of Stage 4 sleep, and supression of REM (Kupfer et al., 1979). Insomnia in children is a frequent symptom and treatment depends on its etiology. Diphenhydramine is effective when used symptomatically for short periods (Russo et al., 1976).

Findings of sleep studies in hyperkinetic children treated with stimulant drugs are variable and inconclusive due to the small number of subjects, individual differences of sleep patterns in response to stimulant drugs and their withdrawal, and the different dosages used. In three hyperactive children treated with d-amphetamine, Small et al., (1971) reported an increase of sleep latencies, a decrease of the number of sleep cycles, and an increase of REM density. Withdrawal of d-amphetamine was associated with decreased sleep latencies, REM latency, REM density and bursts, muscle activity during NREM, and increased REM sleep and number of sleep cycles. In another sleep study, the administration of d-amphetamine to hyperactive children resulted in increases of the eye movement burst index and eye movement density, while d-amphetamine withdrawal resulted in increased sleep time and decreased sleep latency (Feinberg et al., 1974). In seven hyperkinetic children treated with d-amphetamine given in divided daily dosages between 10 mg and 30 mg, there were no significant changes in sleep EEG patterns or sleep-related growth hormone and cortisol secretions, while prolactin was significantly suppressed (Puig-Antich et al., 1978). The administration and withdrawal of methylphenidate in a total of ten hyperactive children was not associated with any significant changes related to sleep EEG and REM (Haig et al., 1974; Nahas and Krynicki, 1977). Small et al. (1971) concluded that the marked clinical improvement with d-amphetamine was associated with only minor changes of the sleep patterns, indicating that the therapeutic efficacy of the drug is probably unrelated to its effects on sleep patterns.

Drug effects on sleep need not be direct, as changes in sleep patterns may occur as a result of drug-induced alterations of brain functions during waking behavior. D-amphetamine is a short-acting drug, and was given in the above studies in a single morning or morning and noon dose. Sleep EEG findings under these conditions may have been a combination of *chronic* d-amphetamine effects, apparently resulting in altered daytime brain functions and behavior, and *acute withdrawal* effects occurring at night. In 19 hyperactive children, daytime EEG digital computer period analysis and visual evoked response (VER) investigations following d-amphetamine therapy withdrawal resulted in statistically significant decreases of the VER latency peaks, in increased theta and alpha EEG activity, and decreased beta activity, average EEG frequency, and frequency deviation (Simeon et al., 1973). While these neurophysiological changes were maximal during the third day after d-amphetamine withdrawal, they occurred also after 24 hours and six days following withdrawal. This may explain the relatively greater sleep EEG changes during d-amphetamine withdrawal following chronic drug

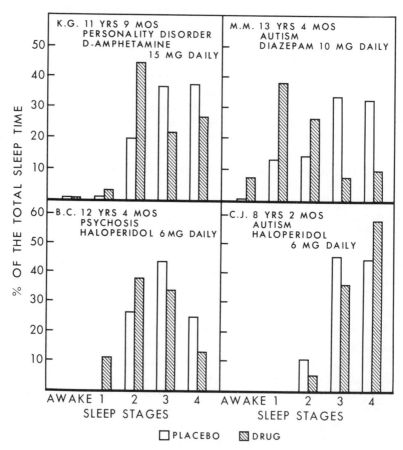

FIG. 3. Changes in the distribution of sleep stages associated with pharmacotherapy. Six weeks of pharmacotherapy in four patients is associated with changes in the distribution of various sleep stages: in patients KG, MM, and BC there is a decrease of Stage 3 and 4, an increase of Stage 2, and an increase of Stage 1 in KG and MM. In contrast, in CJ, Stage 2 and 3 are decreased, and Stage 4 increased. The sleep stage classification is based on computerized sleep prints.

administration, compared to the sleep changes during acute daily drug administration.

In a study of eight hyperactive and eight autistic children—all also suffering from various allergies—parents' ratings showed that most patients had significant sleep difficulties before they were admitted for therapy (Simeon et al., 1979). The patients were treated with cromolyn DSG (Intal), a substance that prevents the release of histamine and histamine-like substances from the mast cells, to determine the effects of this drug on the behavioral and allergy disorders. At the end of the trial, parents had rated the improvement of the sleep disorders in the hyperactive patients as marked in four, moderate in one, mild in two, and none in one patient. Hyperactivity improved in six patients and allergies in five. Following cromolyn administration, five of the eight autistic patients became calmer during daytime, and sleeping difficulties improved in four.

In a study primarily designed to apply quantitative sleep EEG analyses (Itil and Shapiro, 1968) in child psychiatry and psychopharmacology, all-night sleep EEG investigations were undertaken in four patients during a drug-free period and six weeks following pharmacotherapy. Their ages, diagnosis, and drug therapy are shown in Figure 3. The maximum daily dosages indicated were given at the time of the EEG recordings.

The methodology of the sleep EEG investigations is identical to that described in the section on sleep in childhood psychoses. The patients, KG, treated with d-amphetamine, and MM, treated with diazepam, showed decreases of Stage 3 and 4 sleep, and increases of Stage 2 and 1. Patient BC, treated with haloperidol, showed a decrease of Stage 3 and 4 sleep, an increase of Stage 2 sleep, and very little clinical improvement. In contrast, CJ also treated with haloperidol, had an increase of Stage 4 sleep, decreases of Stage 2 and 3, and a significant symptomatic improvement. The computer sleep prints of these four patients before and during pharmacotherapy are shown on Figure 4. These data are shown not to demonstrate specific drug-induced sleep EEG changes, but to illustrate the application and potential usefulness of computerized EEG methods in the investigation of sleep in pediatric psychopharmacology.

The study of associations between drug-induced clinical and sleep EEG changes, especially in the growing organism, is complicated by the fact that different psychotropic agents are clinically effective in the same disorder. At the same time, the same agent can affect target symptoms in different disorders, indicating that different mechanisms underlie similar clinical responses.

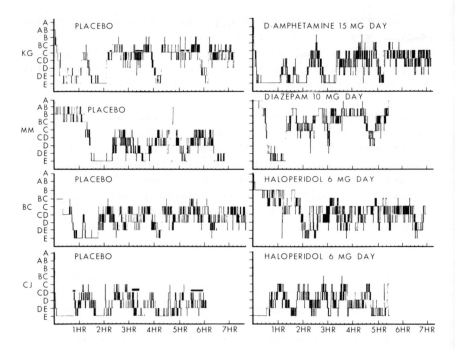

FIG. 4. Computerized sleep prints during placebo and after pharmacotherapy in boys with psychiatric disorders. The patient had received pharmacotherapy for six weeks at the time of the second sleep print. The indicated daily dosage is at the time of the recording. These computerized sleep prints illustrate a nine-stage sleep classification.

CONCLUSION

There are difficulties in the interpretation of many of the published findings on sleep in child psychiatry disorders. In some studies, the various manifestations of sleep were related to one factor only, such as age or psychiatric diagnosis. Others ignore the various degrees of severity of the sleep problems. Most ratings on sleep are based on parental reports, and such information can be misleading. Another complication relates to the population sample, as children treated in child guidance clinics, private institutions, or children's hospitals may differ greatly in the type and frequency of sleep pathology. In psychotic children, individual symptoms, organic pathology and/or etiology, age, IQ, and anxiety may be critical factors in relation to the type and severity of any sleep problems present.

There are many important questions that require further study, such as whether there are any differences in the sleep patterns between different diagnostic groups and normal children, whether the sleep complaints and "disorders" seen in patients are developmental or pathological, and whether any differences in sleep patterns are clinically significant. Finally, it will be necessary to understand the nature of the various sleep manifestations, sleep stages, and REM in relation to brain function, behavior, learning, mood, vigilance, attention, etc. If sleep is indeed needed, it is important to investigate whether sleep is also therapeutic, and if any particular pattern of sleep is more therapeutic in any specific psychiatric disorder. Further progress in this field may open new treatment strategies, and sleep manipulation may also benefit normal growth, functions, and behavior.

REFERENCES

Ames LB: *Sleep and Dreams in Childhood,* New York, MacMillan, 1964

Anders TF, Carskadon MA, Dement WC, Harvey K: Sleep habits of children and the identification of pathologically sleepy children. *Child Psychiatry Hum Dev* 9 (1):56-63, 1978

Anders TF, Sachar E, Kream J, et al.: Behavioral state and plasma cortisol response in the human newborn. *Pediatrics* 46:532-537, 1970

André-Balisaux G, Gonsette R: L'electroencéphalographie dans le somnambulisme et sa valeur pour l'établissement d'un diagnostic étiologique. *Acta Neurol Psychiatr Belg* 56:270-281-1956

Bakwin H: Sleepwalking in twins. *Lancet* 2:446-447, 1970

Bowe TR, Anders TF: The use of the semi-Markov model in the study of the development of sleep-wake states in infants. *Psychophysiology,* 16(1):41-48, 1979

Boyar R, Finkelstein J, Roffwarg H, et al.: Synchronization of augmented luteinizing hormone secretion with sleep during puberty. *N Eng J Med* 287:582-586, 1972

Broughton R: Neurochemical, neuroendocrine and biorhythmic aspects of sleep in man: Relationship to clinical pathological disorders, in Drucher-Colin RR, Myers RD (eds): *Neurohumoral Aspects of Brain Function.* New York, Plenum Press, 1974

Broughton RJ: Sleep disorders: Disorders of arousal? *Science* 159(3819):1070-1078, 1968

Broughton R, Mamelak M: The treatment of narcolepsy-cataplexy with nocturnal gamma-hydroxybutyrate. *Can J Neurol Sci* 6(1):1-6, 1979

Caldwell DF, Brané AJ, Beckett PGS: Sleep patterns in normal and psychotic children. *Arch Gen Psychiatry* 22:500-503, 1970

Cleghorn JM, Brown GM, Kaplan RD: Normalization of sleep and endocrine patterns with gamma-hydroxybutyrate in severe insomnia. *Proc Coll Physicians Surgeons* 12(1):79, 1979

Conners CK: A teacher rating scale for use in drug studies with children. *Am J Psychiatry* 126:152-156, 1969

Conners CK: Symptom patterns in hyperkinetic, neurotic and normal children. *Child Dev* 41:667-682, 1970

Dreyfus-Brisac C: The electroencephalogram of the premature infant and full-term newborn: Normal and abnormal development of waking and sleeping patterns, in Kellaway P, Petersen I (eds): *Neurological and Electroencephalographic Correlative Studies in Infancy*. New York, Grune and Stratton, 1964, pp 186-207

Dreyfus-Brisac C: Neurophysiological studies in human premature and full-term newborns. *Biol Psychiatry* 10(5):485-496, 1975

Dumermuth G, Scollo-Lavizzari G: Analyse spectrale de l'EEG du sommeil du nuit physiologique. *Rev Electroencephalogr Neurophysiol* 2(3):233-240, 1972

Edmonds C: Severe somnambulism: A case study. *J Clin Psychol* 23:237-239, 1967

Feinberg I: Eye movement activity during sleep and intellectual function in mental retardation. *Science* 159 (3820):1256, 1968

Feinberg I, Hibi S, Braun M, et al.: Sleep amphetamine effects in MBDS and normal subjects. *Arch Gen Psychiatry* 31:723-731, 1974

Fisher C, Kahn E, Edwards A, Davis DM: A psychophysiological study of nightmares and night terrors. *Arch Gen Psychiatry* 28:252-259, 1973

Fisher C, Byrne J, Edwards A, Kahn E: A psychophysiological study of nightmares. *J Am Psychoanal Assoc* 18:747-782, 1970

Franks RC: Diurnal variation of plasma 17-hydroxycorticosteroids in children. *J Clin Endocrinol Metab* 27:75-78, 1967

Gastaut H, Broughton R: A clinical and polygraphic study of episodic phenomena during sleep, in J Wortis, (ed): *Recent Advances in Biological Psychiatry vol. 7*. New York, Plenum Press, 1965, pp. 197-221

Gastaut H, Broughton R: *Epileptic seizures: Clinical and Electrographic Features, Diagnosis and Treatment*. Springfield, Illinois, Charles C. Thomas, 1972

Glick BS, Schulman D, Turecki S: Diazepam (Valium) treatment in childhood sleep disorders. *Dis Nerv System* 32(8):565-566, 1971

Guilleminault C, Eldridge FL, Simmons FB, Dement WC: Sleep apnea in eight children. *Pediatrics* 58(1):23-30, 1976

Haig JR, Schroeder CS, Schroeder SR: Effects of methylphenidate on hyperactive children's sleep. *Psychopharmacologia* 37:185-188, 1974

Hauri P: The sleep disorders. *Curr Concepts* Kalamazoo, Michigan, The Upjohn Company, 1977

Hellbrügge T, Lange J, Rutenfranz J, Stehr K: Circadian periodicity of physiological functions in different stages of infancy and childhood. *Ann NY Acad Sci* 117:361-373, 1964

Huapaya LVM: Seven cases of somnambulism induced by drugs. *Am J Psychiatry* 136(7):965-966, 1979

Huber Z: EEG investigations in 200 somnambulic patients abstracted. *Electroencephalogr Clin Neurophysiol* 14:577, 1962

Itil TM, Shapiro DM: Computer classification of all-night sleep EEG (sleep prints), in Gastaut H, Lugaresi E, Berti-Geroni G, Coccagna G (eds.): *The Abnormalities of Sleep in Man.* Bologna, Aulo Gaggi, 1968, pp 45-53

Jacobsen A, Kales A: Somnambulism: All-night EEG and related studies, in Kety SS, Evarts EV, Williams HL (eds): *Research Publication of the Association for Research in Nervous and Mental Disease. Sleep and altered states of consciousness* Vol. 45 Baltimore, Williams & Wilkins, 1967, pp 424-448

Jenkins RL, Nureddin E, Shapiro I: Children's behavior syndromes and parental responses. *Genet Psychol Monogr* 74:261-329, 1966

Kales A, Jacobson A, Paulson M, et al.: Somnambulism: Psychophysiolgical correlates. I: All-night EEG studies. *Arch Gen Psychiatry* 14:586-594, 1966a

Kales A, Kales JD: Sleep Disorders: Recent findings in the diagnosis and treatment of disturbed sleep: *N Eng J Med* 290(9):487-499, 1974

Kales A, Paulson MJ, Jacobson A, Kales JD: Somnambulism: Psychophysiological correlates. II. Psychiatric interviews, psychological testing and discussion. *Arch Gen Psychiatry* 14:595-604, 1966b

Kales A, and Scharf MB. Sleep laboratory and clinical studies of the effects of benzodiazepines on sleep: Flurazepam, diazepam, chlordiazepoxide, and RO 5-4200, in Garattini S, Mussini E, Randall LO (ed): *The Benzodiazepines* New York, Raven Press, 1973, pp 577-598

Kales A, Scharf M, Tan TL, et al.: Sleep laboratory and clinical studies of the effects of Tofranil, Valium and placebo on sleep stages and enuresis, abstracted. *Psychophysiology* 7(2):348, 1970

Kales A, Weber G, Charney DS, et al.: Familial occurrences of sleepwalking and night terrors. *Sleep Res* 6:172 (abstract) 1977

Kupfer DJ, Coble P, Kane J, et al.: Imipramine and EEG sleep in children with depressive symptoms. *Psychopharmacology* 60:117-123, 1979

Macfarlane JW, Allen L, Honzik MP: *A developmental Study of the Behavior Problems of Normal Children Between twenty-one months and fourteen Years.* Berkley, California, University of California Press, 1954

Miller PR, Champelli JW, Dinello FA: Imipramine in the treatment of enuretic school children: A double-blind study. *Am J Dis Child* 115:17-20, 1968

Monroe LJ, Marks PA: Psychotherapists' descriptions of emotionally disturbed adolescent poor and good sleepers. *J Clin Psychol* 33(1):263-269, 1977

Nahas AD, Krynicki V: Effect of methylphenidate on sleep stages and ultradian rhythms in hyperative children. *J Nerv Ment Dis* 164(1):66-69, 1977

Navelet Y, Anders T, Guilleminault C: *Narcolepsy in children, in Advances in Sleep Research 3: Narcolepsy.* Guilleminault C, Passouant P, Dement W (eds): New York Spectrum Publications, 1976 pp 171-177

Onheiber P, White PT, DeMyer MK, Ottinger DR: Sleep and dream patterns of child schizophrenics. *Arch Gen Psychiatry* 12:568-571, 1965

Ornitz EM: Development of sleep patterns in autistic children, in Clemente CD, Purpura DP, Mayer FE (eds): *Sleep and the Maturing Nervous System.* New York, Academic Press, 1972, pp 363-381

Ornitz EM: Neurophysiologic studies, in Rutter M, Schopler E (eds): *Autism: A Reappraisal of Concepts and Treatment.* New York, Plenum Press, 1978, pp. 117-139

Ornitz EM, Forsythe AB, de la Pena A: The effect of vestibular and auditory stimulation on the REMs of REM sleep in autistic children. *Arch Gen Psychiatry* 29:786-791, 1973

Ornitz EM. Ritvo ER, Brown MB, et al.: The EEG and rapid eye movements during REM sleep in normal and autistic children. *Electroencephalogr Clin Neurophysiol* 26:167-175, 1969

Ornitz E, Ritvo ER, Panman LM, et al.: The auditory evoked response in normal and autistic children during sleep. *Electroencephalogr Clin Neurophysiol* 25:221-230, 1968

Ornitz EM, Ritvo ER, Walter RD: Dreaming sleep in autistic twins. *Arch Gen Psychiatry* 12:77-79, 1965

Parmelee AH: Sleep studies for the neurological assessment of the newborn. *Neuropadiatrie* 1(3):351-353, 1970

Parmelee AH, Akiyama Y, Schultz MA, et al.: The electroencephalogram in active and quiet sleep in infants, in Kellaway P, Petersen I (eds): *Clinical Electroencephalography of Children.* Stockholm, Almqvist and Wiksell, 1968, pp 77-88

Passouant P, Cadilhac J: Décharges épileptiques et sommeil, in Niedermeyer E (ed): *Modern Problems of Pharmacopsychiatry: Epilepsy* vol. 4, Basel, S. Karger, 1970 pp 87-104

Pesikoff RB, Davis PC: Treatment of pavor nocturnus and somnambulism in children. *Am J Psychiatry* 128(6):778-781, 1971

Petre-Quadens O: Sleep in mental retardation, in Clemente CD, Purpara DP, Mayer FE (eds): *Sleep and the Maturing Nervous System.* New York, Academic Press, 1972, pp 383-417

Petre-Quadens O, Jouvet M: Sleep in the mentally retarded. *J Neurol Sci* 4:354-357, 1967

Poussaint AF, Ditman KS: A controlled study of imipramine (Tofranil) in the treatment of childhood enuresis. *J Pediatr* 67:283-290, 1965

Poussaint AF, Koegler RR, Riehl JL: Enuresis, epilepsy and the electroencephalogram. *Am J Psychiatry* 123(10):1294-1295, 1967

Prechtl H, Weinmann H, Akiyama Y: Organization of physiological parameters in normal and abnormal infants. *Neuropaediatrie* :101-129, 1969

Puig-Antich J, Greenhill LL, Sassin J, Sachar EJ: Growth hormone, prolactin and cortisol responses and growth patterns in hyperkinetic children treated with dextroamphetamine: Preliminary findings. *J Child Psychiatry* 17(3):457-475, 1978

Ritvo ER, Ornitz EM, Gottlieb F, et al.: Arousal and nonarousal enuretic events. *Am J Psychiatry* 126:77-84, 1969

Ritvo ER, Ornitz EM, LaFranchi S, Walter RD: Effects of imipramine on the sleep-dream cycle: An EEG study in boys. *Electroencephalogr Clin Neurophysiol* 22:465-468, 1967

Ross JJ, Agnew HW, Williams RL, Webb WB: Sleep patterns in pre-adolescent children: An EEG-EOG study. *Pediatrics* 42(2): 324-335, 1968

Russo R, Gururaj V, Allen J: The effectiveness of diphenhydramine HC1 in pediatric sleep disorders. *J Clin Pharmacol* 16:284-288, 1976

Rutter M: Autistic children: Infancy to adulthood. *Semin Psychiatry* 2:435-450, 1970

Rutter M, Greenfield D, Lockyer L: A five to fifteen year follow-up study of infantile psychosis. II. Social and behavoral outcome *Br J Psychiatry* 113:1183-1199, 1967

Saletu B: Psychopharmaka, Gehirntatigkeit and Schlaf: *Neurophysiologische Aspekte der Psychopharmakologie und Pharmakopsychiatrie.* Karger, S. Basel, 1976

Sassin JF, Frantz AG, Weitzman ED, Kapen S: Human prolactin: 24 hour pattern with increased release during sleep. *Science* 177:1205-1207, 1972

Sassin JF, Parker DC, Mace J, et al.: Human growth hormone release: Relation to slow wave sleep and sleep-waking cycles. *Science* 165:513-515, 1969

Satoh T, Harada Y: Tooth grinding during sleep as an arousal reaction. *Experientia* 27:758-786, 1971

Schulman C: Alterations of the sleep cycle in heroin addicted and "suspect" newborns. *Neuropadiatrie* 1:89-109, 1969

Schulte F, Heinze C, Schrempf G: Maternal toxemia, fetal malnutrition and bioelectric brain activity of the newborn in Clemente CD, Purpura DP, Mayer FE (eds): *Sleep and the Maturing Nervous System.* New York, Academic Press, 1972, pp 419-439

Schulte F, Lasson U, Parl U, et al.: Brain and behavioral maturation in newborn infants of diabetic mothers II. Sleep cycles. *Neuropaediatrie* 1(1):36-43, 1969

Schultz MA, Schulte FJ, Akiyama Y, Parmelee AH Jr: Development of electroencephalographic sleep phenomena in hypothyroid infants. *Electroencephalbor Clin Neurophysiol* 25:351-358, 1968

Shirley HF, Kahn JP: Sleep disturbances in children. *Pediatr Clin North Am* 5:629-643, 1958

Simeon J, Itil TM: Computerized electroencephalogram: A model of understanding brain function in childhood psychosis and its treatment. *J. Autism Child Schizphr* 5(3):247-265, 1975

Simeon J, Itil TM: Pediatric psychopharmacology outside the United States, abridged. *Psychopharmacol Bull* 9:50-52, 1973

Simeon J, O'Malley M, Tryphonas H, et al.: Cromolyn DSG effects in hyperkinetic and psychotic children with allergies. *Ann Allergy* 42(6):343-347, 1979

Simeon J, Saletu B, Viamontes G, et al., Clinical and neurophysiological investigations of combined thioridazine-d-amphetamine maintenance therapy and withdrawal in childhood behaviour disorders. *Proceedings of the VIII Congress of the Collegium Internationale Neuropsychopharmacolgicum (CINP),* Copenhagen, 1972 Prague, Avicenum-Czechoslovak Medical Press, 1973, pp 279-292. Abstracted in *Psychopharmacologia* 26 (Suppl), 1972, p 92

Small A, Hibi S, Feinberg I: Effects of dextroamphetamine sulfate on EEG sleep patterns of hyperactive children. *Arch Gen Psychiatry* 25:369-380, 1971

Sours JA, Frumken P, Indermell RR: Somnambulism. *Arch Gen Psychiatry* 9:400-413, 1963

Tennes K, Vernadakis A: Cortisol excretion levels and daytime sleep in one-year old infants. *J Clin Endocrinol Metab* 44:175-179, 1977

Turton EC, Spear AB: EEG findings in 100 cases of severe enuresis. *Arch Dis Child* 28:316-330 1953

Weitzman ED, Graziani L: Sleep and sudden infant death syndrome: A new hypothesis, in Weitzman ED (ed): *Advances in Sleep Research,* vol 1. New York, Spectrum Publications, 1974 pp 327-341

Werry JS: Enuresis—a psychosomatic entity? *Can Med Assoc J* 97:319-327, 1967

White JC: A case of reading epilepsy with observations on the effect of sleep deprivation and fasting on EEG correlates. *Electroencephalogr Clin Neurophysiol* 28:510-513, 1970

Williams RL, Karacan I, Hursch CJ: *Electroencephalography (EEG) of Human Sleep: Clinical Applications.* New York, John Wiley & Sons, 1974

Williams RL, Karacan I: Hursch CJ: *Electroencephalography (EEG) of Human Sleep: Clinical Applications* New York, John Wiley & Sons, 1974

Yoss RE, Daly DD: Narcolepsy. *Arch Intern Med* 106:168-171, 1960

$$6$$

Altered Cognitive Processes in Children: Psychobiological Methods of Approach

HERBERT WEINGARTNER

Psychiatric disorders in children are often reflected by disruptions in some aspect of cognition. These cognitive changes may be a primary expression of the disorder or can be seen as secondary to other psychosocial or biological determinants. Either separately or together these determinants can result in changes in thinking, learning, concept formation, perception, recall, and other processes that we might label cognitive in nature. Experimental strategies that should prove useful in researching the psychobiology of these cognitive behaviors are outlined here.

This paper was formulated as an outline of effective research frameworks that can be used to uncover and describe specific quantitative and qualitative changes in cognition as these appear in behavioral disorders in children or as a response to some treatment manipulation. The research approaches generated by those frameworks are ordinarily not familiar to psychopharmacologists or clinicians who have been interested in behavioral disorders in children. The main point to be emphasized is that cognitions or disruptions in cognitions should not be considered as an undifferentiated behavioral system. Different forms of psychopathology would likely induce very different kinds of changes in component cognitive processes.

These differentiated aspects of cognition can be considered as driven by different mechanisms and underlying psychobiological processes. Likewise, treatments that would remediate cognitive and other aspects of disrupted behavior in the child can alter aspects of cognition in a highly specific manner. These must be considered as separate components if we are to appreciate the effectiveness of some treatment and its implications for our understanding the etiology of the disorder.

SOME GENERAL CONSIDERATIONS

For an experiment to "work" and be replicable requires an appropriate experimental design, measures that are reliable and valid, and effective strategies for analysis of results. However, the experiment as a set of analytic tools should also answer some questions about the nature of cognitive process in children. It would seem that there are three types of research strategies. The first type might be characterized as the demonstration study which usually is characteristic of the initial studies in an area. The demonstration study might be used to test for the presence of some effect (eg, a cognitive effect) in distinguishing between two populations or in response to a drug manipulation. It represents the simplest, perhaps least informative kind of study question. The demonstration study is designed to alert and define new territories which should attract further research and as such can be most exciting and influential; it is not ordinarily an efficient strategy for uncovering the underlying structures or patterns of some phenomena. For example, it would appear that to ask whether a stimulant drug alters cognition in hyperactive children, or whether cognition is different in hyperactive and normal children, is not now an effective hypothesis for experimental study although it may have been a perfectly useful research question a decade ago. A second type of research effort is explicitly designed to examine the pattern or components of cognition that may be altered in children. Here the focus is directed at describing the structure of the cognitive phenomena rather than merely defining the presence of an impairment. The third type of study involves a reductionistic approach where underlying mechanisms are the focus of interest.

It would appear that many of the studies that involve cognitive issues in children are those where the relevance of the cognitive response is not the question. Rather, it is the form, mechanism, processes, components, and other specific aspects of how thinking, learning, remembering, and perceiving are altered in response to some treatment, or in some clinically defined population, which should be a research theme to engage investigations of disorders in children. This would require a research design which explicitly sets out to interrelate a number of facets or patterns of effects as these might appear related to cognitive changes seen in some syndrome. A sample of such factors are illustrated in Figure 1. For example, cognition might be altered along with, but independent of, other aspects of behavior such as mood, arousal, or motor behavior. It is also possible that cognitive changes are either related and linked to these other behaviors through a common third determinant or are directly linked together. Perhaps cognitive factors are codependent on other behavioral changes so that cognitive alterations are never seen without other behavioral factors being present or altered. Furthermore, these behaviors may be seen as interrelated or dependent on these changes in cognition. In some syndromes, cognitive changes may be intimately linked rather than merely correlated with other behaviors in terms of underlying processes. To discern such a relationship requires an experimental design, which in fact permits the specific testing of such interlinking mechanisms rather than relying on post-hoc statistical strategies. One means of accomplishing this is through systematic and independent manipulations of component behaviors. For example, in considering hyperactivity, are the motor aspects of this disorder correlated but independent of some of the cognitive changes seen in this syndrome? Do the two move together in the same child? Are attentional factors effected in hyperactive children because of some deficient filtering or other "early" information processing stage? Are these driven by some underlying change in arousal/activation and is this what is altered by stimulant treatment? Does motor restlessness alter the kinds of search or scanning strategies that are generated from stages of information processing that are dependent on some primary memory store for

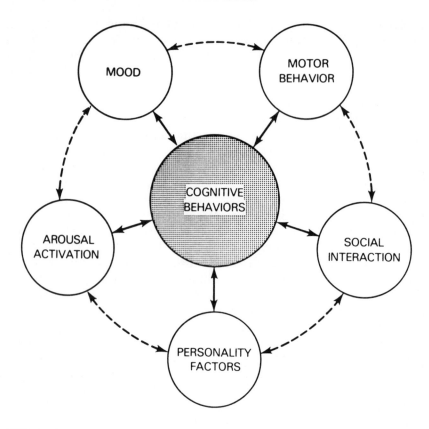

FIG. 1. Independent versus dependent versus process/mechanism linked behaviors. Factors related to cognitive changes in children.

further analysis and eventual learning or storage? Are these components related to some biological factors which determine both the motor restlessness and the inattention? Or are these linked to each? Or are the hyperactivity and the cognitive changes not tied together despite the fact that they move together in the same child? To attack these issues would require research designs that are multivariate, rather than single variate. The potential interrelationship between systems of variables should be tested through appropriate sets of manipulations: designs should be employed that emphasize multiple correlations of many variables which may or may not be relevant in considering some syndrome or treatment strategy.

Similar issues are relevant in considering the possible component changes that might occur within the domain of cognition. These are outlined in Figure 2. A treatment may affect everything that is cognitive in nature irrespective of complexity, type of cognitive process, or the kind of stimuli that must be processed. It is difficult to think of a variable whose effects are that simple or ubiquitous, but perhaps an intense treatment (dose) by some central nervous system depressant drug would be an example of such an effect (example A in Fig. 2). A somewhat more complex effect might be one in which cognitive processes and operations are significantly altered as a

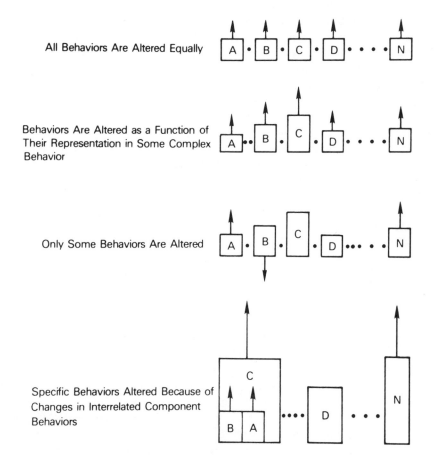

FIG. 2.   Altered cognitive behaviors. Components of cognitive processes and their interrelationships.

function of how these are represented in some complex cognitive behavior. The more completely a given component is represented in that behavior, the more likely we are to see expressed changes in that component in response to a drug in the expression of some clinical syndrome (example B in Fig. 2). However, it is also possible that some treatment variable can alter some aspects of cognition without changing other cognitive components (example C in Fig. 2). For example, language processing may be altered without affecting pattern processing (as in dominant temporal lobe lesion), or attentional components may be affected leaving unaltered retrieval processes, or the consistency of retrieval may be particularly compromised but not the shift of information from some short-to long-term memory store (as described below). The point again is that cognition is not represented as one undifferentiated system but must be considered in terms of component mechanisms. Finally we may see some change in some aspect of cognition because of some underlying effect on component processes which drive that particular cognitive behavior. For example, attention might be particularly susceptible to change by stimulant treatment because of changes in the orienting strategies, defined by long-term memory structures, that subsequently determine how a child searches through and filters incoming information. Although we note a change in what is considered attention, it does not imply that this represents the focus of some cognitive change. Regardless of which pattern of cognitive factors might adequately account for what we observe altered, we must consider that pattern of cognition in relation to the clinical features of a disorder. Therefore, this would require a design in which such factors are explicitly built into a study design and thereby tested experimentally rather than inferred by post-hoc statistical analysis.

COGNITIVE MODELS AND FRAMEWORKS

Outlined below are three broadly defined conceptualizations which are useful in defining how experiences are perceived, attended, stored, transformed, learned, and retrieved from memory. These are characterized in summary fashion in Figure 3. These approaches each represent a variety of somewhat different but specific models of storage, learning, memory, and retrieval of events. Each position has been worked out in great detail outside a clinical arena but should provide some important new knowledge for our understanding of the

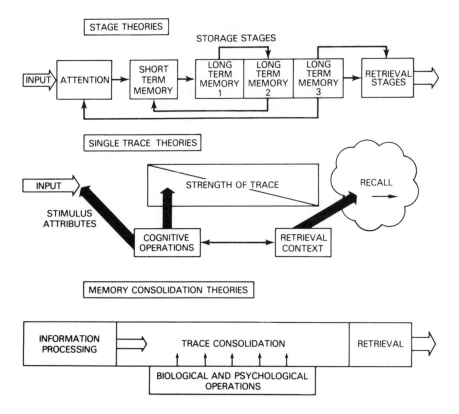

FIG. 3.   Features of stage, single process, and consolidation theories of cognition.

psychobiology of cognitive disturbances in children. In exploring these models, the reader is first introduced to an outline of the traditional use of these approaches, then to instances where these have been used clinically, and finally, to how these approaches might be used in future research.

The multitude of cognitive approaches have been reduced to three classes of models. These are now contrasted and then integrated. Each approach is examined by the way it defines how experiences are processed and learned, and how trace events are represented and retrieved from memory. Together they afford perspectives for understanding the cognitive aspects of psychiatric syndromes, drug altered states, and neurobehavioral disorders.

Although specific information processing theories have been frequently employed in the study of clinical populations, their value has only recently been realized for defining changes in language, thinking, learning, remembering, and other aspects of experience processing. Three explanations are apparent:

1. Many of the techniques used to study cognitive processes in clinical studies represent an unnecessarily simple rendering of information processing systems. They often represent dated versions of some theory which has long since been modified by its initial proponents.

2. Investigators using models of cognition to test characteristics of a syndrome frequently fail to integrate or bridge divergent theoretical positions. This may be caused by the insularity or unique terminology used to define each theory of memory, learning, or retrieval. In addition, the techniques used to study and test each cognitive hypothesis are often theory bound. They limit broader interpretation and application of findings.

3. Generally, the clinical investigators have failed to appreciate the relevance of the clinical data base as a source of experimental findings for modifying, elaborating, and comparing present theories of learning-memory or formulating new explanations that would account for the variety of mental operations that make up cognition. Clinical studies should be as central to the enterprise of testing theories of cognition as the findings generated from research constructed for the human learning laboratory.

THREE THEORETICAL APPROACHES TO INFORMATION PROCESSING STAGE THEORIES (BIN THEORIES)

Stage theories of information processing were first developed as computer simulation models of cognition. They define event processing as occurring in either serial or parallel stages. Information is represented differently in distinct stages of storage, processing, and retrieval (Simon, 1976; Atkinson & Shiffrin, 1968; Glanzer, 1971; Wickelgren, 1973; Bower, 1967). Each stage also involves the use of different cognitive operations. Disruptions and decay of stored trace events are characterized in a stage specific manner (Glanzer and Schwartz, 1971). Information is described as moving from one stage to another, where each step involves different cognitive processes. These theories were initially elaborated to describe components of storage, but later, theorists postulated similar component retrieval stages for accessing events in memory (Kintsch, 1970). A typical model of this kind views information as flowing through some attentional system (a sensory register), a short-term memory store, one or several long-term memory stores, and either one or several retrieval stages. When learning takes place, information is said to be shifted from short- to long-term memory, a necessary condition for the establishment of a permanent record in memory.

This theoretical position can also be classified as a multiple trace model of memory and learning, since the representation of previously processed events is different at each stage of information processing. In each stage of storage or retrieval an event is represented uniquely, decays at different rates, and is unequally susceptible to interference effects. Stage theories have generally ignored the "dynamics" of information processing and issues of encoding.

Clinically, this cognitive framework has served as a basis for much of the research in (1) memory effects of lateralized brain lesions in man (Drachman and Arbit, 1966; Baddley and Warrington, 1970; Milner, 1971), (2) defining some of the cognitive deficits seem in depression (Henry et al., 1973), and (3) measuring cognitive responses to psychoactive drugs (Murphy and Weingartner, 1973; Weingartner and Murphy, 1977a, 1977b). This theoretical framework has not been often used to characterize schizophrenic-like thought disorders where qualitative aspects of encoding operations appear to be a particularly relevant concern (Weingartner et al., in press).

SINGLE TRACE THEORIES OF MEMORY AND LEARNING (SPECIFIC EFFORT THEORIES)

Single trace models of memory/learning have been developed as a contrasting and competitive system to the stage theories (Jenkins, 1974). This alternative view of cognition postulates that information does not exist in different representational forms and/or strengths in different stages of memory. Rather, cognitive processing, as in remembering, is described along a strength continuum (Craik and Lockhart, 1972; Craik and Tulving, 1975; Lockhart et al., 1975). Strength of memory traces is defined by retrieval probability and/or by the operations performed at time of stimulus processing (Hyde, 1973; Hyde and Jenkins, 1973). Orienting tasks (Hyde, 1973; Hyde and Jenkins, 1973), stimulus relevance, familiarity, rehearsal strategies, and the informational context that surrounds input are a few of the variables considered to influence how "deeply" or "completely" an event is processed. This determines the "salience," "elaborateness," or strength (probability of recall) of the memory representations of trace events. Stated simply, we remember an event not because it has been shifted or transformed from short- to long-term memory, but because we have attended to the "meaning" of that event, related it to past information (rehearsed it), and found it more pertinent and compelling than other ongoing events.

Another aspect of single trace or depth of processing theories has been the consideration of the *qualitative* nature of trace events. This view of memory emphasizes that the encoding of an event is set by the context in which input processing occurs. Retrieval of information is dependent on both the depth of processing (at the time of storage) and the similarity of retrieval context with storage context. Events in memory may be stored but not recalled because the retrieval context is inappropriate. This would be an instance of memory failure where stored information was potentially "available" but "inaccessible." One form of this theory has considered the specificity of encoding operations and retrieval operations as being context dependent. What has been stored is considered necessarily linked to the retrieval conditions used to test for the presence of the trace event in memory (Tulving and Thomson, 1973; Eich et al., 1975; Weingartner, 1978).

Single trace theories have not been used very much to explore cognitive disturbances in psychiatric syndromes, despite the fact that they are particularly useful in defining encoding operations and the uniqueness of input processing. They have been important, however, in the development of cognitive theories of drug altered changes in brain state, particularly for those drugs that induce dissociations in memory, a phenomena defined as state dependent learning (Weingartner, 1978). This has been observed in hyperactive children treated with stimulant medication (Swanson and Kinsbourne, 1976), as well as in other instances that involve clinically defined populations (Weingartner et al., 1977; Reus et al., 1979).

MEMORY CONSOLIDATION THEORIES (SOLIDIFICATION THEORIES)

Trace consolidation or memory consolidation theory has been investigated almost exclusively in animal learning paradigms (McGaugh and Herz, 1972; Gibbs and Mark, 1973). Theories of memory consolidation can be defined in terms of a series of experimental operations that include: (1) acquisition or learning of some behaviors, (2) biologic treatments following learning, such as with the use of drugs, electroconvulsive shock, or other treatments for altering neurochemical milieu, brain state arousal, etc in a time and intensity dependent manner *after processing,* and (3) retrieval at some later time, either just after either similar treatments or in an unaltered brain state. Treatments that disrupt brain state arousal after information processing are viewed as altering the likelihood of translating transient trace events into a permanent (consolidated) record of experience (Bloch, 1976; Weingartner et al., 1976). This view of memory has not often been applied to information processing in man.

SOME SIMILARITIES AND DIFFERENCES IN THESE THEORETICAL APPROACHES

Staging theories of information processing share much in common with concepts used to define consolidation. This is not immediately apparent because staging theorists, unlike investigators of memory consolidation, ignore biological events and have limited their research to studies of human learning rather than animal learning experiments. On the other hand, consolidation theory is described biologically, both in terms of defining operations (eg, treatment, dose, or intensity, time of treatment, central nervous system locus of treatment) and presumed underlying mechanisms (eg, change in the biological structure of a trace event, in forming a chemical template from some transient neuroelectrical event). Consolidation theory emphasizes the context and content of internal stimuli (eg, drives, motivation, arousal) as these might affect ongoing learning processes. In contrast, staging theories emphasize differences in the characteristics of stimuli (eg, language versus pattern information, organized versus random stimuli), mode of presentation, sequencing of events, and the time between storage and retrieval as determinants of what might be stored in memory. Internal state variables are ignored by staging theorists. Staging theories and concepts of memory trace consolidation imply the existence of several complementary, parallel, and changing representations in memory.

Single trace theories of memory and learning can be viewed as contextual theories of cognition. They emphasize conditions that are present when experiences are processed and stored in memory. Structural characteristics of stimuli are considered as important as in staging theories, but these are also used to link information storage and retrieval. Single trace theories specify strength of trace by relating retrieval probability with storage processes performed at the time information is laid down in memory. These orienting and encoding strategies can also determine the qualitative characteristics of the trace events, which are ignored in both consolidation and multiple stage theories of memory. These operations are defined almost exclusively in terms of an informational context or behavioral sets rather than as biological determinants. The one exception to this psychological rather than biological description of context is in studies of state dependent learning (Weingartner, 1978). In these investigations, the context for learning derives from a manipulation of brain state, rather than from structuring a field of information or providing an instructional set. Nonetheless, recent state dependent learning studies have also neglected to focus on the neuropharmacological specificities of different drugs. The salient features of each of these approaches to memory, learning, storage and retrieval are outlined in Table 1.

Differences in the language and terminology used to describe the theoretical structures of these three different cognitive approaches accounts for much of the apparent disparity between them. Furthermore, the consensually agreed upon manipulations used by researchers of each mode, the types of cognitive responses of interest, and the kinds of subjects studied all help to insulate these potentially overlapping and complementary approaches from one another. For example, researchers studying consolidation processes, using post-processing treatments to affect changes in output measures, such as response probability or response rate, do not infer anything about mediational processes or change structures in long-term memory. The choice of learning tasks is guided more by factors such as whether the

TABLE 1. Features of Theories of Learning and Memory

Stage Theories	Context Theories	Consolidation Theory
Different trace events at different stages of storage	Single trace that varies in strength	Performance is a function of learning and the time $\times$ intensity of post-learning treatment

TABLE 2. Experimental Findings Used to Explore Modes of Memory and Learning

	Stage Theories	Context Theories	Consolidation Theory
Type of subject	Human	Human	Animal
Type of learning	Primarily verbal learning; relatively meaningless items	Meaningful information; manipulate encoding operations	Operant learning, conditioning
Type of data	1. Serial position curve 2. Recall = a function of retrieval × time, eg, immediate vs delayed recall; short-term memory decay	1. Encoding context vs retrieval context 2. Test recall probabilities = retrieval test	1. Response latency 2. Probability of correct responses
Type of manipulation	1. Time 2. Rehearsal 3. Amount, form, and position of information	1. Storage and retrieval context 2. Processing operations 3. Processes that occur between storage and retrieval	1. Drugs and other brain-state manipulation, post-processing 2. Arousal/activation

behavior is rapidly acquired than theoretical concerns about the nature of memory traces. Furthermore, in responding, the animals do not think or generate retrieval strategies or access memory; they respond correctly or incorrectly with some response latency.

Nevertheless, it is quite possible to view consolidation in terms akin to trace change, or shift from short- to long-term memory. Depth or elaborateness of event processing can be viewed similarly by considering how much information has been shifted from short- to long-term memory. Conversely, it is plausible to reflect storage stages and trace consolidation in terms of depth of processing factors.

An example may clarify this further. The "serial position effect" has been used to explore short- versus long-term memory and has been analyzed in the following manner. To be recalled later, the initial input items must be stored in long-term memory while the last presented items must, if remembered, represent output from short-term memory. Alternatively, the same phenomena and findings are explained in terms of single trace concepts of storage, where initially presented items are processed more deeply because of a lack of interference from previously presented items and more opportunity for rehearsal. The last items are not followed by other items that would retroactively interfere with processing (eg, rehearsal). It follows that the first and last items are remembered better than the items in the middle of a sequence because they have been processed more completely and effectively.

All these theoretical positions differentiate between storage and retrieval. Although they all focus ultimately on the same functions, ie, learning and recalling, none has yet been integrated effectively into a comprehensive explanation of the biological and psychological determinants which modulate information processing. Some of the experimental strategies and findings used to explore and test these different learning-memory systems are outlined in Table 2.

CLINICAL APPLICATION

Clinical investigators must systematically consider the implications of these different theories of cognition. Failure to do so prevents the selective application of a particular explanation or model to a carefully chosen research problem. Staging theory was dominant ten years ago. Currently, studies exploiting single trace, "levels of processing" methods are multiplying rapidly. There has been little consideration of the potential interplay of these approaches. Collectively, these approaches would provide powerful explanations of many features found in disorders of intellectual function (ie, neurochemically or neuropathologically based diseases).

The clinical and psychopharmacological findings that have emerged from studies using the different approaches to information storage and retrieval are outlined in Table 3. Those studies derived from staging theories have focused primarily on disturbances in the shift of information from short- to long-term memory (eg, described as the central deficit in Korsakoff's syndrome at one time). Also, disruption in the development of a long-term memory trace was described as stimulus specific (eg, impairment of learning verbal items — as opposed to visual ones — after partial removal of the left temporal lobe). Memory research in depression related the failure in shifting information from short- to long-term memory to the intensity of depression.

Clinical investigators have attended to the nature of encoding operations only in the last few years (Weingartner et al., 1979; Caine et al., 1978). For example, the methods and techniques associated with single trace theories have proved fruitful in studying Huntington's

TABLE 3. Clinical and Psychopharmacological Findings and Models
of Learning and Memory

Stage Theories	Context Theories	Consolidation Theory
1. Amnesia syndromes (Korsakoffs' syndrome, temporal lobe lesions)	1. Drug manipulations at storage/retrieval (state dependent learning)	1. Behavioral and pharmacological manipulations after acquisition changes recall probability (animals)
2. Depression	2. Mood disturbances	2. Cholinergic state dependent learning (human)—combined with context theory
3. CNS Depressants	3. Dementia and amnesia syndromes	
4. Drugs that reverse cognitive deficits (eg, 1-dopa in depression)	4. Drugs that facilitate learning	

disease. Patients demonstrate an inability to differentially retrieve words with unique stimulus properties (eg, high versus low imagery words) (Weingartner et al., 1979). This kind of approach has also proved useful in elucidating the psychological properties of specific amnesia-producing drugs. Scopolamine, for example, prevents individuals from recalling words processed for their meaning more efficiently than words processed for sound properties. These same subjects show the normal "semantic processing" advantage after administration of placebo (Caine et al., 1978). But single trace theories, like the stage theories before them, have traditionally tended to ignore neurochemical and neurophysiological mechanisms which must mediate brain function. Issues as defined by single trace theories may be particularly pertinent for defining differences between children with learning problems and those who learn normally. Specific cognitive strategies that children use to operate on information processing may be particularly pertinent in uncovering specific cognitive changes in the hyperactive syndrome in children (Weingartner and Ferguson, in press).

Similarly, the animal learning research literature is replete with parallel kinds of studies demonstrating the amnesic effects of post-learning electroconvulsive therapy, but investigators have only recently asked whether such "forgetting" might be retrieval cue-dependent. In fact, these apparently unconsolidated or disrupted memory traces can be retrieved when the animal is treated with a reminder or cue shock. This raises a parallel issue that is rarely considered in disrupted cognition in children, namely, what is the nature of the events succeeding input processing that may play a major role in altering cognition and trace formation.

Other problems arise when reviewing clinical investigations. Neuropsychiatric syndromes have been studied as a static problem, where diseased patients are considered as constant over time and are compared to a matched, "normal" control group. There has been little consideration that many of these disorders are dynamic, evolving conditions. Most studies have ignored the potential of acute, "diagnostic" drug treatments or prolonged therapeutic trials as tools to further study a syndrome. Also, we know that an individual's motivational state can dramatically alter the recall probability of processed events. The motivational variable is often considered an undesirable artifact, one that is allowed to remain uncontrolled and vary randomly. It could serve as an independent variable worthy of systematic study, particularly in studies of altered cognition in children. Such research would necessarily involve investigations of arousal and activation. In turn, this would lead to a consideration of the reticular activating system and the limbic system, and their respective roles in modulating motivation, learning, and remembering. Future efforts to study clinical syndromes systematically using some of these "experimental" cognitive approaches might include: (1) serial evaluations of cognitive functions during the evolution of specific neuropathologically or nosologically defined syndromes; (2) studies in which treatments are introduced at defined stages during an illness; (3) acute trials in healthy people who are administered neurotransmitter agonists and antagonists before, during, and after learning of verbal as well as nonverbal information; and (4) direct manipulations of encoding processes in the context of pharmacological studies.

After having briefly considered the major, current theoretical themes developed by experimental psychologists who study learning and memory, what might be useful in defining a psychobiology of cognition in children? It should be possible to define which stages of information processing are particularly disrupted in some syndrome and how this may be related to other aspects of the disorder. For example, are hyperactive children primarily unable to attend to information but quite capable of accessing information which we know they have stored in memory? Having attended information, are these children as effective in shifting information into some more permanent memory register? It is quite possible to measure aspects of arousal/activation. Perhaps changes in some aspects or stages of information storage or retrieval are related to focal changes in information processing, and these same components are altered by stimulant treatment of these children. It may also be useful to ask whether such children fail to form elaborated or salient trace events in memory and for this reason fail to learn normally. Here single trace context theories may be quite useful in exploring the psychobiology of disrupted cognition and its remediation. If hyperactive children fail to consolidate information in memory it may prove particularly useful to explore the behavioral and biological events that precede information storage. Would some post-processing drug treatments normalize cognitive processes in the hyperactive child? And how would this alter our view of this disorder?

These are but a few of the issues that can be considered in research strategies and might reflect current conceptualization about the nature of cognitive processes and the varieties of ways in which these might be altered. Precisely because we have available powerful biological measures and tools for altering behavior, and because so much of our thinking has turned to biological explanations of disordered children, we are dependent on more precise methods of evaluating the behavior of such children. The precision of our methods of behavioral analysis must be commensurate with the precision of our biological measures if we are to make good use of the power of our biological tools.

REFERENCES

Atkinson RC, Shiffrin RM: A proposed system and its control processes, in Spence KW, Spence JT (eds): *The Psychology of Learning and Motivation: Advances in Research and Theory,* vol 2. New York, Academic Press, 1968, pp 890-921

Baddley AD, Warrington E: Amnesia and the distinction between long and short-term memory. *J Verb Learn Verb Behav* 9:176-189, 1970

Bloch U: Brain activation and memory consolidation, in Rosenzweig ME, Bennett EC (eds): *Neural Mechanisms of Learning and Memory.* Cambridge, Massachusetts, MIT Press, 1976, pp 583-590

Bower GH: A multicomponent theory of the memory trace, in Spence KW, Spence JT (eds): *The Psychology of Learning and Motivation: Advances in Research and Theory,* vol 1. New York, Academic Press, 1967

Caine ED, Hunt RD, Weingartner H, et al.: Huntington's dementia: Clinical and neuropsychological features. *Arch Gen Psychiatry* 35:377-384, 1978

Craik FIM, Lockhart RS: Levels of processing: A framework for memory research. *J Verb Learn Verb Behav* 11:671-684, 1972

Craik FIM, Tulving E: Depth of processing and the retention of words in episodic memory. *J Exp Psychol [Gen]* 104:268-294, 1975

Drachman DA, Arbit J: Memory and the hippocampal complex: Is memory a multiple process? *Arch Neurol* 15:52-61, 1966

Eich J., Weingartner H, Stillman RC, et al.: Statedependent accessibility of retrieval cues in the retention of a categorized list. *J Verb Learn Verb Behav* 14:408-417, 1975

Gibbs ME, Mark RF: *Inhibition of Memory Formation.* New York, Plenum Press, 1973

Glanzer M: Short-term storage and long-term storage in recall. *J Psychiatr Res* 8: 423-438, 1971

Glanzer M, Cunitz AR: Two storage mechanisms in free recall. *J Verb Learn Verb Behav* 5:351-360, 1966

Glanzer M, Schwartz A: Mnemonic structure in free recall: Differential effects on STS and LTS. *J Verb Learn Verb Behav* 10:194-198, 1971

Henry G, Weingartner H, Murphy DL: Influence of affective states and psychoactive drugs on verbal learning and memory. *Am J Psychiatry* 130:966-971, 1973

Hyde TS: Differential effects of effort and type of orienting task on recall and organization of highly associated words. *J Exp Psychol* 79:111-113, 1973

Hyde TS, Jenkins, JJ: Recall for words as a function of semantic, graphic and syntactic orienting tasks. *J Verb Learn Verb Behav* 12:471-480, 1973

Jenkins JL: Remember that old theory of memory? Well, forget it. *Am Psychol* 7:785-794, 1974

Kintsch W: Models for free recall and recognition, in Norman DA (ed): *Models of Human Memory*. New York, Academic Press, 1970, pp 331-373

Lockhart RS, Craik FIM, Jacoby LL: Depth of processing in recognition and recall: Some aspects of a general memory system, in Brown J (ed): *Recognition and Recall*. London, Wiley, 1975

McGaugh JC, Herz MJ: *Memory Consolidation*. San Francisco, Albion Publishing Co, 1972

Milner B: Memory and the medial temporal regions of the brain, in Pribram KH, Broadbent DO (eds): *Biology of Memory*. New York, Academic Press, 1971, pp 29-50

Murphy DL, Weingartner H: Catecholamines and memory: Enhanced verbal learning during L-Dopa administration. *Psychopharmacology* 27:319-326, 1973

Peterson LR, Peterson MJ: Short-term retention of individual verbal items. *J Exp Psychol* 58: 193-198, 1959

Raymond B: Short-term storage and long-term storage in free recall. *J Verb Learn Verb Behav* 8:567-574, 1969; 276-284, 1977

Reus V, Weingartner H, Post R: Clinical implications of state-dependent learning. *Am J Psychiatry* 136:927-931, 1979

Simon HE: Different traces in STM and LTM. The information storage system called "human memory," in Rosenzweig ME, Bennett EC (eds): *Neural Mechanisms of Learning and Memory*. Cambridge, Massachusetts, MIT Press, 1976, pp 79-96

Swanson J, Kinsbourne M: Stimulant related state-dependent learning in hyperactive children. *Science* 192:1754-1757, 1976

Tulving E, Thomson DM: Encoding specificity and retrieval process in episodic memory. *Psychol Rev* 80:352-373, 1973

Weingartner H: Human state-dependent learning, in HO BT, Richards DW, Chute DC (eds): *Drug Discrimination and State-Dependent Learning*. New York, Academic Press, 1978, pp 361-382

Weingartner H, Caine ED, Ebert MH: Imagery, encoding and the retrieval of information from memory: Some specific encoding-retrieval changes in Huntington's disease. *J Abnorm Psychol* 88:52-58, 1979

Weingartner H, Ferguson B: Learning disabilities in children. *Psychol Bull* (in press)

Weingartner H, Miller HA, Murphy DL: Affect state-dependent learning. *J Abnorm Psychol* 86:276-284, 1977

Weingartner H, Miller H, Murphy DL: Mood state-dependent retrieval of verbal associations. *J Abnorm Psychol* 86:276-284, 1977

Weingartner H, Murphy DL: Brain states and memory. *Psychopharmacol Bull* 13(1):66-68, 1977a

Weingartner H, Murphy DL: State-dependent storage and retrieval of experience, in Birnbaum IM, Parker ES (eds): *Alcohol and Human Memory*. New York, John Wiley & Sons, 1977b, pp 159-176

Weingartner H, Murphy DL, Weinstein S: Imagery, affective arousal and memory consolidation. *Nature* 263:311-312, 1976

Weingartner H, Van Kammen DL, Docherty J: The schizophrenic thought process: Structure, storage and retrieval of information from memory. *J Abnorm Psychol* (in press)

Wickelgren WA: The long and the short of memory. *Psychol Bull* 80(6):425-437, 1973

$$7$$

Stimulant Related Growth Inhibition in Children: A Review

LAURENCE L. GREENHILL

This chapter will review the literature describing stimulant related growth inhibition in hyperkinetic children. The approach will be critical, emphasizing worthwhile data while spotlighting the methodological pitfalls which appear in most of the work. The best data can be found in papers that have utilized standard clinical doses of stimulants continuously over long periods of time to generate dose-response curves, relating stimulant dose to growth suppressant effects.

Since Bradley's report (1937) that amphetamines (Benzedrine) could calm some hyperactive children, the stimulant medications have become the most controversial and best studied of the psychoactive drug treatments for children's behavior disorders. Stimulants, and in particular, methylphenidate, appear to be the treatment of choice (Shopsin and Greenhill, 1976) for children who fit criteria (APA, 1980) for the attention deficit disorder of childhood with hyperkinesis

(ADDH). Multiple short-term drug trials have shown that methylphenidate and d-amphetamine are significantly superior to placebo in improving the behavior of children with ADDH on parent and teacher global rating forms (Gittelman-Klein, 1975). The reduction of inattentiveness and hyperactivity and the improvement on psychological tests following stimulant administration (Greenhill, 1977) is also seen in normal children (Rapoport et al., 1980), so this drug response is not diagnostically specific for any psychiatric disorder (Shaffer and Greenhill, 1979).

There is no way of predicting, however, which child is likely to respond or how long treatment will be helpful. Long-term follow-up of children treated with stimulants show that they suffer persistent academic difficulties (Weiss et al., 1975). Children with learning disabilities but no hyperactivity are not helped on achievement tests by methylphenidate or by other stimulants (Gittelman-Klein and Klein, 1976).

The side-effects reported in these short-term drug studies appeared to be mild and well-tolerated. Stimulants cause children to fall asleep later than usual, but this initial insomnia may be handled by changing the time of dosage, and no drug-related changes in sleep architecture have been reported (Greenhill et al., 1981). A dose dependent depression of food intake may be seen initially (Bradley, 1950), enough to cause weight loss, but the anorexia diminishes with time (Rapoport and Quinn, 1974). Methylphenidate may increase blood pressure and pulse rate, both at rest and during exercise (Greenhill, 1977; Werry et al., 1980). Irritability, tearfulness, and sensitivity to criticism, which can resemble a minor depressive episode, may be seen. Other rarer short-term treatment emergent symptoms include abdominal pain, hyperacusis, the appearance of tics (Denckla et al., 1976), outbursts of aggressiveness, visual hallucinations, psychosis, allergic reactions, and periods of fearfulness (Greenhill, 1977); these symptoms generally respond to a reduction or cessation of dosage. Although there was general concern that psychological dependence to stimulants could develop after chronic treatment (Goyer et al., 1979; Schrag and Divoky, 1975), long-term follow-up (Laufer, 1971) has indicated that substance abuse does not occur in children previously treated with stimulants, even when compared to nonhyperactive controls (Beck et al., 1975; Hechtman et al., 1978).

It was not until Daniel Safer reported drug related growth inhibition that stimulants were known to have long-term side-effects. His data suggested that a dose related growth suppression of weight and height attainment occurred in children treated continuously with stimulants for one year (Safer and Allen, 1973; Safer et al., 1975). ADDH children, whose measured height and weight had been assigned percentiles on the age-corrected normative growth charts (Vaughan, 1969), showed significant weight percentile losses in comparison with untreated ADDH children. Although Safer's work suffered from retrospective data collection without prior standardization of measurement techniques, it was impressive that no growth inhibition was present in the group of children on the low dose of methylphenidate and that the growth rates of children discontinued from the medicine returned to near normal levels (Safer et al., 1975).

Safer's reports were a cause for concern. A significant retardation of growth would be a serious side-effect (Eisenberg, 1972). Wender (1971) has estimated that ADDH may occur in five percent of the primary school population, and up to one percent of primary school age children may be taking stimulants (Krager and Safer, 1974). Methods should be developed to avoid growth suppression in such a large group of treated children, especially if the effect were not reversible. Even if a subgroup of children were vulnerable, temporary suppression of height velocity could be serious for the child of short stature and for the child who remains on the drug past the point in development when his long-bone epiphyses close, limiting further height growth.

This chapter will begin with a brief survey of the literature of stimulant related growth disturbance, emphasizing the various methodological approaches used to study both treated and untreated children. Hypothesized mechanisms of the growth problem will be explored. This chapter will close with a description of a stimulant administration method which will avoid growth problems.

STIMULANT RELATED GROWTH SUPPRESSION

The stimulant growth literature is troubled by its diversity and the irregularity of general methodological approaches. These studies display a general absence of standardized drug dosages, of growth measurement techniques, and of controlled study time periods. Some lack adequate baseline growth measures and others follow subjects on multiple psychoactive drugs. Even a short-term drug trial with a handful of subjects can produce complex tables of growth data (Puig-Antich et al., 1978) which introduce new terms ("expected height velocity") to the reader. Often the actual mean growth losses seem small, eg, 0.8 inches of height growth less than expected per year (Greenhill et al., 1981), but these effects may be cumulative during prolonged therapy.

The stimulant-growth literature was surveyed initially by Overall (1977) in consultant papers written for the Pediatric Subcommittee of the Federal Drug Administration and the Psychopharmacologic Drugs Advisory Committee (Roche et al., 1979). Growth parameters, types of normative growth charts, methodological approaches of individual studies, and the specific drugs and their growth effects were carefully assessed.

Their review revealed that the literature on untreated children with ADDH demonstrated no general evidence of abnormal growth patterns. Hyperactive children before treatment are near published medians for stature and weight. Longitudinal data of untreated hyperactive children followed normative growth curves in both a one-year prospective study (Rapoport and Quinn, 1974) and in a two-year retrospective study (Safer et al., 1972). Overall (1977) has concluded that the baseline data from multiple drug studies show normal growth parameters for untreated hyperactive children, making it unlikely that the growth problems in children with ADDH arise from other causes than the stimulants.

GROWTH PARAMETERS AND NORMATIVE GROWTH DATA

There are three different ways of expressing data on a child's growth: the actual height (in centimeters) or weight (in kilograms); the child's percentile, when his height or weight is plotted on the age-corrected normative growth charts; or his growth velocity in cm/yr for height or in kg/yr for weight.

Many investigators have tracked the maturity and the longitudinal growth of their treated hyperactive children by using percentile charts and curves derived cross-sectionally from normal children. Often these curves are based on a single growth measure taken from a group of children of many different ages. Curve smoothing techniques are used to generate group growth curves to approximate the growth of children followed longitudinally (Hamill et al., 1976). One must realize that these curves are generated from many bits of cross-sectionally derived data and are probably unreliable for predicting the true longitudinal course of an individual child's growth (Gittelman-Klein, personal communication).

Investigators tend to use a number of growth charts. Some (Puig-Antich et al., 1978; Safer et al., 1977; Greenhill et al., 1981; Gross, 1976) have employed the Iowa or Boston charts (Vaughan, 1969), which are based on cross-sectional measures collected from very small child groups studied over 40 years ago. The best available reference data for United States children currently comes from the National Center for Health Statistics (NCHS), which has detailed growth percentile tables. Unfortunately, even the NCHS data is cross-sectionally derived. Age, race, sex, and a large number of other variables are also included (Malina, 1974). The NCHS tables have been adopted in the most recent studies (Mattes and Gittelman-Klein, 1979; Satterfield et al., 1979).

Why use these cross-sectional controls, which only serve as approximations of longitudinal data? The percentile charts are convenient for they can adjust for age differences when comparing growth data among a large diverse sample of children. Of course, there can be complexities in the interpretation and analysis of this data. Roche (1977) has commented on the need to match any controls employed for age and sex. Changes in the percentile ranks of treated children have been difficult to interpret without the mean and variance of corresponding growth changes in the control children. Hoeffler (1974) suggests that the use of parametric statistics to test the significance of percentile rank changes (Puig-Antich et al., 1978; Safer et al., 1972; Greenhill et al., 1981) may be inaccurate for other reasons since the percentile ranking is ordinal data and it requires nonparametric analysis. Most studies use parametric Student's t tests in data analysis, however.

Growth velocity data is more reliable than percentile ranks since the numbers are not derived from normative percentile charts. Throughout the pre-pubertal period, the growth velocities are reasonably stable. The velocity data can be generated by subtracting the mean growth height or weight from the mean values one year earlier in the same percentile column in either the Iowa Tables or in the NCHS Tables. Growth velocity data is only accurate when readings are taken at least nine months apart (Jose, 1975). Tanner (Tanner et al., 1966a, 1966b) has developed a series of age-corrected height and weight velocity curves, based on the British school children, which have proven useful in our studies. Although these velocity norms are cross-sectionally derived, they will serve as approximations for tracking any individual children's growth patterns longitudinally. Only two authors (Puig-Antich et al., 1978; Greenhill et al., 1981) have identified the source of their growth velocity norms, though many use them (Dickinson et al., 1979; Safer and Allen, 1973; Safer et al., 1972, 1975).

METHODOLOGICAL APPROACHES IN GROWTH STUDIES

Control data have been extremely critical for the full interpretation of the growth inhibition side-effect. Statistically significant growth rate inhibition in stimulant-treated hyperactive children (STHC) has been demonstrated by combining the data of multiple studies, as shown in a recent review (Roche et al., 1979). Five different control techniques (Overall, 1977) have been used in this literature to study growth deficits.

1. Comparison of STHC with Published Age-Corrected Normative Data

STHC of different ages and with different duration of treatment has produced individual cross-sectional growth measures which have been plotted onto percentile charts in a variety of studies (Roche, 1977). This technique is the weakest for analyzing growth data, for published age-corrected normative charts do not give reliable norms for longitudinal growth. Gross (1976), for example, analyzed longitudinally collected growth data on STHC of different ages and converted the data to percentiles at the end of treatment using cross-sectional tables. He could have achieved greater precision by using the many cross-sectional individual height and weight measures, obtaining the percentiles, and analyzing the group data nonlongitudinally as if each measure represented a different child.

2. STHC Used As Their Own Controls (Serial Growth Data) Using Percentile Changes On Published Normative Data

This technique is highly popular, and it involves plotting a child's repeated measures serially on age-corrected growth charts. It has been utilized in much of the literature (Dickinson et al., 1979; Greenhill et al., 1981; Gross, 1976; Millichap and Millichap, 1975; Oettinger et al., 1977; Page et al., 1974; Puig-Antich et al., 1978; Safer and Allen, 1973; Safer et al., 1972, 1975; Satterfield, 1979; Weiss et al., 1975). Gross (1976) has commented that individual serial growth curve irregularities can be smoothed out by looking at group data. All published tables, as mentioned before, are based on cross-sectional data, which limit the accuracy of analyses to attained size rather than to velocities of growth for the individual patients in these studies (Malina, 1974).

3. Comparison of Attained Size in STHC with Untreated Nonhyperactives

The procedure compares actual growth measures rather than percentiles and basically involves cross-sectional data (Beck et al., 1975; McNutt et al., 1976; 1977; Oettinger et al., 1977) obtained simultaneously from STHC and from nonhyperactive children followed in the same clinic. One must take care to match the two groups for age, season of measurement, and activity level. McNutt (1977) weakened her analysis by comparing older hyperactives measured in the spring and fall with younger normals measured in the summer during an exercise program. Growth rates of children are faster in summer, and this could have complicated the results. Roche (1977) has commented on the complexities of comparison when the hyperactives and normals differ in age or in activity level.

4. Comparison of STHC with Untreated Hyperactives

This method controls for any as yet undiscovered growth delays associated with ADDH itself. Overall (1977) has been concerned that untreated hyperactive children may be a poor control for STHC because of hidden sampling errors. Untreated hyperactive children could represent a milder form of the disorder than the children taking drugs. Even with these reservations, growth inhibiting effects of stimulants are significant for STHC when compared with the growth rates of untreated patients (Safer and Allen, 1973; Safer et al., 1972; Weiss et al., 1975, 1979).

5. Comparison of STHC On Drug All Year With STHC On Drug Nine Months (Off Summer)

The final method examines the phenomenon of "catch-up" growth when stimulants are discontinued. Growth rates of STHC on drugs continuously are compared with those of STHC who stop treatment for the summer(Dickinson et al., 1979; Mattes and Gittelman-Klein, 1979; Safer et al., 1972, 1975; Satterfield et al., 1979). Although some of these studies were retrospective (Safer et al., 1972, 1975) or involved prospective methods with missing data (Satterfield et al., 1979), the relatively large total number of children from all these studies (N = 188) is impressive. Clearly, height and weight growth velocities suddenly accelerate soon after stimulants are discontinued.

METHODOLOGICAL PROBLEMS

There are other methodological problems besides the issue of controls. Puig-Antich and colleagues (1978) have drawn attention to the field's reliance on retrospective rather than prospective data. In addition, studies had been started on children who were receiving stimulant treatment before baseline growth measures (Gross, 1976) and may have experienced their velocity deaccelerations before baseline measurements had been taken. In other articles (Beck et al., 1975), the subjects were taking other drugs simultaneously with the stimulants.

Only a few workers have carefully standardized their measures (McNutt et al., 1977) or have taken care to use multiple repeated measurements of recumbent length (Greenhill et al., 1977; Puig-Antich et al., 1978; Greenhill et al., 1981). Judging compliance is also critical, for studies that report no growth inhibition (Gross, 1976) may not supply compliance data showing that the children actually took the pills. A range of stimulant doses is rarely published in any study, in order to find a dose-response curve. Few investigations have bothered to study the mechanism of the disorder, either by *in vitro* studies (Kilgore et al., 1979) or by neuroendocrine or sleep determinations (Dickinson et al., 1979; Greenhill et al., 1981). These study features are more carefully explicated in Table 1.

THE GROWTH DATA ITSELF

Actual growth decrements have been expressed in a variety of ways. Some authors (Satterfield et al., 1979; Safer and Allen, 1973) list mean centimeter or kilogram "deficits" from expected final height or weight attainments. Others list drops in percentile ranks (Puig-Antich et al., 1978). Infrequently, growth velocities are compared statistically with ideal velocities for that age derived from growth tables (Dickinson et al., 1979). Both Safer, Allen, and Barr (1975) and Satterfield and his colleagues (1979) speak of a growth velocity deficit, which is given as a percent of the extent of the difference from the ideal growth velocity. This leads to some confusion when the subject gains *more* than expected.

In this review, an attempt has been made to speak of the percent of expected velocity of "%E" (actual growth velocity divided by the ideal growth velocity multiplied by 100). Thus, if 100% represents a normal growth rate, 120% E would mean the subject is growing 20 percent faster than expected; if he is growing at 80% E, he would have a growth deficit of 20 percent. This "index" is also listed in Table 1.

GROWTH EFFECTS OF INDIVIDUAL DRUGS

D-Amphetamine

D-amphetamine appears to have the most powerful growth inhibiting action, milligram for milligram, of all pharmacological agents used in the treatment of ADDH (See Table 1). Safer, Allen, and Barr (1972) treated 11 children for one year with a mean dose of 11.7 mg/day and saw a 60% E of weight velocity, with an acceleration of weight to 130% E when d-amphetamine was discontinued. Although there were no effects on height velocity in the first 1972 study, in two later studies, he reported that 29 children taking 12 mg of d-amphetamine grew at 75% E of height velocity (Safer and Allen, 1973) and at 68% E of height velocity (Safer et al., 1975); during drug discontinuation, height velocity rose to 123% E. Unfortunately, Safer's studies were retrospective, and standardized measurment techniques ere not utilized.

Puig-Antich and colleagues made a preliminary report on seven children followed prospectively for one year on a higher mean d-amphetamine dose of 22.8 mg/day. These children displayed a

TABLE 1. Studies of Psychoactive Drug Effects on Growth

Drug Type	Study	N	Methodology	Height Growth (% Ex)	Weight Growth (% Ex)	Mean Time Period of Treatment	Mean Dose mg/Day
D-Amphetamine	1. Safer et al., 1972	3M 8M,DC 9M × 7(C)	1,14 1,5,14 1,4,14	No Change No Change –(htpc)	60%E* 130%R* 56%E (−1.3kg)*	12 Months 9 Months 24 Months	11.7 mg/day 11.8 mg/day NG
	2. Safer and Allen, 1973	29M,14C	2,5,14	75%E (−1.5cm)* (−13pc)*	62%E (−0.5kg)* (−20pc)T*	35 Months	NG
	3. Safer et al., 1975	8M 26M,DC	5,7 5,7	68%E* 123%E(R)*	53%E* 150%E(R)*	12 Months 9 Months	12 mg/day 12 mg/day
	4. Gross, 1976	24M	1,14	(+10.9pc)*	(+16.0pc)*	81 Months	19.6 mg/day
	5. Oettinger et al., 1977	25M	1,6	100%E	—	54 Months	17.5 mg/day
	6. Puig-Antich et al., 1978	7M (8M)	1,2,7,8,10,19 11,12,13,14, 16	58%E* (−2.3cm)	28%E* (−1.79kg)	12 Months	22.8 mg/day (0.88mg/kg)
	7. Greenhill et al., 1981	13M	1,2,7,8,10 11,12,13,14, 16	68%E* (−1.8cm)	13%* (−2.6kg/gr)	Up To 21 Months	21 mg/day (0.88mg/kg)

Drug	Study	Sample	Codes			Duration	Dose
Imipramine	1. Gross, 1976	16M,84A	1,14,19	(+8.1pc)*	(−10.4pc)*	57 Months	105 mg/day
	2. Rapoport and Quinn, 1975	12M,12C,23A	2,12,14,16	(−2.2pc) NS	+(−7.6pc) NS	12 Months	65 (2 mg/kg)
	3. Werry, 1980	30M	2,7,8,10,16	NG	(−0.36kg)*	1 Month	54 (2 mg/kg)
Methylphenidate	1. Safer et al., 1972	4M / 5M,DC,9A / 9M×7C	1,12,14 / 1,5,12,14 / 1,4,14	No Change / No Change / No Change	60%E*(X) / 130R*(X) / 56%E* (−1.3kg)	12 Months / 9 Months / 24 Months	37.5 mg / 24 mg / NG
	2. Safer and Allen, 1973	10M,DC / 10M,DC	2,5,12,14 / 2,5,14	(−9pc)*R / (−1pc)	(−10)* / (−3)	35 Months / 35 Months	>20 mg(X) / <20 mg
	3. Safer et al., 1975	8M / 24M,DC	5,7 / 5,7	71%E* / 115%E(R)*	75%E* / 168%E(R)*	12 Months / 9 Months	27 mg/day / 27 mg/day
	4. Beck et al., 1975	30M,30C	3,6,13,18	No Change	No Change	6 Months	NG
	5. Satterfield (in Overall, 1977)	63M (32DC), 100C	4,5,7,10,12, 13,16	75%E*	63%E*	12 Months	25 mg/day

(continued)

TABLE 1. Studies of Psychoactive Drug Effects on Growth (Continued)

Drug Type	Study	N	Methodology	Height Growth (% Ex)	Weight Growth (% Ex)	Mean Time Period of Treatment	Mean Dose mg/Day
	6. Satterfield et al., 1979	72M (41DC)	2,5,7,8,10,14	83%E—(80%ER)	66%E (76%ER)	12 Months	17.4 mg
		48M (24DC)	16	108%E (110%ER)	90%E (102%ER)	24 Months	22 mg
	7. Rapoport and Quinn, 1975	5M × 12C, 12A	2,12,14,16	(−3.0pc)	(−15.4pc)	12 Months	>20 mg
		18M × 12C, 12A		(+5.1pc)	(−6.9pc)	12 Months	≤20 mg
	8. Weiss et al., 1975	13M	1,2,14,16	7/13<E; (−2.4cm)	NG	60 Months	>20 mg
		3M		2/3<E (−2.3cm)	NG	60 Months	≤20 mg
	9. Schain and Reynard, 1975	94M	2,16	NG	(40SS ↓ WT −0.9kg)	4 Months	26.5 mg
	10. Gross, 1976	135M	1,14,19	(+12.8pc)*	(11.4)*	69 Months	43.8 mg
	11. McNutt et al., 1977	28M,24C, 47N	3,4,7,8,10, 13,16,17	No Difference	No Difference	12 Months	24 mg
		13M,10C, 14N	3,4,7,8,10, 16,17	No Difference	No Difference	24 Months	22 mg

Drug	Study	N				Duration	Dose
Methylphenidate (continued)	12. Mattes and Gittelman-Klein, 1979	39M	1,2,3,5,7,8,10,15,16	(−17pc, −0.5cm)	(−20pc, −3kg)	27 Months	40 mg
	13. Millichap and Millichap, 1975	38M	1,2	−(34/50> 68pc)	(29/50> 50pc)	30 Months	≤20
		12M					>20
	14. Werry, 1980	30M	2,7,8,10,16	0	(−0.18kg)	1 Month	11 mg (0.4 mg/day)
Pemoline	1. Page et al., 1974	111M × 105C	3,7,8,13,16	—	(−0.59kg)	13 Months	75 mg (1.9 − 2.5 mg/kg)
		288M	1,2,15,7,8, 13,16	94.4%E	—	19.5 Months	75 mg (1.9 − 2.5 mg/kg)
	2. Dickinson et al., 1979	7M	1,2,16,11,5	66%E(−2cm)	100%E	26 Months	104 mg (3.7 mg/kg)

1 = Index Subject × Published Norms
2 = Subjects As Own Controls
3 = Hyperactives Taking Drug × Untreated Hyperactives
4 = Hyperactives Taking Drug × Untreated Normals
5 = Hyperactives Taking Drug Full Year × Hyperactives On Nine Months (Off Summer)
6 = Follow-up of Adults Who Had Taken Drug
7 = Standardized Reliable Growth Measures
8 = Reliable Baseline Growth Measures
9 = Random Controls Selected
10 = Objective Compliance Measures
11 = Sleep Endocrine Measures
12 = Stimulant Dose—Growth Effect Relationship
13 = Off of Drugs At Baseline
14 = Iowa Norms (1940)
15 = NCHS Norms (1974)

16 = Prospective
17 = Body Composition Measures
18 = Taking More Than One Drug Simultaneously
19 = Control Group Taking Another Drug

M = Children Medicated
N = Normals
C = Hyperactives Off Drug
R = "Rebound" Off Drug
X = "High Dose" Methylphenidate (>20 Mg)
E = Expected Growth Velocity
NG = Not Given
T = Tolerance
DC = Discontinued Drug in Summer
SS = Subjects
* = p<0.05

decreased height (58% E) velocity and very depressed weight velocity (28% E). Greenhill et al. (1981) reported on the full sample of 13 STHC from Puig-Antich's study, and showed more evidence of a significant depression of height velocity (60% E) and weight velocity (13% E) for these children treated for up to 21 months on 21 mg/day. These two studies presented evidence for a dose dependent growth inhibition effect.

Data from seven studies suggest d-amphetamine has a significant effect on weight velocity and may have a depressant effect on height velocity in a sensitive subgroup.

Methylphenidate

Methylphenidate is currently the most popular psychoactive drug for children in the United States (Greenhill, 1977). Safer described, in all three publications (Safer and Allen, 1973; Safer et al., 1972, 1975), a clear dose-response effect with children taking more than 20 mg/day showing significant depressant effects on percentiles, and on height (71% E) and weight (75% E) velocities for eight children taking 27 mg./day for one year. This resulted in deficits of 0.9 cm/yr and 0.5 kg/yr respectively. Rebound growth accelerations occurred for height (115% E) and for weight (168% E) when 24 STHC were discontinued from 27 mg/day of methylphenidate during the summer; however, catch-up was incomplete.

In spite of these observations on the dose-effect of methylphenidate, many workers used subthreshold methylphenidate doses in their growth studies. Satterfield and his colleagues (1979) used 17.4 mg/day for two years in his study of 48 STHC and found height and weight velocities were near normal; McNutt and colleagues (1977) studied 28 STHC taking a mean dose of 24 mg/day of methylphenidate for one year and found no significant differences in body composition measures or height and weight attainments when controlled by a group of untreated hyperactives and untreated normals. Werry, Aman, and Diamond (1980) also found small weight losses when studying 30 STHC for one month on 11 mg/day. Millichap and Millichap (1975) also found most of their sample of 50 STHC children measuring greater than the 50th percentile in height and weight after 30 months of taking 20 mg or less of methylphenidate.

Higher dosage studies do report some positive findings for methylphenidate. Schain (1975) reported a 0.9 kg. weight loss in 40 STHC taking 26.5 mg/day for four months; Mattes and Gittelman-

Klein (1979) reported a 17th percentile height loss and a 20th percentile weight loss in 39 STHC followed for 27 months receiving 40 mg of methylphenidate/day. Satterfield (1975) reported that 63 STHC were growing at lower height velocities (76% E) and weight velocities (63% E) with a one-year treatment with a mean dose of 25 mg/day.

The reports, mainly on prepubertal children, show a variable picture of methylphenidate's actions on growth. Therapy either produces no effect on growth or a gain of from 0.4–0.9 cm/yr less height than expected. Although Mattes' report (1979) suggests cumulative losses may reach as high as three inches from expected height, other reports show reversals in growth (Gross, 1976). These inconsistencies may be due to poor compliance or to methylphenidate's very short plasma half-life of 2.5 hours (Hungund et al., 1979).

Magnesium Pemoline (Cylert)

Page and colleagues (1974) reported an initial loss of weight in 111 STHC receiving a mean dose of 75 mg/day over the first three months. In one of the longest prospective follow-up studies (77 months) of drug treatment, Page found 288 STHC children growing at 94% E of height velocity at 19.5 months of taking 75 mg of pemoline. Dickinson, Lee, and Ringdahl (1979) found seven children had attained 2 cm less height than expected on a higher dose—104 mg/day—after 26 months. The small sample of children makes Dickinson's data difficult to interpret, especially since it is the only report showing height losses without weight losses.

CRITIQUE OF THE GROWTH STUDIES

The majority of research on growth effects in STHC is plagued with severe methodological deficits. Safer's reports are retrospective, used no standardization of measurement methodology (Safer and Allen, 1973; Safer et al., 1972, 1975), and used the Iowa norms for percentile norms. Gross (1976) utilized the Iowa norms, had no compliance checks on whether the children took the medication, had no standardized measurement techniques, and no controls. Beck and colleagues (1975) studied 30 STHC compared with a group of controls, but the dosages of methylphenidate were not given. The children had taken marijuana concomitantly, and the treatment period of six months was probably too short for a drug-growth effect. Millichap and Millichap (1975) and Schain (1975) were uncontrolled anecdotal reports, with little standardization and scanty growth and dosage data, and the subjects were treated for highly variable amounts of time. McNutt, Ballard, and Boileau (1977) used highly sophisticated growth measures and standardized periods of drug exposure in a large number of STHC but utilized relatively low doses of methylphenidate (22 mg/day), and featured control children from an exercise program measured at different times of the year; both factors may explain why they found a minimal effect on growth. Werry et al (1980) utilized low methylphenidate dosages (11 mg/day) for only one month, so growth effects were not reported.

Several studies demonstrated growth suppressant effects when rigorous methodology was used. Individual children who are treated for a year or more with good clinical dosages of the drug show growth suppression. Puig-Antich et al. (1978) and Greenhill et al. (1981) studied small numbers of STHC children on d-amphetamine, had a contrast group on another drug (chlorpromazine) rather than controls, and did not randomize drug assignment. Yet, standardized measurement techniques were used along with prospective data collection, reliable baseline data collection, objective compliance measures, and sleep endocrine measures. These factors make their positive findings of growth suppression more certain. Mattes and Gittelman-Klein utilize NCHS standards, routine methylphenidate dosages (40 mg/day), random selection, controls (STHC and untreated hyperactives), reliable growth measures, objective compliance techniques, and a prospective methodology. Although Satterfield (1979) used prospective methodology, his subjects were treated with small methylphenidate dosages (17.4 mg/day, mean dose).

The growth suppressant effect of stimulants may be related to the pharmacokinetics of the drug. Higher dosages of longer-acting drugs such as d-amphetamine require a shorter exposure (12 months) to see higher suppression. D-amphetamine, in our investigations, shows a mean half-life of 10.5 hours (Ebert, personal communication) in STHC, compared to 2.5 hours for methylphenidate (Perel, personal communication). In addition to our earlier work (Puig-Antich et al., 1978) and that of others (Dickinson et al., 1979; Rapoport et al., 1975; Safer et al., 1972; Safer and Allen, 1973; Satterfield, 1975), other investigators have shown a stimulant dose-growth suppressant effect.

FUTURE STUDIES

The major shortcomings of previously published studies include inadequate stimulant doses, poor design, no compliance measures, retrospective data collections, inadequate controls, and absence of nutritional data. Questions about the true prevalence of growth disorders in STHC, the mechanism involved, and its nutritional component will only be answered by a dual study design. A retrospective investigation of adults who had been STHC must be carried out. In addition, there has to be a prospective, controlled study of STHC with nutritional assessments taken regularly, both for the hyperactive children taking drugs and those on nonpharmacological (behavior modification) therapies. Both studies should utilize family controls (parents and siblings) to obtain some estimate of predicted adult height (Roche, 1975; Oettinger et al., 1975; Kalachnik et al., 1982). Family controls will allow the investigation to estimate the "growth future" of the individual child, as if the child were his own control.

MECHANISMS OF GROWTH EFFECTS

The mechanisms by which stimulant drugs produce slight to moderate growth inhibition, particularly towards the beginning of treatment, are unknown. A variety of hypotheses have been advanced.

1. Nutritional

Anorexia is common and dependent on the amount of stimulant taken (Gross, 1976). Poor nutrition could lead to growth losses, but this seems unlikely, since tolerance to the drug's anorexic effects develops rapidly in adults (FDA, 1979). Still, no studies of nutritional intake of children on long-term stimulant treatment has been carried out, and this nutritional deficiency mechanism must be studied in the population of drug-treated children at risk.

2. Interference with Human Growth Hormone (HGH) Secretion

Reduced growth rates could result from a drug-induced HGH deficiency. Although d-amphetamine and methylphenidate cause insomnia, we found no effect of this stimulant on the secretion of HGH in 13 STHC during slow wave sleep, a portion of sleep physiologically linked to the main secretion of HGH in the growing child (Greenhill et al., 1981). Responses to insulin-induced hypoglycemia (the insulin tolerance test) were also normal in all STHC we treated. Mean sleep-related HGH plasma concentrations were unaffected by stimulants. Dickinson et al. (1979) reported normal HGH levels in STHC treated with magnesium pemoline.

3. Suppression of Prolactin (PRL) Secretion

Mean sleep-related prolactin has been reported to be significantly ($p <$ 0.015) suppressed by d-amphetamine in 13 STHC (Greenhill et al., 1981). Height velocity inhibition was significantly correlated with PRL suppression (Pearson $r = 0.57$, $p < 0.05$) in the STHC taking d-amphetamine. Since PRL has yet to be shown to be a powerful growth factor in humans, the authors concluded that the PRL suppression and growth losses were correlated, but not causally related.

4. Somatomedin Deficiency or End-Organ Resistance to Growth Factors

HGH acts on skeletal tissues indirectly by stimulating the hepatic production of serum peptides called somatomedins (Van Wyck, 1974). Somatomedin abnormalities are present in malnutrition (Pimstone et al., 1973). Kilgore and coworkers (1979) have demonstrated, through in vitro studies, that metamphetamine suppresses somatomedin and interferes with enzymes responsible for cartilage synthesis. In vitro studies have shown that amphetamines alter growth by depressing somatomedin and by inhibiting cartilage cell growth (Kilgore et al., 1979). Clinical studies of somatomedin responses in STHC have yet to be done.

CONCLUSIONS AND RECOMMENDATIONS

Overall (1977) has concluded that, despite methodological problems, these clinical studies provide general evidence that stimulants moderately suppress weight velocity. Drugs appear to have differential growth effects. D-amphetamine probably causes the most intense weight losses and some height velocity decreases; tolerance to its growth suppression was given in one report (Gross, 1976). Methylphenidate causes dose dependent weight losses, but major height velocity decrements were only recently shown by Mattes and Gittelman-Klein (1979) for a sensitive subgroup of children receiving high doses for three to four years. Tolerance to methylphenidate's growth suppression has been discussed in two papers (Gross, 1976; Satterfield et al., 1979). Pemoline has a brief minor effect on weight (Dickinson et al., 1979), but tolerance has been seen by one year (Page et al., 1974).

Clinicians will continue to treat children with stimulant medication because these drugs constitute one of the most effective treatments for the disorder available (Gittelman-Klein, 1975). Incomplete "catch-up" growth during summer drug vacations appears to be useful early in treatment (Safer et al., 1975).

The stimulant-related growth inhibition is not a complete contraindication to their use in the *well diagnosed hyperkinetic child*. A good clinical drug response should be determined initially, before long-term treatment. These studies should, however, provide a further caution to the indiscriminate use of stimulants in children. Since there is no way of identifying those children who might experience marked growth suppression, all pediatric patients treated with these drugs should be followed with regular tri-monthly height and weight measures. The collected data can be plotted on the NCHS curves now available on standard growth charts.

REFERENCES

American Psychiatric Association: *Diagnostic and Statistical Manual of Mental Disorders,* ed. 3. Task Force on Nomenclature and Statistics, Spitzer RL, Washington, DC American Psychiatric Association, 1980, pp 41-45

Beck L, Langford WS, MacKay M, Sum G.: Childhood chemotherapy and later drug abuse and growth curve: A follow-up study of 30 adolescents. *Am J Psychiatry* 132(4):436-438, 1975

Bradley C: The behavior of children receiving benzedrine. *Am J Psychiatry* 94:577, 1937

Bradley C: Benzedrine and Dexedrine in the treatment of children's behavior disorders. *Pediatrics* 5:24, 1950

Dickinson LC, Lee J, Ringdahl IL: Impaired growth in hyperkinetic children receiving pemoline. *J Pediat* 94(4):538-541, 1979

Denckla MB, Bemporad JR, MacKay MC: Tics following methylphenidate administration: A report of 20 cases. *JAMA* 235:1349-1351, 1976

Eisenberg L: The hyperkinetic child and stimulant drugs. *N Eng J Med* 287:249-250, 1972

Federal Drug Administration: Update on amphetamine abuse and labelling. *FDA Drug Bull* 9(4):23, 1979

Gittelman-Klein R, Klein DF: Methylphenidate effects in learning hyperkinesis, in Klein of, Gittelman-Klein R (eds): *Progress in Psychiatric Drug Treatment,* New York, Brunner Mazel, 1975, pp 661-674

Gittelman-Klein R, Klein D F: Methylphenidate effects in learning disabilities. *Arch Gen Psychiatry* 33:655-664, 1976

Goyer PF, Davis GL Rapoport JL: Abuse of prescribed stimulant medication by a 13-year-old hyperactive boy. *J Am Acad Child Psychiatry* 18:170-175, 1979

Greenhill LL: Methylphenidate (Ritalin) and other drugs for treatment of hyperactive children. *Med Lett Drugs Ther* 19(13):53-55, 1977

Greenhill LL: Puig-Antich J, Chambers W, et al.: Growth hormone, prolactin and growth response in hyperkinetic males treated with d-amphetamine. *J Acad Child Psychiatry* 20(1): 71-84, 1981.

Greenhill L, Puig-Antich J, Sachar E: Hormone and growth responses in hyperkinetic children on stimulant medication. *Psychopharmacol Bull* 13(2):33-35, 1977

Greulich W, Pyle SI: *Radiographic Atlas of Skeletal Development of the Hand and Wrist.* Stanford, California, Stanford University Press, 1959

Gross MD: Growth of hyperkinetic children taking Ritalin, Dexedrine, or imipramine/desimipramine. *Pediatrics* 58(3):423-431, 1976

Hamill PVV, Drizd TA, Johnson CL, et al.: *NCHS Growth Charts 1976, Monthly Vital Statistics Report.* Examination Survey Data, National Center for Health Statistics (HRA) 76-1120, 25 (Suppl 3):1-22, 1976

Hechtman L, Weiss G, Perlman T: Growth and cardiovascular measures in hyperactive individuals as young adults and in matched normal controls. *Can Med Assoc J* 118:1247-1250, 1978

Hoeffler DF: The misuse of statistics (continued) letter to the editor. *Pediatrics* 53(4):586-587, 1974

Hungund BL, Perel JM, Hurwic MJ, et al.: Pharmacokinetics of methylphenidate in hyperkinetic children. *Br J Clin Pharmacol* 8:571-576, 1979

Jose EE: Growth hormone deficiency in childhood: Evaluation of diagnostic procedures, in: Falkness F, N. Kretchmer N, Rossi E (eds): *Monographs in Paediatrics,* New York, S. Karger, 1975

Kalachnik J, Sprague R, Sleator E, et al: Effect of methylphenidate hydrochloride on stature of hyperactive Children. *Dev Med Child Neurol* 24:586-595, 1982

Kilgore B, Dickinson L, Burnett C, et al.: Alterations in cartilage metabolism by neurostimulant drugs. *Pediatrics* 94:542-545, 1979

Krager JM, Safer DJ: Type and prevalence of medication used in treatment of hyperkinetic children. *N Eng J Med* 291:118-120, 1974

Laufer MW: Long-term management and some follow-up findings on the use of drugs with minimal cerebral syndromes. *J Learn Dis* 153:518-522, 1971

Loeb JN: Corticosteroids and growth. *N Eng J Med* 295(10):547-552, 1971

McNutt BA, Ballard JE, Boileau R: The effects of long-term stimulant medication on the growth and body composition of hyperactive children. II. Report on two years. *Psychopharmacol Bull,* 13(2):36-38, 1977

McNutt BA, Boileau RA, Cohen MN, et al.: The effects of long-term stimulant medication on the growth and body composition of hyperactive children: First report on two years. Presented at the Meeting of Early Clinical Drug Evaluation Unit of the National Institute of Mental Health, Key Biscayne, Florida, May 1976

Malina RM: Body dimensions and proportions, white and negro children, 6-11 years (United States): National Center for Health Statistics, Vital and Health Statistics. Series 11. Data from the National Health Survey, No. 143, DHEW Publication No. (HRA) 75-1625. Washington, DC, Superintendent of Documents, US Government Printing Office, 1974, pp 22-23

Mattes J, Gittelman-Klein R: Drug linked to growth problem in children. *Psychiatr News* 14(17), 1979

Millichap JG, Millichap M: Growth of hyperactive children. *N Eng J Med* 292:1300, 1975

Oettinger L, Gauch RR, Majousky LV et al.: Bone age in children with minimal brain dysfunction. Percept Mot Skills 39:1127-1131, 1977

Overall J: Evaluation of studies concerning growth of children treated with stimulant drugs. Letter to Jay Cinque, executive secretary, Pediatric Advisory Subcommittee, Federal Drug Administration, 1977

Page JG, Bernstein JE, Janicki RS, Michelli FA: A multi-clinic trial of pemoline in childhood hyperkinesis, in Conners CK (ed): *Clinical Use of Stimulant Drugs in Children.* Netherlands, Excerpta Medica, 1974, pp 98-124

Pimstone BL, Decker JJ, Hansen JDL: Human growth hormone and sulfation factor in protein-calorie malnutrition, in Gardner L, Amocher P (eds): *Endocrine Aspects of Malnutrition.* KROC Foundation Symposia, No. 1. Santa Ynez, California, KROC Foundation, 1973, pp 73-90

Puig-Antich J, Greenhill LL, Sassin J, Sachar EJ: Growth hormone, prolactin, and cortisol responses and growth patterns in hyperkinetic children treated with dextroamphetamine: Preliminary findings. *J Am Acad Child Psychiatry* 17(3):457-475, 1978

Rapoport JL, Quinn PO: One-year follow-up of hyperactive boys treated with imipramine or methylphenidate. *Am J Psychiatry* 132:241-245, 1975

Rapoport JL, Buchsbaum MS, Weingartner H et al.: Dextroamphetamine: Cognitive and behavioral effects in normal and hyperactive boys and normal adult males. *Arch Gen Psychiatry* 37:933-943, 1980

Roche AF: The RWT method for the prediction of adult stature. *Pediatrics* 56:1026, 1975

Roche AF, Davila GH, Eyman, SL: A comparison between Greulich-Pyle and Tanner-Whitehouse assessments of skeletal maturity. *Radiology* 98: 273, 1971

Roche AF, Lipman RS, Overall JE, Hung W: The effects of stimulant medication on the growth of hyperkinetic children. *Pediatrics* 63(6): 847-849, 1979

Roche AF: Possible growth suppression effects of long-term stimulant medication. Presented to the FDA Pediatric Advisory Panel on Hyperkinesis, January 19, 1977

Safer DJ, Allen R: Factors influencing the suppressant effects of two stimulant drugs on the growth of hyperactive children. *Pediatrics* 51: 660-667, 1973

Safer D, Allen R, Barr E: Depression of growth in hyperactive children on stimulant drugs. *N Eng J Med* 287:217-220, 1972

Safer DJ, Allen R, Barr E: Growth rebound after termination of stimulant drugs. *J Pediat* 86:113-116, 1975

Satterfield JA: Data presented to the FDA Pediatric Advisory Panel on Hyperkinesis. January 19, 1977. MH 17039-09

Satterfield JH, Cantwell DP, Schell A, Blaschke T: Growth of hyperactive children with methylphenidate. *Arch Gen Psychiatry* 36:212-217, 1979

Schain RJ, Reynard CL: Observation on effects of a central stimulant drug (methylphenidate) in children with hyperkinetic behavior. *Pediatrics* 55:709-716, 1975

Schrag P, Divoky D: *The Myth of the Hyperactive Child.* New York, Dell Publishing Company, 1976

Shaffer D, Greenhill L: A critical note on the predictive validity of "the hyperkinetic syndrome." *J Child Psychol Psychiatry* 20:61-72, 1979

Shopsin B, Greenhill L: The psychopharmacology of childhood: Profile, in Siva Sanka DV (ed): *Psychopharmacology of Childhood.* Westbury, New York, PJD Publications, Ltd, 1976, pp 179-207

Snyder SH, Banerjee SP, Yanamura HI, Reinburg D: Drugs, neurotransmitters, and schizophrenia. *Science* 184:1243-1253, 1974

Tanner JM, Whitehouse RH, Takaishi M: Standards from birth to maturity for height, weight, height velocity, and weight velocity. British children, 1965, Part I. *Arch Dis Child* 41:454-471, 1966a

Tanner JM, Whitehouse RH, Takaishi M: Standards from birth to maturity for height, weight, height velocity, and weight velocity. British children, 1965, Part II. *Arch Dis Child* 41:613-635, 1966b

Van Wyck J: Somatomedin. *Rec Pro Horm Res* 30:259, 1974

Vaughan V: Growth and development, in Nelson WE (ed): *Textbook of Pediatrics,* ed. 9. Philadelphia, W. B. Saunders Co. 1969, pp 15-57

Weiss G, Hechtman L, Perlman T, et al.: Hyperactives as young adults. *Arch Gen Psychiatry* 36(6):675-681, 1979

Weiss G, Kruger E, Danielson U, Elman M: Effect of long-term treatment of hyperactive children with methylphenidate. *Can Med Assoc J* 112:159-165, 1975

Wender PH: *The Minimal Brain Dysfunction in Children*. New York, John Wiley & Sons, 1971

Werry JS, Aman M, Diamond E: Imipramine and methylphenidate in hyperactive children. *J. Child Psychol Psychiatry* 21:27-35, 1980

$$\boxed{8}$$

Subclassification of Hyperactive Children on the Basis of Minor Physical Anomalies and Plasma Dopamine-Beta-Hydroxylase Activity: An Attempted Replication

JEFFREY A. MATTES,
RACHEL GITTELMAN,
and MORTON LEVITT

It is generally accepted that the hyperactive reaction of childhood (Attention Deficit Disorder with Hyperactivity in DSM-III) probably represents several discrete disorders which, though similar in manifest symptomatology, differ with regard to etiological antecedents. Attempts to subclassify hyperkinetic children have been few.

In 1974, Rapoport et al. reported that a subgroup of hyperactive children seemed to differ from the overall clinical group. In a group of 76 previously unmedicated hyperactive boys (15 percent of whom were more distractible than hyperactive per se) Rapoport et al. rated obstetrical complications and history of hyperactivity in the father (rated as present or absent), and categorized the children as having few (none to four) or many (five or more) minor physical anomalies. The authors found a significant association between severity of hyperactivity and conduct problems and number of minor physical anomalies (stigmata). Furthermore, children with five or more stigmata were significantly more likely to have a history of obstetrical complications or of paternal hyperactivity. The number of stigmata in hyperactive children was also significantly associated with activity of the plasma enzyme dopamine-beta-hydroxylase (DBH). Consequently, Rapoport et al. hypothesized the existence of a subgroup of hyperactive boys characterized by a combination of the following: a genetic component (through their fathers) for hyperactivity, relatively severe symptoms, a relatively large number of stigmata, and high levels of DBH activity. The authors suggest that this genotype can be mimicked phenotypically by obstetrical complications.

Rapoport et al. did not find a significant correlation between DBH activity and severity of hyperactivity, though both variables were significantly correlated with stigmata. Furthermore, these authors found that both methylphenidate and imipramine significantly increased DBH activity.

The physical anomalies investigated by Rapoport et al. were first observed and noted in children with chromosomal abnormalities (such as Down's syndrome). Subsequently, Waldrop conducted several investigations concerning the significance of these stigmata in children without known chromosomal abnormalities. In a series of five studies, Waldrop et al. (1968) and Waldrop and Halverson (1971) showed that the prevalence of stigmata in both normal and disturbed children was positively correlated with gross motor activity level. Firestone et al. (1976) also found that hyperkinetic children had significantly more anomalies than normals, but Sandberg et al. (1978) failed to obtain a significant correlation between activity level and anomalies in children with a variety of psychiatric diagnoses. Waldrop et al. (1978) and Berg et al. (1978) reported that newborn minor physical anomalies predicted difficult temperamental traits such as irritability and impulsivity. Steg and Rapoport (1975) have reviewed the relationship of minor physical anomalies to a number of psychopathological states in children.

The presence of stigmata may be helpful in understanding cerebral developmental defects and genetic factors in illnesses with which they are associated. Smith and Bostian (1964) present evidence indicating that minor physical anomalies are more closely associated with idiopathic mental retardation than they are with major anomalies (such as cleft lip or ventricular septal defect), suggesting that minor anomalies may parallel central nervous system developmental deviation.

Dopamine-beta-hydroxylase (DBH) is the enzyme that converts dopamine to norepinephrine (Kaufman and Friedman, 1965). The implication of both these catecholamines in etiological theories of hyperkinesis (Wender, 1971) makes the measurement of DBH activity in hyperkinetic children a rational undertaking. Plasma DBH is believed to be derived almost entirely from peripheral sympathetic neurons being released concomitantly and proportionately with norepinephrine during sympathetic nervous system activity (Gerwitz and Kopin, 1970), but plasma DBH activity has been found to correlate significantly with cerebrospinal fluid (CSF) DBH activity (Okada et al., 1976; Lerner et al., 1978; Fijita et al., 1977). The relationship between DBH and hyperactivity is provocative partly because DBH activity is largely under genetic control (Ross et al., 1973; Levitt and Mendlewicz, 1975; Levitt et al., 1976; Mendlewicz et al., 1975); the correlation of DBH activity in same-sex siblings is high (Weinshilboum et al., 1973).

The present study was designed to replicate and extend the Rapoport et al. findings by examining the relationships among physical anomalies, DBH activity, severity of hyperactivity, methylphenidate administration, obstetrical complications, and paternal hyperactivity in a group of hyperactive boys and a group of nonhyperactive boys with reading disorders. Both short-term and chronic methylphenidate effects on DBH activity were studied.

In keeping with the findings of Rapoport et al., it was posited that number of physical anomalies would be associated with severity of hyperactivity and conduct problems, history of obstetrical difficulties, history of hyperactivity in the father, and DBH levels. In addition, given the Rapoport et al. report, plasma DBH activity levels were expected to increase significantly with methylphenidate treatment.

METHODS

Subjects

Two groups of children were included: one consisted of 62 hyperactive boys (mean age, 9.3 years) the other of 21 boys with reading disabilities (mean age, 10.4 years). The children were predominantly lower middle class; 71 were white and 12 were black (11 hyperactive, one reading disabled).

The criteria for hyperactivity and reading disability have been described elsewhere (Gittelman-Klein and Klein, 1976; Gittelman-Klein et al., 1976). Briefly, hyperactive children were between 6 and 12 years of age, had IQs above 85, clinical evidence of cross-situational hyperactivity, and a hyperactivity factor score on the Conners Teacher Rating Scale (Conners, 1969) of at least 1.8 (out of a possible 3.0). Children with other gross psychopathology were excluded.

Children with reading disabilities were between 6 and 12 years of age and had IQs of at least 85, no clinical history of hyperactivity, no significant emotional difficulties, a hyperactivity factor score of less than 1.5, and significant reading lags.

The 62 hyperactive children fell into two research groups: one group of 41 children had participated in previous experimental drug studies and had received methylphenidate (but no other medication) for varying periods of time. Another group of 21 children had not received medication before this study.

To replicate the study by Rapoport et al. (1974) the sample was limited to boys. However, five hyperactive girls were available, as were five normal male siblings (between 6–12 years of age) of the hyperactive boys. Data from the hyperactive girls and siblings are presented separately.

Assessments

Children were evaluated before and after methylphenidate treatment. Since the timing of assessments in previously treated and untreated children differed, these procedures are presented separately for each group.

Assessments Before Methylphenidate Treatment

Previously Treated Children. The evaluation schedule for the 41 previously treated hyperactive children is presented in Table 1. Upon

TABLE 1. Schedule of Assessments for Previously Treated Children*
(N = 41)

Time 1**	Time 2†
Teacher hyperactivity factor	Initial DBH assay
Stigmata examination	Abbreviated teacher questionnaire
Obstetrical history	(estimate of Teacher hyperactivity
Paternal history of hyperactivity	factor)

*Previously untreated children had all assessment concurrently, when they
  began treatment at the clinic.
**Time 1 = time of entry into the clinic.
 †Time 2 = time of the initial DBH assay. The mean difference between Time
  1 and 2 was 27 months.

entry into the clinic, the Teacher Rating Scale (Conners, 1969) was
obtained, a neurological examination which included minor physical
anomalies was performed, and any history of obstetrical complications
or family history of hyperactivity was elicited in systematic
interviews, usually with the mother. The obstetrical complications
analyzed in this study are similar to those evaluated by Rapoport et al.
(1974) and are listed in Table 2. Data elicited from the stigmata
examination and the history were recorded in uniform tabular form.
The above procedure spanned from September 1971 to May 1976 (Time
1).

The children's scores on the hyperactivity factor of the Teacher
Rating Scale were used as estimates of severity of hyperactivity at the
time of the examination for stigmata. The scores on the conduct
disorder factor of the Teacher Rating Scale were used as measures of
severity of conduct problems.

TABLE 2. Obstetrical Complications

Bleeding
Toxemia
Birth by caesarean section (except if the reason was a previous caesarean section)
Premature birth (less than 30 weeks)
Threatened abortion
Rh incompatability
Severe edema, salt-free diet, high blood pressure, or proteinuria
Other

TABLE 3. Physical Stigmata and Scoring Weights*

Stigmata	Scoring Weight
Head	
Head circumference	
More than 1.5 standard deviations	2
1 to 1.5 standard deviations	1
"Electric" hair	
Very fine hair that won't comb down	2
Fine hair that is soon awry after combing	1
Eyes	
Epicanthus	
Where upper and lower lids join at the nose point of union is:	
Deeply covered	2
Partly covered	1
Hypertelorism	
Approximate distance between tear ducts:	
More than 1.5 standard deviations	2
1.25 to 1.5 standard deviations	1
Ears	
Low-set	
Top of ears lower than outercanthus	
More than 0.5 cm.	2
Less than 0.5 cm.	1

Beginning in September 1976, DBH assays were obtained (Time 2). The previously treated children had all received methylphenidate, from 5 to 68 months (mean, 27 months) before the DBH assays.

To obtain teacher ratings of hyperactivity concurrently with the DBH assays, all children were removed from medication for two weeks and the Conners' Abbreviated Teacher Questionnaire (US DHEW, 1976) was obtained for each child during this drug-free period.

The Abbreviated Teacher Questionnaire contains three of the six items of the hyperactivity factor of the Teacher Rating Scale: "restless (overactive)," "excitable-impulsive," and "disturbs other children." The correlation between the mean of these three items and the Teacher Rating Scale hyperactivity factor score in 49 hyperactive and reading disabled children was 0.97. Given this very high association, the mean of these three items was used as an estimate of the Teacher hyperactivity factor score.

Children were evaluated for physical anomalies in the manner described by Rapoport et al. (1974). Table 3 lists anomalies and their

TABLE 3. (Continued)

Stigmata	Scoring Weight
Adherent lobes	
Lower edges of ears extend:	
Up and back toward crown of head	2
Straight back toward rear of neck	1
Malformed	1
Asymmetrical	1
Mouth	
High palate	
Roof of mouth:	
Definitely steppled	2
Flat and narrow at the top	1
Furrowed tongue	1
Smooth-rough spots on tongue	1
Hands	
Fifth finger	
Markedly curved inward toward other fingers	2
Slightly curved inward toward other fingers	1
Single transverse palmar crease	1
Feet	
Third toe	
Definitely longer than second toe	2
Appears equal in length to second toe	1
Partial syndactyly of two middle toes	1
Gap between first and second toe (approximately ¼ inch)	1

*Scoring weights are summed to give total sum stigmata.

ratings. For black children, the evaluation for "electric" hair could not be made and the measurement for hypertelorism was adjusted for racial differences (Waldrop and Halverson, 1971). Thirteen hyperactive children were evaluated before the Rapoport et al. paper appeared and a slightly different list of physical anomalies was assessed; ratings of five of the 18 anomalies included by Rapoport et al. were missing in these 13 children. Therefore, data concerning physical anomalies for these 13 children were analyzed separately.

Venous blood samples (5 ml) for the measurement of DBH activity were put immediately on ice and centrifuged in the cold. The cells were discarded and the supernatant plasma frozen until assayed. Duplicate aliquots of each plasma sample were assayed for DBH activity using the method described by Nagatsu and Udenfriend (1972). The laboratory assay of enzyme activity was completely independent of all other measures and was done without knowledge of type of patient or medication.

Previously Untreated Children. The children who had never been treated received all the above evaluations (Teacher Rating Scale, stigmata examination, perinatal history, family history of hyperactivity, and DBH) concurrently before treatment.

Assessments After Methylphenidate Treatment

All previously treated children were placed back on methylphenidate after the off-medication assessment. Dosage was regulated clinically, up to a maximum of 80 mg/day. Previously untreated children received methylphenidate or placebo, double-blind, up to 60 mg/day; 13 received methylphenidate, eight received placebo. The mean methylphenidate daily dose for all children on methylphenidate was 42.7 mg/day (range, 20 to 80 mg/day).

After six to eight weeks of methylphenidate or placebo treatment, teacher ratings and blood samples for repeat DBH assays were collected.

SPECIFIC AIMS

The specific questions below were investigated:

Are stigmata more prevalent in hyperactive children than in nonhyperactive reading-disabled children?

In hyperactive children, is the number of stigmata positively related to:

1. the severity of hyperactivity and conduct problems?
2. a history of obstetrical difficulties?
3. a history of childhood hyperactivity in the father?

Is DBH activity (a factor in catecholamine synthesis) higher in hyperactive children than in:

1. nonhyperactive reading-disabled children?
2. their siblings?

In hyperactive children, is DBH activity related to:

1. the number of stigmata?
2. severity of hyperactivity?

Is DBH activity increased by methylphenidate treatment, thereby indicating a drug effect on catecholamine synthesis?

Is any methylphenidate-induced change in DBH activity positively associated with behavioral improvement?

Do hyperactive boys differ from hyperactive girls in number of stigmata and DBH levels?

Since the sample of hyperactive boys included a group of children who were defined as hyperactive at one point in time, according to uniform strict criteria (Time 1), and reassessed from 5 to 68 months later (mean 27 months) (Time 2), it was possible to examine whether severity of subsequent hyperactivity was associated with the other variables. The specific question in this group of children was:

Is severity of continued hyperactivity, or degree of chronicity, associated with stigmata, with a history of obstetrical complications, and with a history of childhood hyperactivity in the father?

To permit an evaluation of the above questions regarding DBH, the association between DBH level and age was examined (though DBH has been reported to be relatively stable after the age of five (Freedman et al., 1972). If DBH levels were significantly associated with age, the age factor would have to be controlled.

RESULTS

Behavioral Ratings

The behavioral ratings and other characteristics of the hyperactive boys are summarized in Table 4. The mean baseline Teacher hyperactivity factor score was 2.52 (on a 0–3 scale in which 0 = not at all, 1 = just a little, 2 = pretty much, 3 = very much). Parent ratings on the same scale averaged 1.94 on the item "restless-overactive," indicating restlessness at home as well as at school.

Mean ratings of improvement for children taking methylphenidate rated at the time of the on drug/placebo DBH assay was 2.77, 2.83, and 2.91 for psychiatrist, parent, and teacher, respectively, on an eight point, 1–8 scale. The means fall between 2 = "much improved" to 3 = "improved."

Not all measures were obtained for all subjects. The reasons for missing data were all due to factors unrelated to the relationships studied. The number of subjects included in each analysis is indicated in Table 4.

TABLE 4. Patient Characteristics

	Hyperactive			Reading Disabled		
Variable	N	Mean	SD	N	Mean	SD
Baseline Teacher Rating						
Hyperactivity factor score	54	2.52	0.41	20	0.62	0.47
Conduct disorder factor score	54	1.01	0.68	20	0.93	0.30
Selected Parent Ratings						
Restless-overactive	62	1.94	0.78	12	0.83	0.94
Excitable-impulsive	62	1.95	0.69	12	0.75	0.62
Disturbs other children	62	1.85	0.83	12	0.41	0.51
Temper outbursts	62	1.61	0.96	12	0.25	0.45
Three-Item Estimate of Teacher Rating						
Hyperactivity factor at Time 2*	40	2.05	0.84	—	—	—
Sum stigmata	42	2.60	1.78	17	2.59	2.24
Percent with obstetrical complications	51	51%	—	16	42%	—
Percent with paternal history of hyperactivity	44	48%	—	16	47%	—
Ratings of Global Improvement on Methylphenidate**						
Parent	41	2.83	0.97	—	—	—
Teacher	44	2.91	1.49	6	3.33	1.21
Psychiatrist	48	2.77	0.75	—	—	—

*Includes only children previously in treatment at clinic, rated before first DBH assay.

**Ratings on an eight point, 1–8 scale, with 1 = completely recovered and well to 8 = much worse; 2 = much improved, and 3 = improved. These ratings were made at the time of the second DBH assay and include only children taking methylphenidate at that time.

Stigmata

Reliability of Stigmata Ratings

Ratings of stigmata have been shown to be reliable (Waldrop and Halverson, 1971). To evaluate reliability in this study, the psychiatrist who examined the children for stigmata reexamined 21 children on an average of eight months after the first evaluation without having access to his original examination. It was unlikely that the psychiatrist could remember the original stigmata ratings at the time of the reexamination since the evaluations were embedded in a lengthy neurological evaluation of 1½ hours duration. Between the first stigmata evaluation and the retest the physician had performed the examination on about 150 other children.

The correlation between the two sum stigmata scores was 0.58. This is lower than the correlation of 0.71 found by Waldrop and Halverson (1971) when evaluating the stability of stigmata by reexamining at age 7½ children who had been examined at 2½. The relatively lower reliability is probably not attributable to changes in stigmata over time, and is likely due to measurement error. The reliability coefficient obtained, however, is high enough to enable the detection of significant relationships between sum stigmata and other variables if relatively strong relationships exist.

If the stigmata ratings are dichotomized at the level of five or more, as in Rapoport et al. (1974), the scores are highly reliable; there was complete categorical agreement in 20 of the 21 children. In the one exception the child was rated as having five stigmata on one testing and four on the other.

Stigmata Scores and Severity of Behavior Problems

Stigmata scores for both hyperactive and reading-disabled boys ranged from 0 to 9 with an overall mean of 2.59. (SD = 1.90). The mean stigmata score for the hyperactive group was 2.60 (SD = 1.78), and that for the reading-disabled group was 2.59 (SD = 2.24) (Table 4). There was no difference in number of stigmata between the hyperactive and reading-disabled children.

No significant association between stigmata scores and Teacher Factor scores of hyperactivity and of conduct disorder was found for the hyperactive sample (r = 0.07 and 0.17, respectively); correlations between the major variables are shown in Table 5.

Analyses including only the 13 children with the shortened anomaly evaluations also yielded no significant correlations between stigmata and behavior ratings.

TABLE 5. Correlations for Hyperactive Boys
Between Stigmata, DBH, and Clinical Characteristics*

Variable Number	Variable Name	1	2	3	4
1	Sum stigmata		0.10	−0.07	0.16
			(40)	(42)	(42)
2	Initial DBH level			−0.01	−0.18
				(52)	(52)
3	Teacher hyperactivity factor**				0.49
					(54)
4	Teacher conduct disorder factor**				
5	Three-item estimate of Teacher hyperactivity factor at Time 2†				
6	Presence/absence of paternal hyperactivity				
7	Presence/absence of obstetrical difficulties				
8	DBH change with methylphenidate				
9	DBH percent change with methylphenidate				
10	Teacher improvement rating††				
11	Parent improvement rating††				
12	Psychiatrist improvement rating††				

*N in parentheses. Ns vary partly because of missing data.
**Rated at time of examination for stigmata.
 †Includes only children previously in treatment at clinic, rated before first DBH assay.
††Includes only children taking methylphenidate, rated at the time of the second DBH assay.
Higher scores indicate less improvement.
−p<0.05
=p>0.001

TABLE 5. (Continued)

5	6	7	8	9	10	11	12
0.42	−0.11	0.10	0.06	−0.11	0.23	−0.19	−0.04
(21)	(29)	(37)	(24)	(23)	(23)	(26)	(32)
0.20	−0.02	0.09	−0.04	−0.17	0.25	−0.07	0.01
(40)	(42)	(52)	(38)	(37)	(43)	(41)	(47)
0.21	−0.13	−0.14	−0.28	−0.13	−0.13	−0.10	−0.18
(33)	(39)	(47)	(32)	(31)	(39)	(35)	(42)
0.36	−0.21	0.11	−0.18	−0.12	−0.07	0.00	0.01
(33)	(39)	(47)	(32)	(31)	(39)	(35)	(42)
	−0.18	0.32	0.03	−0.09	0.15	−0.20	−0.12
	(30)	(50)	(29)	(28)	(31)	(30)	(34)
		−0.16	−0.18	−0.15	−0.27	0.34	−0.11
		(43)	(28)	(27)	(32)	(29)	(36)
			0.27	0.14	0.11	0.09	0.14
			(30)	(29)	(36)	(33)	(40)
				0.82	0.19	0.21	0.26
				(37)	(36)	(36)	(38)
					0.29	0.22	0.31
					(35)	(35)	(37)
						0.05	0.58
							(44)
							0.43
							(41)

Stigmata Scores and Obstetrical Complications
Obstetrical histories were available for 51 of the hyperactive boys.
They were dichotomized into present versus absent (percentages were
51 percent and 49 percent, respectively).

No significant relationship was found between presence of
obstetrical complications and number of stigmata ($r = .10$). Mean
stigmata scores for the groups with and without histories of obstetrical
complications were 2.78 and 2.47, respectively ($t = 0.42$, ns). Each
obstetrical complication, as well as various clinically meaningful
combinations (eg, bleeding plus threatened abortions, toxemia plus
severe edema, salt-free diet, high blood pressure, or proteinuria), were
correlated with stigmata scores. None of the a posteriori analyses
yielded a significant relationship between obstetrical complications
and stigmata.

Stigmata Scores and Paternal History of Hyperactivity
The father's childhood history was obtained for 44 of the hyperactive
boys. The paternal history of childhood hyperactivity was dichotomized
into present or absent (percentages were 48 percent and 52 percent,
respectively). No significant relationship between a positive history
and number of stigmata was found ($r = 0.11$). The mean stigmata
scores for children with and without paternal histories of hyperactivity
were 2.50 and 2.93, respectively ($t = 0.58$, ns).

Plasma DBH

The range of plasma DBH activity for children off medication was
0–1179 units, (mean = 412, SD = 323). These values are similar to
those previously reported (Goldstein et al., 1974; Horwitz et al., 1973).
Reliability and stability of DBH activity was excellent: the correlation
between the first and second DBH for children receiving placebo was
0.99 ($p < 0.001$), and the mean difference was only 38.7 units (not
significantly different from zero). Age was not significantly related to
DBH level ($r = -0.05$).

DBH, Stigmata and Hyperactivity Ratings
No significant relationship between initial DBH activity and stigmata
scores was found ($r = 0.10$).

The hyperactive and reading-disabled children did not differ in
mean initial DBH levels (means were 412 and 418, respectively).
(Table 6).

TABLE 6. DBH Activity in Hyperactive and Reading-Disabled Children "Off" and "On" Methylphenidate

DBH Activity		Hyperactive			Reading Disabled			t*	p
		Mean	SD	N	Mean	SD	N		
Off medication		412	323	60	418	268	21	0.08	ns
On methylphenidate	Change**	−4.5**	11.6	38	−48.3**	63.1	8	1.03	ns
	Percent change**	−4.1**	24.8	37	−11.4**	12.0	8	0.81	ns

*Between-group t-tests.
**Change = off medication minus on methylphenidate DBH activity. For both Hyperactive and Reading Disabled groups, neither the change nor the percent change in DBH activity with methylphenidate were significantly different from zero.

In addition, DBH levels were not significantly associated with the teacher ratings of hyperactivity (Table 5).

Methylphenidate Effect on DBH

The results pertaining to methylphenidate effects on DBH are presented in Table 6. The children's mean DBH activity level was not significantly affected by methylphenidate. Methylphenidate did not increase DBH activity; if anything, there was a trend towards a decrease in DBH activity with the drug.

There was no difference in methylphenidate effect on DBH activity between the hyperactive and reading -disabled children using absolute differences in DBH activity or percent change in DBH activity between the off and on drug conditions (Table 6).

In addition, measures of DBH activity change did not correlate with the teacher, parent, or psychiatrist ratings of improvement (Table 5).

Since children previously treated with methylphenidate might have chronic changes in DBH activity which could prevent acute changes in DBH with methylphenidate treatment, previously treated and previously untreated children were compared on initial DBH activity. Results are shown in Table 7. Mean DBH activity was 427 and 380 in each group, respectively ($t = 0.52$, ns).

Furthermore, the absolute difference and percent change in DBH activity with methylphenidate for previously treated and untreated children were compared. Previously treated patients had an average

TABLE 7. Comparison of Previously Treated and Previously Untreated Patients on DBH Measures

		Initial DBH	Change in DBH with Methylphenidate	Percent Change in DBH with Methylphenidate
Previously treated	Mean	426.6	27.1	8.7%
	SD	314.4	111.2	25.3%
	N	(41)	(30)	(29)
Previously untreated	Mean	379.7	−80.4	−12.6%
	SD	346.6	96.0	14.5%
	N	(19)	(8)	(8)
t		−0.52	2.49	2.27
p		ns	($p < 0.02$)	($p < 0.03$)

increase of 27.1 units in DBH activity, while previously untreated patients had an average decrease of 80.4 units ($t = 2.49$, $p < 0.02$) (Table 7). The percent change in DBH activity was 8.7 percent and -12.6 percent in the previously treated and untreated children ($t = 2.27$, $p < 0.03$). Thus, with methylphenidate, previously untreated patients had a significantly greater decrease in DBH than previously treated children.

DBH Activity in Hyperactive Boys and Siblings

DBH activity levels were obtained on the five available same-sex siblings of the hyperactive children. As shown in Table 8, the patients' mean initial DBH activity was significantly greater than that of their normal brothers ($t = 3.55$, $p < .05$). The mean age of siblings was 9.0 years versus 8.4 for their hyperactive brothers, a nonsignificant difference.

Relationship Between Chronicity of Hyperactivity and Other Measures

As shown in Table 4, the mean of the three-item estimate of the hyperactivity factor for previously treated children reassessed at Time 2 was 2.05 on a 0–3 scale (SD = 0.84, range = 0.63 − 3.0). Using this three-item estimate, only 10 of the 41 previously treated children still met the original cutoff criteria on the hyperactivity factor of 1.8.

The Time 2 ratings of hyperactivity did not correlate significantly with the Time 1 hyperactivity factor scores (r = 0.21), but did with the ratings of conduct problems (r = 0.36, $p < 0.05$).

TABLE 8. DBH Activity in Hyperactive Boys and Siblings*

	DBH Activity	
Pair No.	Patient	Sibling
1	887	559
2	1060	584
3	401	252
4	322	270
5	416	000
Mean	617	333
SD	333	242

*Correlated $t = 3.55$, $p < 0.05$, two-tailed.

The number of stigmata and Time 2 hyperactivity ratings showed a trend toward a significant positive association ($r = 0.42$, $p < 0.06$). This subgroup of 41 previously treated boys was indistinguishable from the total sample with regard to number of stigmata. Furthermore, their Time 1 Teacher hyperactivity factor scores did not correlate significantly with sum stigmata.

The presence of obstetrical difficulties was also significantly positively correlated with the Time 2 ratings of hyperactivity ($r = 0.32$, $p < 0.05$).

Paternal history of hyperactivity was not significantly associated with the Time 2 hyperactivity ratings ($r = -0.18$).

Analyses by Sex and Race

Comparing the five available hyperactive girls with the *sample* of boys on initial DBH and sum stigmata showed no significant differences, although females tended to have higher DBH levels (mean = 453 versus 412 for males) and less stigmata (mean = 2.0 versus 2.6 for males). Repeating many of the major analyses lumping males and females together did not change the results substantially, except for the fact that the correlation between stigmata and the three-item estimate of the hyperactivity factor for previously treated children reached significance ($r = 0.40$; $p < 0.05$).

Similarly, analyses comparing white to black children on these two variables showed no significant differences, though black children had lower DBH activity (mean = 393 versus 413 for whites) and fewer stigmata (mean = 1.70 versus 2.66 for whites). Repeating the major analyses excluding blacks did not alter the results.

DISCUSSION

The overall mean stigmata score of 2.60 is lower than the mean score of 3.58 in the Rapoport et al. study. It is also lower than the mean of 5.59 for hyperactive elementary school boys in the Waldrop and Halverson study and the mean of 3.8 in Sandberg et al. and 4.0 in Firestone et al. The lower values may indicate a real difference in study samples or a different threshold for identifying anomalies. This issue is not addressed by reliability data, and only a direct comparison across samples would identify the source of variability.

Overall, the results did not confirm most of the Rapoport et al. (1974) findings. Thus, we failed to obtain significant relationships between number of stigmata and history of obstetrical complications or paternal hyperactivity, between plasma DBH and stigmata, and between methylphenidate administration and change in DBH activity.

The only result that was to some extent replicated was the relationship between hyperactivity and stigmata score using the later ratings of hyperactivity, and this became significant only when the sample size was increased by including girls. The effect of including girls is surprising in that Waldrop and Bell (1976) and Berg et al. (1978) suggest that stigmata may not be associated with hyperactivity in girls. It is likely that restricted variance in the initial ratings of hyperactivity due to the use of a relatively high minimum criterion score for the diagnosis of hyperactivity limited the ability to detect the full magnitude of the relationship between severity of hyperactivity and stigmata scores.

The nonsignificant trend between later ratings of hyperactivity (which may be viewed as an index of chronicity) and stigmata suggests that hyperactive children who have a relatively high number of stigmata may be more likely to retain high levels of hyperactivity over time. Furthermore, these children, with more chronic hyperactivity, were more likely to have had obstetrical complications. This agrees with the findings of Pasamanick et al. (1956), Pasamanick and Knoblock (1960), Knoblock and Pasamanick (1962), and Wolff (1967) of a relationship between obstetrical complications and childhood behavior problems, though this relationship has not been consistently confirmed (Werry, 1968, 1972). These findings need replication; if substantiated in other samples, a subgroup of hyperactive children might emerge—one in which the presence of stigmata and obstetrical complications predict a chronically severe form of hyperactivity. Consistent with this finding is the Rapoport and Quinn (1975) observation that children with stigmata scores of five or more were characterized by an earlier onset of difficulties. Thus, the two sets of data are consistent in suggesting that a high number of stigmata may identify a subgroup of hyperactive children whose severity of hyperactivity is relatively stable.

The expectation that obstetrical complications are related to stigmata is considerably weakened by the prospective study of newborns by Rapoport et al. (1977) in which no relationship between stigmata and obstetrical complications was found. It may be that there exist relationships among paternal history of hyperactivity, obstetrical complications, stigmata, and activity level, but that these relationships are weak and measurement unreliability and relatively small sample sizes make them difficult to detect.

It has been reported that DBH activity is higher in males than in females (Horwitz et al., 1973); Waldrop and Halverson (1971) found that boys had more physical anomalies than girls. The differences between girls and boys in this study were nonsignificant, but the small number of females restricted the power to detect differences between the sexes.

Similarly, blacks have been found to have lower DBH activity than whites (Horwitz, et al., 1973); our results showed only a trend in this direction.

The lack of association between stigmata and DBH activity suggests that the Rapoport et al. finding may have been chance. Also supporting this interpretation is the fact that patients with Down's Syndrome, who are known to have more physical anomalies than normals, have been reported to have lower DBH activity than normal children (Wetterberg et al., 1972; Goldstein et al., 1974).

The only noteworthy finding regarding DBH activity in this study was that hyperactive children had significantly lower DBH activity than their same-sex siblings. This finding demonstrates the usefulness of sibling or other genetically related control groups when measuring a largely genetically determined variable with a large variance. These results, based on ten subjects, require confirmation. Rapoport et al. (1977) found significant positive correlations between newborn DBH activity and items evaluating negative mood and "fussiness" rated at five months and one year of age; however, no significant correlations between DBH activity and behavioral ratings were obtained in their previous sample of hyperactive boys (Rapoport et al., 1974).

Speculation is certainly premature, but if the findings regarding siblings are replicated one could theorize that the genetic, perinatal, or extrauterine factors that cause hyperactivity might also result in elevated DBH activity which might affect catecholamine metabolism in the central nervous system. One might further speculate that low levels of dopamine could lead to induction of the enzyme DBH in order to produce sufficient norepinephrine with resultant high levels of DBH activity.

It might also be argued that increased physical activity caused the increased DBH activity found in hyperactive patients compared with their siblings. There is some evidence, though not consistent (Lovenberg et al., 1974), that physical activity can increase DBH activity (Frewin et al., 1973) presumably due to increased sympathetic activity. However, the studies in this area have involved extreme amounts of activity, eg, pedaling an exercise bicycle enough to increase the pulse to 150 beats per minute. Okoda et al. (1976) reported a diurnal rhythm to plasma DBH activity, related possibly to changes in physical activity during the day. The complexity of DBH regulation has been reviewed by Molinoff (1974).

Unlike Rapoport et al. (1974), we did not find that methylphenidate increased DBH activity. Our sample, unlike that of Rapoport et al., included children previously treated with methylphenidate. However, this factor cannot account for the discrepant findings since several analyses comparing previously treated and untreated children yielded no evidence that previous methylphenidate treatment obscured any DBH augmenting effects of methylphenidate. In fact, the data suggest the opposite of the Rapoport et al. finding, indicatiing that methylphenidate can reduce DBH activity in previously unmedicated hyperactive boys.

The similarity in the methylphenidate effect on DBH activity in hyperactive and reading-disabled children argues against the notion that the drug has a diagnostically specific effect on catecholamine metabolism, at least with regard to the measure used in this study.

Furthermore, the lack of difference in DBH levels in the hyperactive and learning-disabled children fails to give support to the theory positing a deficiency of dopamine in hyperactive children. It should be noted, however, that the learning-disabled children were not a "normal" control group, and while they differed from the hyperactive sample in hyperactivity per se, they may have been similar in other respects.

ACKNOWLEDGMENTS

The authors wish to thank Sidney Katz, MD, who examined all children. This study was supported in part by Grant No. MH-18579.

REFERENCES

Berg C, Hart D, Quinn P, Rapoport J: Newborn minor physical anomalies and prediction of infant behavior. *J Aut Child Schizophr* 8:427–439, 1978

Cantwell DP: Familial-genetic research with hyperactive children, in Cantwell DP (ed): *The Hyperactive Child.* New York, Spectrum Publications, 1975, pp. 93–105.

Connors CK: A teacher rating scale for use in drug studies with children. *Am J Psychiatry* 126:884–888, 1969

Freedman LS, Ohuchi T, Goldstein M, et al.: Changes in human serum dopamine-beta-hydroxylase activity with age. *Nature* 236:310–311, 1972

Frewin DB, Downey JA, Levitt M: The effect of heat, cold and exercise on dopamine-beta-hydroxylase activity in man. *Can J Physiol Pharmacol* 51:986–989, 1973

Fijita K, Maruta K, Teradaira R, et al.: Dopamine-beta-hydroxylase activity in human cerebrospinal fluid and serum. *J Neurochem* 29:1141–1142, 1977

Firestone P, Lewy F, Douglas V: Hyperactivity and physical anomalies. *Can Psychiatr Assoc J* 21: 23–26, 1976

Gerwirtz GP, Kopin IJ: Release of dopamine-beta-hydroxylase with norepinephrine during cat splenic stimulation. *Nature* 227:406–407, 1970

Gittelman-Klein R, Klein DF: Methylphenidate effects in learning disabilities. *Arch Gen Psychiatry* 3:655–664, 1976

Gittelman-Klein R, Klein DF, Abikoff H, et al.: Relative efficacy of methylphenidate and behavior modification in hyperkinetic children: An interim report. *J Abnorm Child Psychol* 4:361–379, 1976b

Goldstein M, Freedman LS, Ebstein RP, et al.: Human serum dopamine-beta-hydroxylase: Relationship to sympathetic activity in physiological and pathological states, in Usdin E (ed): *Neuropsychopharmacology of Monoamines and Their Regulatory Enzymes*. New York, Raven Press, 1974, pp 105–119

Horwitz DR, Alexander RW, Lovenberg W, Keiser H: Human serum dopamine-beta-hydroxylase. *Circ Res* 32:594–599, 1973

Kaufman S, Friedman H: Dopamine-beta-hydroxylase. *Pharmacol Rev* 17:71–100, 1965

Knobloch R, Pasamanick B: The developmental behavioral approach to the neurologic examination in infancy. *Child Dev* 3:181–198, 1962

Lerner P, Goodwin FK, van Kammen DP, et al.: Dopamine-beta-hydroxylase in the cerebrospinal fluid of psychiatric patients. *Biol Psychiatry* 13:685–693, 1978

Levitt M, Dunner DL, Mendlewicz J, et al.: Plasma dopamine-beta-hydroxylase activity in affective disorders. *Psychopharmacologia (Berlin)* 46:205–210, 1976

Levitt M, Mendlewicz J: A genetic study of plasma dopamine-beta-hydroxylase in affective disorder, in Mendlewicz J (ed): *Genetics and Psychopharmacology*. Basel, Brussels, S. Karger, 1975, pp 89–98

Lovenberg W, Bruckwick EA, Alexander RW, et al.: Evaluation of serum dopamine-beta-hydroxylase activity as an index of sympathetic nervous activity in man, in Usdin E (ed): *Neuropsychopharmacology of Monoamines and Their Regulatory Enzymes*. New York, Raven Press, 1974, pp 121–128

Mendlewicz J, Levitt M, Fleiss JL: A genetic study of plasma dopamine-beta-hydroxylase activity in man. *Acta Genet Med Gemellol (Roma)* 24:105–110, 1975

Molinoff PB, Nelson DL, Orcutt JC: Dopamine-beta-hydroxylase and the regulation of the noradrenergic neuron, in Usdin E (ed): *Neuropsychopharmacology of Monoamines and Their Regulatory Enzymes.* New York, Raven Press, 1974, pp 95–104

Nagatsu T, Udenfriend S: Photometric assay of dopamine-beta-hydroxylase activity in human blood. *Clin Chem* 18:980–983, 1972

Okada T, Ohta T, Shinoda T, et al.: Dopamine-beta-hydroxylase activity in serum and cerebrospinal fluid in neuropsychiatric diseases. *Neuropsychobiology* 2:139–144, 1976

Pasamanick B, Knobloch H: Brain damage and reproductive casualty. *Am J Orthopsychiatry* 30:298–305, 1960

Pasamanick B, Rogers M, Lilienfeld A: Pregnancy experience and the development of behavior disorders in children. *Am J Psychiatry* 112:613 (1956)

Rapoport J, Prandoni C, Renfield M, et al.: Newborn dopamine-beta-hydroxylase, minor physical anomalies, and infant temperament. *Am J Psychiatry* 134:676–678, 1977

Rapoport JL, Quinn PO, Lamprecht F: Minor physical anomalies and plasma dopamine-beta-hydroxylase activity in hyperactive boys. *Am J Psychiatry* 131:386–389, 1974

Rapoport JL, Quinn PO: Minor physical anomalies (stigmata) and early developmental deviation: A major biologic subgroup of "hyperactive children." *Int J Ment Health* 4:29–44, 1975

Ross SB, Wetterberg L, Myrked M: Genetic control of plasma dopamine-beta-hydroxylase. *Life Sci* 12:529–532, 1973

Sandberg ST, Rutter M, Taylor E: Hyperkinetic disorder in psychiatric clinic attenders. *Dev Med Child Neurol* 20:279–299, 1978

Smith D, Bostian K: Congenital anomalies associated with idiopathic mental retardation. *J Pediatr* 65:189–196, 1964

Steg JP, Rapoport JC: Minor physical anomalies in normal, neurotic, learning disabled, and severely disturbed children. *J Aut Child Schizophr* 5:299–307, 1975

US Department of Health, Education, and Welfare: *ECDEU Assessment Manual for Psychopharmacology.* Washington, DC, US DHEW Publication ADM-76-338, 1976, pp 300–303

Waldrop M, Bell R: Minor physical anomalies and inhibited behavior in elementary school girls. *J Child Psychol Psychiatry* 17:113–122, 1976

Waldrop M, Bell R, McLaughlin B, Halverson C: Newborn minor physical anomalies predict short attention span, peer aggression, and impulsivity at age three. *Science* 199:563–565, 1978

Waldrop M, Halverson CE: Minor physical anomalies and hyperactive behavior in young children, in Hellmuth J (ed): *The Exceptional Infant.* New York, Brunner/Mazel, 1971, pp 343–380

Waldrop M, Pedersen F, Bell RQ: Minor physical anomalies and behavior in preschool children. *Child Dev* 39:391–400, 1968

Weinshilboum RM, Raymond FA, Weidman WH: Serum dopamine-beta-hydroxylase activity: Sibling-sibling correlation. *Science* 181:943–945, 1973

Wender J: *Minimal Brain Dysfunction in Children.* New York, Wiley-Interscience, John Wiley & Sons, 1971

Werry J: Developmental hyperactivity. *Pediatr Clin North Am* 15:581–598, 1968

Werry JS: Organic factors in childhood psychopathology, in Quay HC, Werry JS (eds): *Psychopathological Disorders of Childhood.* New York, John Wiley & Sons, 1972, p 83

Wetterberg L, Gustauson KH, Backstrom M, et al.: Low dopamine-beta-hydroxylase in Downs syndrome. *Clin Genet* 3:152–153, 1972

Wolff S: The contribution of obstetric complications to the etiology of behavior disorders in childhood. *j Child Psychol Psychiatry* 8:57–66, 1967

9

Methylphenidate in Hyperactive and Enuretic Children

JOHN S. WERRY and MICHAEL G. AMAN

In 1937, Charles Bradley reported a study of a stimulant, Benzedrine, in a mixed group of children presenting with emotional, behavioral, and academic problems. A number of immediate improvements were noted within the group, including an apparent improvement in school performance, a reduction in aggressive and domineering behavior, and a reduction in inappropriate motor activity. Bradley described the children as more "subdued" and referred to the effects of the stimulant drug as "paradoxical." Whether he meant to imply this pharmacologically or whether Bradley was using literary license is immaterial, since it is clear that the term *paradoxical,* to describe the effects of the stimulant drugs in hyperactive children, has become widespread. This seems to assume that hyperactive children become subdued under medication whereas normal and nonhyperactive disordered children would presumably become activated.

183

While considerable research with hyperactive children indicates stimulants consistently improve conduct, reduce motor activity, and often enhance performance on cognitive tasks as assessed in the laboratory (Cantwell and Carlson, 1978), proof that this is indeed paradoxical and unique has never been forthcoming. Indeed, there is considerable evidence to the contrary. In his review of the stimulants, Sroufe (1975) concluded that their effects on learning, physiology, and motor activity in hyperactive children appear to be generally consistent with effects observed in normal adults. He noted that there was no data on their effects in psychiatrically normal children. Conners and Werry (1979) also drew attention to the lack of evidence that stimulants were even specifically effective for hyperactive children, there being some suggestion (including Bradley's original study) that they may be effective in conduct, oppositional, and even sometimes in anxious, withdrawn children.

More recently, Rapoport and her associates (1978; 1980) investigated the effects of dextroamphetamine (Dexedrine) in both hyperactive and normal children, using a wide array of measures including motor activity, learning performance, mood, and speech parameters. In general, the changes were consistent over both groups, and they showed a general pattern of improvement.

Although the study by Rapoport et al. (1978; 1980) was carefully conducted, some problems remain in resolving the issue of paradoxical effects. First, the generality of their findings is somewhat attentuated by the fact that all children in the normal group were from professional families within a biomedical research institute. Second, the size of this group necessarily had to be limited (n=14). Third and most serious, however, was the fact that the statistical analysis employed did not actually resolve the issue of whether the stimulant had a *quantitatively* greater impact in the hyperactive group, since it did not allow for interactive effects between group and drug.

The present study was begun about the same time, but in ignorance of Rapoport's investigation to help resolve the issue of whether stimulants have an action in hyperactive children which is different from that in psychiatrically normal children and if so whether it is paradoxical. Like the Rapoport et al. study, cognitive and motor activity measures were employed to compare group response to a stimulant drug. In addition, physiological, motor, and self-report measures were derived in the normal group to increase our knowledge regarding drug action in psychiatrically normal children. A related issue addressed in the current study was whether hyperactive children show a more dramatic response to the stimulants. Thus, this study extends and, in a limited sense, at least serves as a replication of the Rapoport investigation.

METHOD

Subjects

Children were accepted into the study only after a thorough discussion with their parents of the possible adverse effects of methylphenidate. Informed consent from all parents and, where appropriate, assent of the child was obtained.

Normal Children

Because of ethical problems, it was decided to use psychiatrically normal, enuretic children. Since the New Zealand Health Department recommended the use of stimulants in enuresis, it also afforded an opportunity to test its paradoxical effects as well as its benefits in enuresis. Three criteria were applied for admission to this group. First, the bedwetting had to be severe enough to merit treatment. Second, the child had to be free of behavioral and academic problems as determined by a nonblind psychiatric interview (by JSW). Regrettably, because of shortage of child psychiatrists in Auckland, it was not possible to test the reliability of this judgment, but the Teacher Questionnaire scores (below) serve as validation. Third, the child had to obtain normal scores on both the Inattention and Hyperactivity factors as rated by teachers on Conners (1969) Teacher Questionnaire (TQ).

Sixteen children (13 boys and three girls) were selected, ranging in age from 5.3 to 12.1 years, with a mean age of 8.4 years. TQ scores on Factors I to IV were 1.27, 1.73, 1.70, and 1.60, respectively, with nonoccurrence of symptoms being scored as 1.0. All these scores are normal (Werry and Hawthorne, 1976; Werry et al., 1975).

Hyperactive Children

Suitable cases were selected from about 50 children who had participated in previous trials of methylphenidate in this laboratory, so as to match the enuretic subjects closely on age and sex. However, those selected were simultaneously extreme on both the Inattention and Hyperactivity factors of the TQ. Care was also exercised to ensure that drug orders were properly counterbalanced (ie, equal numbers of

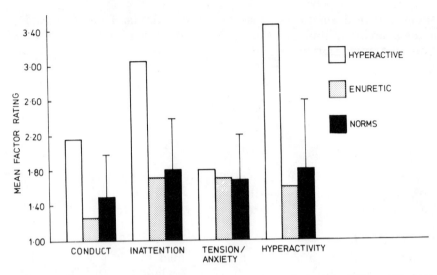

FIG. 1.   Mean scores on Conners TQ for hyperactive and enuretic children. (Markers indicate one standard deviation.)

placebo first, methylphenidate second, and vice versa) within this group.

The 16 hyperactive children ranged in age from 7.3 to 12.8 years, with a mean age of 8.5 years. Their scores on Factors I to IV of Conners TQ were 2.16, 3.04, 1.80, and 3.45, respectively. Thus, the two groups were closely matched on age and sex, but differed dramatically on the rating scale dimensions known to signify hyperactivity (Fig. 1).

Unfortunately, however, it was not possible to match the groups for the period on medication because the authors did not feel that the enuretic children should be given stimulants for longer than a week, by which time any benefit would be obvious. On the other hand, hyperactive children had been on medication for three or four weeks.

Procedure

This was a double-blind, placebo controlled study in which each subject acted as his own control. As noted, the enuretic children received placebo and methylphenidate for one week each, whereas hyperactive children received each for longer periods. Half of each group received placebo first and drug second, the remaining subjects receiving the opposite order.

Each child was tested approximately 90 minutes (range, 60–120 minutes) after taking his pill. The enuretic children received a larger battery of tests than did the hyperactive subjects due to the fact that they were tested relatively later in the sequence of studies conducted in this laboratory. All tests which were administered to both groups were controlled by modular programming equipment, thereby ensuring highly uniform testing procedures.

Tests on Both Groups

A. The Short-Term Memory (STM) Task, used commonly in pediatric psychopharmacology (Aman, 1978), involved the presentation of an array of pictures followed a few seconds later by a test picture. Arrays were presented in sizes of one, three, or nine pictures. The children had to decide whether the test item appeared within the previous array and their responses were indicated by depressing either a "Same" or a "Different" response lever.

The relevant measures on this task included the accuracy of responding and mean speed of responding.

B. The Continuous Performance Task (CPT), developed by Rosvold, et al. (1956), is a vigilance-type task and is commonly regarded as an index of attention span. The child was required to monitor a screen on which letters of the alphabet were presented sequentially. If the letter "X" appeared, the child was to respond by depressing a lever, but otherwise he was to refrain from pressing. The relevant measures included errors of omission (failures to detect), errors of commission (false detections), and mean response time. This test is used widely in pediatric psychopharmacology research (Aman, 1978).

C. Seat activity was recorded during each of the above using a ballistographic chair (Sprague and Toppe, 1966). The children were not aware that there was anything unusual about the seat.

Tests on Enuretic Group Only

A. Cardiovascular Function. Heart rate and blood pressure were sampled in a standardized fashion which required a mandatory five minute rest, while lying supine, before recording. Blood pressure was then sampled a second time immediately after the child was requested to stand.

TABLE 1. Effects of Diagnostic Group and Drug Treatment on Measures
of Cognition and Seat Activity

Variable	$\overline{X}$ Placebo	$\overline{X}$ Methylphenidate	F Values	
STM Accuracy (%)				
Enuretic	91.67	88.89		
Hyperactive	82.95	86.55		
			Group	6.47*
			Drug	0.08
			G × D	4.86*
STM Speed (Σ 1/sec)				
Enuretic	0.480	0.475		
Hyperactive	0.554	0.553		
			Group	4.33*
			Drug	0.10
			G × D	0.07
CPT Omissions[a]				
Enuretic	2.12	2.00		
Hyperactive	3.25	1.56		
			Group	1.10
			Drug	5.53*
			G × D	4.67*
CPT Commissions[a]				
Enuretic	0.94	0.88		
Hyperactive	4.25	3.69		
			Group	8.68**
			Drug	1.76
			G × D	0.32

B. Motor Function. The test of motor steadiness described by
Knights and Moule (1968) was comprised of two parts. During the
Maze Task, the child was required to traverse a complex route with a
metal stylus while attempting not to touch the sides. The Graduated
Holes task was similar in concept except that steadiness was sampled
under static conditions. The child was asked to hold a stylus in a series
of holes, for ten seconds each, while attempting not to touch the sides.
The relevant measures for both tasks included the total number of
contacts and the total time of contact, recorded separately for dominant
and nondominant hands.

C. Self-Report Measures. The items from the Piers-Harris Self
Concept scale (The Way I Feel About Myself) (Piers and Harris, 1969)

TABLE 1. (Continued)

Variable	$\bar{X}$ Placebo	$\bar{X}$ Methylphenidate	F Values	
CPT Response Time				
Enuretic	37.89	36.50		
Hyperactive	39.90	37.00		
			Group	0.72
			Drug	15.94†
			G × D	1.97
Seat Movement (STM)				
Enuretic	134.19	83.69		
Hyperactive	128.30	79.30		
			Group	0.04
			Drug	8.10**
			G × D	0.00
Seat Movement (CPT)				
Enuretic	21.06	25.88		
Hyperactive	27.20	8.80		
			Group	0.38
			Drug	1.01^{b}
			G × D	2.94††

Note: Degrees of freedom = 1,30 for the cognitive measures and 1,24 for seat
   movement.
[a]In order to normalize the data which were badly skewed, a square root transformation was applied. For clarity the untransformed means are presented here.
[b]When the data were normalized (square root transformation) this factor showed
   a significant drug effect.
   *$p < 0.05$
   **$p < 0.01$
   †$p < 0.001$
   ††$p < 0.10$

were recorded on tape to provide a uniform situation. The 80 items are
scored to render six independent dimensions, each relating to an aspect
of self-image, plus a total self-concept score.

RESULTS

Measures Common to Both Groups

The measures taken on both groups were analyzed using a two-factor
ANOVA model. One factor was a between-groups factor—diagnostic

group (enuretic or hyperactive), and the other a within-subjects factor — drug treatment (methylphenidate or placebo).

The results from these comparisons are presented in Table 1. In general, the diagnostic group comparisons suggest differences which are in predictable directions: on the STM task, which tends to tax both memory and attention span, hyperactive subjects performed more poorly than their enuretic counterparts. Furthermore, the hyperactive children were significantly more impulsive as indicated by faster response times. Similarly, on the CPT, the hyperactive children made more errors of commission, also suggesting a more impulsive style and poorer attention span. On the other hand, it is somewhat surprising that these children did *not* show more seat activity than the psychiatrically normal children, although differences in activity have been shown to be somewhat situation specific in the past (Werry, 1978).

The main effects due to drug treatment are those classically known to occur in hyperactive children in laboratory settings (Aman, 1978). Omission errors and mean latency were reduced on the CPT, suggesting an enhancement of attention span. Also, seat activity was generally reduced for both groups, particularly during the STM task. The failure to obtain a main drug effect on STM accuracy is not too unusual (Aman, 1978), but in this case may well have been due to ceiling effects within the enuretic group.

With respect to the issue of paradoxical effects, the critical value is that expressed in the diagnostic group by drug treatment interaction. The significant interaction for STM accuracy is probably misleading due to the ceiling effect noted earlier. That is, there was little room for the enuretic to improve because they were already performing at a very high level. However, the interaction for CPT omissions and the emergence of a trend for CPT seat movement favoring the hyperactive group must be taken more seriously. The direction of the means suggests that hyperactive children show a quantitatively *greater* response to methylphenidate, not a qualitatively different or paradoxical one.

Measures in Enuretic Group Only

A two-factor ANOVA model was used in which one factor accounted for drug order (placebo-methylphenidate or vice versa) and the other assessed the main effect of drug treatment. Occasionally, where a third dimension was inherent in the measure, another within-subjects factor was employed.

The cardiovascular and motor performance measures are presented in Table 2. The cardiovascular measures indicate a significant increase in diastolic and systolic blood pressure and a nonsignificant increase in heart rate. This latter is probably explained by the small number of subjects employed rather than by a genuine lack of effect. While no direct comparisons could be made with the hyperactive group, these cardiovascular effects appear to be entirely consistent in type with those found in hyperactive children by a number of investigators (Aman and Werry, 1975a, 1975b; Boileau, et al., 1976; Cohen et al., 1971; Greenberg and Yellin, 1975).

The tests of motor function were relatively insensitive to drug action in this case. The only measure substantially influenced was error time on the Graduated Holes, which showed a nonsignificant improvement due to drug treatment. These trends are generally similar in direction but much smaller in degree than those obtained with hyperactive and learning disabled children (Knights and Hinton, 1969; Werry et al., 1980).

Thus, the cardiovascular and motor performance changes are generally in the same direction as those seen in hyperactive children.

TABLE 2. Effects of Methylphenidate on Cardiovascular and Motor Function in Enuretic Group

Measure	Placebo	Methylphenidate	F Values
Heart beats/min	82.88	87.31	3.01
Diastolic blood pressure[a]	75.28	78.03	10.06*
Systolic blood pressure[b]	110.38	114.88	25.24**
Maze errors[c]	12.03	11.33	0.29
Maze error time (secs)[c]	1.66	1.70	0.10
Holes errors[c]	61.34	56.78	0.88
Holes error time (secs)[c]	8.88	7.70	2.96

Note: Degrees of freedom = 1,14 for all measures except Maze, where df = 1,13.
[a]Three-way ANOVA, in which position (lying vs standing) represented third dimension. Lying resulted in significantly lower blood pressure ($p < 0.05$).
[b]Three-way ANOVA, as above; not significant.
[c]Three-way ANOVA, in which dominant and nondominant hand comprised third dimension. All measures, except Maze error time, showed superior performance with dominant hand.
*$p < 0.01$
**$p < 0.001$

TABLE 3.   Effects of Methylphenidate on Self-Esteem Measures
in Enuretic Group

Factor		Placebo	Methylphenidate	F Values
I	Behavior	12.44	13.25	2.60
II	Intellectual status	11.31	11.88	0.70
III	Physical appearance	8.12	8.56	0.54
IV	Anxiety	10.75	10.75	0.00
V	Popularity	7.88	7.69	0.41
VI	Happiness	8.25	8.62	0.70
Total		58.50	61.38	2.65

Note: Degrees of freedom = 1,14.

The self-report measures presented in Table 3 showed little evidence of drug effect. We have argued elsewhere (Werry, 1978; Werry et al., 1980) that there is an inexplicable absence of such data addressing the question of how children themselves perceive the effects of drugs. However, the limited data that exist on hyperactive children (Conners and Werry, 1979; Werry et al., 1980), suggest that changes are modest and furthermore that they tend to emphasize behavioral (ie, conduct) effects as they are perceived by the children involved.

DISCUSSION AND CONCLUSIONS

The first point to be established is that of the diagnostic normality of the enuretic group. Two lines of evidence support this—the independent teacher assessments and the differences on the laboratory tests between enuretic and hyperactive children. The second point is whether or not the difference in length of administration of medication (one versus three to four weeks) could explain differences observed. This seems improbable since stimulants are generally immediately effective and there is no evidence of a cumulative effect, but it cannot be eliminated entirely.

In addressing the major questions in this chapter, that of the validity of the concept of paradoxical effects, the answer seems quite straightforward, especially since data from this and the Rapoport et al. (1978; 1980) studies are similar. The response of both hyperactive and psychiatrically normal children is generally consistent and singular in direction. In yet another study with normal adults, we found that methylphenidate tended to cause slight improvements, but most of these were not statistically significant (Aman et al., in press). The greatest lesson in this issue would seem to be the fact that the concept of the "paradoxical" response in hyperactive children was based upon an assumption — namely, that we knew how *normal* children would respond and furthermore that this response would be stimulating, that is, one of physical activation, anxiety, and generally poor psychological integrity. Instead, the typical human pharmacological response to low doses of stimulants appears to be one of increased alertness and concomitantly reduced physical activity with little evidence of induction of anxiety (Martin et al., 1971; Rapoport et al., 1980). Consequently, the response of hyperactive children cannot be said to be paradoxical at all, but rather represents changes in the expected direction.

A related issue, not so easily resolved, is whether hyperactive children show an exaggerated or more dramatic response to stimulant medication. The current study revealed a group of measures (STM accuracy, CPT omissions, and possibly CPT seat movement) on which the hyperactive children were apparently more responsive. The analysis employed by Rapoport and her associates did not permit an examination of such interaction effects. However, informal analysis of their data also suggests that certain measures, such as motor activity, may well be more susceptible to drug action in hyperactive children. This is an exceedingly difficult issue to resolve conclusively, however, because of the "law of initial values"; this law states that the degree of change resulting from a given treatment may be determined in part by the relative levels of subjects on the given dimension before intervention even begins.* For example, it may be easier to modify attention span in hyperactive children who are notoriously poor on such tasks, merely because there is more room for improvement. It is also quite possible that hyperactive children show a genuinely greater response to medication; however, this remains to be demonstrated.

Finally, it might be mentioned that this study fails to support or detract from the more popular biological theories of hyperactivity, namely, reduced catecholamine and/or arousal levels (Cantwell and

---

*Robbins and Sahakian (1979) have presented an elegant model of drug response bearing the label "rate-dependency." Based upon pharmacological studies with stimulants in animals and man, they have shown that there is generally a direct relationship between the control rate of spontaneous motor activity and the response to drug treatment. This relationship, which appears to hold across species and categories of behavior, may be a far more valid explanation of stimulant effects in hyperactive children than the popular notion of "paradoxical effects."

Carlson, 1978). Although it is clear that stimulant treatment, being both dopaminergic and adrenergic (and, incidentally, cholinergic too), might alleviate such disorders, it is also apparant that improvement is not specific to hyperactive children, but rather represents a typical response for most children. At best, any unique effect in hyperactive children is merely quantitative — at least in the functions tested.

ACKNOWLEDGMENTS

This research was supported in large part by a grant from the Medical Research Council of New Zealand to Professor J.S. Werry. The authors would like to thank Joan Mayhew and Eileen Diamond for assistance in the collection and analysis of data.

REFERENCES

Aman MG: Drugs, learning and the psychotherapies, in Werry JS (ed): *Pediatric Psychopharmacology: The Use of Behavior Modifying Drugs in Children.* New York, Brunner/Mazel, 1978

Aman MG, Vamos M, Werry JS: Effects of methylphenidate in normal adults with reference to drug action in hyperactivity. *Aust NZ J Psychiatry,* in press.

Aman MG, Werry JS: The effects of methylphenidate and haloperidol on the heart rate and blood pressure of hyperactive children with special reference to time of action. *Psychopharmacologia* 43:163–168, 1975a

Aman MG, Werry JS: Methylphenidate in children: Effects upon cardiorespiratory function on exertion. *Int J Ment Health* 4:119–131, 1975b

Boileau RA, Ballard JE, Sprague RL, et al.: Effect of methylphenidate on cardiorespiratory responses in hyperactive children. *Res Q* 47:590–596, 1976

Bradley C: The behavior of children receiving benzedrine. *Am J Psychiatry* 94:577–585, 1937

Cantwell DP, Carlson GA: Stimulants, in Werry JS (ed): *Pediatric Psychopharmacology: The Use of Behavior Modifying Drugs in Children.* New York, Brunner/Mazel, 1978

Cohen NJ, Douglas VI, Morgenstern G: The effect of methylphenidate on attentive behavior and autonomic activity in hyperactive children. *Psychopharmacologia* 22:282–294, 1971

Conners CK: A teacher rating scale for use in drug studies with children. *Am J Psychiatry* 126:152–156, 1969

Conners CK, Werry JS: Pharmacotherapy of psychopathology in children, in Quay HC, Werry JS (eds): *Psychopathological Disorders of Childhood.* New York, John Wiley & Sons, 1979

Greenberg LM, Yellin AM: Blood pressure and pulse changes in hyperactive children treated with imipramine and methylphenidate. *Am J Psychiatry* 132:1325–1326, 1975

Knights RM, Hinton G: The effects of methylphenidate (Ritalin) on the motor skills and behavior of children with learning problems. *J Nerv Ment Dis* 148:643–653, 1969

Knights RM, Moule AD: Normative data on the motor steadiness battery for children. *Percept Mot Skills* 26:643–650, 1968

Martin WR, Sloan JW, Sapira JD, Jasinski DR: Physiologic, subjective, and behavioral effects of amphetamine, methamphetamine, ephedrine, phenmetrazine, and methyphenidate in man. *Clin Pharm Ther* 12:245-258, 1971

Piers EV, Harris DB: *Manual for the Piers Harris Children's Self Concept Scale (The Way I Feel About Myself).* Nashville, Counselor Recordings and Tests, 1969

Rapoport JL, Buchsbaum MS, Weingartner H, et al.: Dextroamphetamine: Cognitive and behavioral effects in normal and hyperactive children and normal adults. *Arch Gen Psychiatry* 37:933-946, 1980

Rapoport JL, Buchsbaum MS, Zahn TP, et al.: Dextroamphetamine: Cognitive and behavioral effects in normal prepubertal boys. *Science* 199:560–563, 1978

Robbins TW, Sahakian BJ: "Paradoxical" effects of psychomotor stimulant drugs in hyperactive children from the standpoint of behavioral pharmacology. *Neuropharmacology,* 18:931-950, 1979

Rosvold A, Mirsky A, Sarason I, et al.: A continuous performance test of brain damage. *J Consult Psychol* 20:343–350, 1956

Sprague RL, Toppe LK: Relationship between activity level and delay of reinforcement. *J Exp Psychol* 3:390–397, 1966

Sroufe L: Drug treatment of children with behavior problems, in Horowitz F (ed): *Review of Child Development Research,* vol 4. Chicago, University of Chicago Press, 1975

Werry JS: Measures in pediatric psychopharmacology, in Werry JS (ed): *Pediatric Psychopharmacology: The Use of Behavior Modifying Drugs in Children.* New York, Brunner/Mazel, 1978

Werry JS, Aman MG, Diamond E: Imipramine and methylphenidate in hyperactive children. *J Child Psychol Psychiatry* 21:27-36, 1980

Werry JS, Hawthorne D: Conners teacher questionnaire—norms and validity. *Aust NZ J Psychiatry* 10:257–262, 1976

Werry JS, Sprague RL, Cohen MN: Conners teacher rating scale for use in drug studies with children—an empirical study. *J Abnorm Child Psychol* 3:217–229, 1975

$$\boxed{10}$$

Pilot Trial of Mianserin Hydrochloride for Childhood Hyperactivity

DENNIS H. LANGER,
JUDITH L. RAPOPORT,
MICHAEL H. EBERT,
C. R. LAKE,
and LINDA E. NEE

Stimulant drug treatment of children with attention deficit disorder with hyperactivity (ADDH) is often dramatically successful in controlling impulsive, distractible, and even antisocial behaviors. Although this increased vigilance and decreased motor restlessness has been shown to be a nonspecific effect of stimulants (Rapoport et al., 1978), the mechanism of action of stimulants may still be of considerable importance in understanding the biological basis of restless and inattentive behavior in children. Recent reports suggest a link between alteration in central nervous system norepinephrine

(NE) metabolism and the therapeutic action of stimulants in hyperactive children. Urinary 3-methoxy-4-hydroxyphenylglycol (MHPG) is decreased with amphetamine treatment in hyperactive children (Shekim et al., 1977, 1979; Brown et al., 1979), and this decrease may correlate with clinical response to the drug.

Moreover, a number of recent studies have related depletion of central NE to attentional deficit in animal models (Mason and Fibiger, 1978, 1979; Lorden et al., 1980). As attentional deficit is postulated to be a key pathological feature in hyperactive children, these studies have relevance to a possible mechanism of drug response.

Mianserin hydrochloride is a tetracyclic compound which has been reported to be an effective antidepressant for adults, with relatively few side-effects (Brogden et al., 1978; Coppen and Kopera, 1978), although some sedation has been described (Perry et al., 1978). Only weak NE uptake blockade has been found in animal studies (Zis and Goodwin, 1979), but mianserin has pronounced presynaptic alpha-adrenergic receptor blocking activity and antihistaminic properties, without central anticholergic activity and with little effect on central serotonergic mechanisms (Brogden et al., 1978).

Mianserin increases NE turnover (Leonard and Kafoe, 1976) without appreciably impeding NE re-uptake in vivo (Leonard, 1974). The most plausible explanation is that mianserin inhibits presynaptic alpha-adrenergic receptors (Bauman and Maitre, 1977), an effect that would lead to enhanced release of NE from the nerve terminal (Starke, 1977). In contrast, tricyclic antidepressants also block both pre- and post-synaptic adrenergic receptors, but probably inhibit mainly post-synaptic alpha-adrenergic receptors (Svensson and Usdin, 1977; Fludder and Leonard, 1978).

The present report describes an open clinical trial of mianserin in doses up to 60 mg/day in five hyperactive prepubertal boys. The purpose of the study was to evaluate clinical efficacy, testing whether increasing NE at the nerve terminal by mechanisms other than acute release would be clinically effective in children with ADDH.

SUBJECTS

Five male children treated with mianserin (mean age of 8.4 years; range 6–12 years) and five male children treated with placebo (mean age of 8.2 years; range 6–10 years) were evaluated as day patients on a research unit at the National Institute of Mental Health (NIMH). The boys were referred by area practitioners and clinics for longstanding restless and inattentive behavior at home and at school. All subjects were greater than two standard deviations from norms for hyperactivity on the 28-item revised Conners' Teacher Rating Scale (CTRS) (Connors, 1969, Goyette et al., 1978). All of the patients were "good responders" to stimulant medication treatment either by history or as established after the conclusion of the study. All met the DSM-III criteria for ADDH. Informed consent was obtained from both parents and children.

Exclusion criteria were "hard" neurological findings, ie, clinical seizure disorder or any other medical disorder; psychiatric disorder other than conduct disorder or specific developmental disorder (312.00 and 315.00, respectively, in DSM-III); or full scale IQ less than 80 on the WISC-R. Four of the boys also qualified for another DSM-III diagnosis, in addition to attention deficit disorder: specific developmental disorder (two) and conduct disorder, undersocialized aggressive type (two).

PROCEDURE

Following a one week baseline evaluation, children received either two or three weeks of placebo or a two or three week trial of mianserin. Mianserin (or placebo) was given in tablets of 10 mg, starting at one tablet per day and increasing the dose by one tablet every other day, so that by the end of the second week, each child received the maximum dose of 60 mg/day, as tolerated. The placebo group was taken from a double-blind study reported elsewhere (Langer et al., 1981), while the mianserin group was administered the drug in a single-blind fashion. Thus, the two comparison groups presented here, the pilot mianserin trial and the placebo contrast group, were studied on the same ward, but under somewhat different circumstances.

Side-effects were monitored weekly using both a self-report scale—the Subject's Treatment Emergent Symptoms Scale (STESS), and the Emergent Symptoms Scale (ESS), completed by the physician (Guy, 1976). Classroom behavioral ratings were completed weekly by the NIMH teacher using the CTRS. Motor activity was measured weekdays during the baseline evaluation and each treatment period.

BEHAVIORAL AND PHYSIOLOGICAL MEASUREMENTS

Activity

Motor activity was measured for a two-hour period (between 10 a.m. and 12 noon while the children were in school) by an acceleration-sensitive device that has a solid state memory and can store data on number of movements per unit time over a 48-hour period (Colburn et al., 1976).

Sustained Attention Measure (CPT)

Rosvold's Continuous Performance Test (CPT) (Rosvold et al., 1956) was modified to allow a greater performance range. The task is described elsewhere (Rapoport et al., 1978).

Memory and Learning Task

A paired associate verbal learning task was used, which is described elsewhere and has previously been found to be sensitive to a single-dose amphetamine administration in ADDH and normal children (Rapoport et al., 1978, 1980).

Blood Pressure, Pulse, and Plasma NE

Studies of plasma NE were done as described in detail elsewhere (Lake et al., 1976). Pulse was measured by radial palpation and blood pressure by auscultation. Blood pressure, pulse, and blood samples were obtained from subjects in the supine position 20 minutes after venipuncture and again after five minutes of standing.

24-Hour Urine MHPG and VMA

All the children were on a low monoamine, low xanthine, normal salt diet. MHPG and vanillylmandelic acid (VMA) were assayed in urine by a gas chromatographic-mass spectrometric method previously described (Gordon et al., 1974; Karoum et al., 1975). In these assays, deuterated internal standards for MHPG and VMA are utilized.

RESULTS

Five children completed the mianserin trial. One subject dropped out of the study after the first day of drug treatment because of orthostatic hypotension and an epileptic seizure confirmed by EEG and is not included in this analysis. Because of excessive drowsiness and orthostatic hypotension, the dosage of medication was limited to a maximum of 40 mg/day in one of the boys who completed the trial.

Group *t*-tests between baseline and week 3 of the trial were performed on each of the dependent measures to compare the effects of placebo and mianserin. Results are shown in Table 1.

Teacher Rating (CTRS)

During mianserin treatment there was no change in Factor I (conduct) or Factor II (hyperactivity). This is in contrast to the significant decrease in Factor I and Factor II scores usually seen with amphetamine treatment (Arnold et al., 1972), and obtained on our inpatient unit with comparable small samples.

Motor Activity

Mianserin treatment was not associated with an effect on total motor activity. In contrast, there was a significant decrease in motor activity (about 40 percent) during dextroamphetamine treatment during a comparable time period (Rapoport et al., 1980).

Sustained Attention Measure (CPT)

There was no significant improvement on any of the vigilance measures (mean interstimulus interval, errors of commission, errors of omission) during mianserin treatment compared to placebo. These effects of mianserin on vigilance are in contrast to the improved performance of boys with ADDH treated with dextroamphetamine (Rapoport et al., 1980).

TABLE 1. Cognitive and Behavioral Effects of Mianserin or Placebo
in Hyperactive Boys

Measure	Baseline (Mean ± SD)	Week 3 (Mean ± SD)	Paired t	df	p
	Mianserin (n = 5)				
Conners Teacher Rating Scale (CTRS)					
Factor I (Conduct)	0.84 ± 1.24	0.31 ± 0.16	−0.85	3	NS
Factor II Hyperactivity	0.90 ± 0.76	0.61 ± 0.21	−0.95	3	NS
Vigilance CPT					
Commission errors	*25.20 ± 17.05	12.60 ± 8.50	−2.20	4	0.10
Omission errors	*10.00 ± 4.18	11.80 ± 8.23	0.58	4	NS
Interstimulus interval	*994.50 ± 439.73	719.50 ± 290.42	−2.12	4	NS
Motor Activity	239.10 ± 76.59	283.26 ± 193.77	0.61	4	NS
Memory-Learning					
Semantic Bushke	7.45 ± 2.15	8.23 ± 1.28	0.58	3	NS
Acoustic Bushke	8.25 ± 1.50	7.53 ± 2.03	−0.60	3	NS
Serial Learning (number correct/trial)	6.35 ± 3.14	6.85 ± 4.41	0.28	3	NS

Memory and Learning Task

Mianserin treatment was not associated with an effect on free or
cued-recall testing, in clear contrast to the improved performance on
these measures in ADDH boys treated with dextroamphetamine
(Rapoport et al., 1980). Subjects treated with placebo had improved
scores on one of the tasks, suggesting a learning effect not seen with
mianserin subjects.

Blood Pressure and Pulse

Chronic mianserin, like chronic (two weeks) dextroamphetamine
treatment (Langer et al., in press) did not cause any change from

TABLE 1. (Continued)

Measure	Baseline (Mean ± SD)	Week 3 (Mean ± SD)	Paired t	df	p
		Placebo (n = 5)			
Conners Teacher Rating Scale (CTRS)					
Factor I (Conduct)	1.03 ± 0.30	1.75 ± 0.67	2.22	4	NS
Factor II Hyperactivity	1.53 ± 0.70	2.12 ± 0.95	1.39	4	NS
Vigilance CPT					
Commission errors	47.00 ± 29.63	38.00 ± 31.68	−0.93	3	NS
Omission errors	13.25 ± 3.86	14.00 ± 7.12	0.34	3	NS
Interstimulus interval	815.75 ± 281.26	785.50 ± 313.47	−1.35	3	NS
Motor Activity	249.31 ± 94.94	279.30 ± 154.87	0.55	3	NS
Memory-Learning					
Semantic Bushke	6.23 ± 1.47	8.03 ± 0.83	5.06	3	<.02
Acoustic Bushke	6.70 ± 1.32	6.77 ± 2.30	0.08	2	NS
Serial Learning (number correct/trial)	4.71 ± 3.85	5.00 ± 4.29	0.31	2	NS

*Different versions of the CPT were used for different groups, therefore scores are not directly comparable across groups.

medication-free values in any of these measures. This did not reflect the periodic postural hypotension (systolic and diastolic) during mianserin treatment described below.

Plasma NE

Table 2 shows plasma NE levels (picograms per ml plasma) for mianserin and placebo groups. There was an increase ($p < 0.05$) in supine NE values between baseline and week 3 values during mianserin treatment. Because only two placebo subjects completed the NE measure during this study, no meaningful comparison is possible.

TABLE 2. Effects of Mianserin on Norepinephrine and Metabolites

Measure	Baseline (Mean ± SD)	Week 3 (Mean ± SD)	Paired t	df	p
	Mianserin (n = 5)				
Total MHPG (ng/24 h)	751.00 ± 481.08	1004.2 ± 682.97	2.24	4	NS
MHPG (µg/ng creatinine)	2.85 ± 1.68	3.95 ± 3.28	1.08	4	NS
VMA (ng/24 h)	4.35 ± 0.62	4.16 ± 1.90	−0.26	4	NS
VMA (µg/mg creatinine)	8.59 ± 3.62	9.83 ± 4.89	0.76	4	NS
Plasma norepinephrine					
Supine	328.60 ± 70.56	517.60 ± 135.62	3.21	4	<0.05
Standing	792.00 ± 232.07	1020.6 ± 372.07	1.52	4	NS
	Placebo (n = 5)				
Total MHPG (ng/24 h)	801.50 ± 293.14	720.50 ± 335.80	−0.68	3	NS
MHPG (µg/ng creatinine)	1.78 ± 0.74	2.13 ± 0.85	0.93	3	NS
VMA (ng/24 h)	5.40 ± 3.30	5.95 ± 3.13	0.94	3	NS
VMA (µg/mg creatinine)	7.47 ± 1.20	9.14 ± 4.59	0.97	3	NS
Plasma norepinephrine					
Supine	159.00 ± 66.47	212.50 ± 57.28	8.23	1	NS
Standing	325.00 ± 32.53	410.00 ± 132.94	1.20	1	NS

Urinary MHPG and VMA

Table 2 shows the urine values for 24-hour MHPG and VMA, as well as the urine values for micrograms MHPG per mg creatinine and micrograms VMA per mg creatinine. There was no difference between baseline and week 3 values in any group. This is in contrast to the significant decrease in 24-hour urinary MHPG values seen following treatment with dextroamphetamine (Shekim et al., 1977, 1979; Brown et al., 1979).

Side-Effects

Severe drowsiness in two subjects, postural hypotension in two subjects (one of whom dropped out of the study after the first day of treatment), and tachycardia in three subjects brought about discontinuation of the trial.

Side-effects were increased on the physician's weekly ratings (ESS) during mianserin compared to placebo (p < 0.01). Significant increases in drowsiness, orthostatic hypotension, and tachycardia were noted. Children, however, did not complain of side-effects on the self-rating scale (STESS) when taking mianserin. This is similar to the lack of self-reported side-effects we have observed in other clinical drug trials (Langer et al., in press) and supports the contention that ADDH children may be relatively poor raters of drug side-effects.

Global Impression

The clinical impression of all study investigators was that mianserin, at least at the doses used in this study, was not clinically beneficial. In contrast, dextroamphetamine produces such clear changes in ADDH children that staff participants in our inpatient dextroamphetamine studies are seldom truly "blind." Moreover, drowsiness, orthostatic hypotension, and tachycardia, even at doses as low as 10–20 mg/day, caused serious clinical concern in three of the children, and were the basis for discontinuing the trial.

DISCUSSION

Mianserin does not appear to be a useful therapeutic agent for the treatment of ADDH. It is difficult to evaluate the significance of the tendency for the placebo group to deteriorate on several measures (Table 1) as the placebo contrast group had been studied at an earlier time and in a double-blind study. However, the *lack* of significant effect on motor activity, most vigilance tasks, and the memory and learning tasks during mianserin treatment are in marked contrast to the clear improvement seen with equally small samples during dextroamphetamine treatment on our inpatient unit.

Studies in animals (Mason and Fibiger, 1978, 1979; Handley and Thomas, 1978a, 1978b; Pycock, 1977; Lorden et al., 1980; Kostowski et al., 1978) and in children (Shekim et al., 1977, 1979; Brown et al., 1979) suggest a link between alteration in NE metabolism and improvement in restless and/or inattentive behavior following dextroamphetamine treatment. A single dose of dextroamphetamine significantly elevates plasma NE in children during at least the first three hours after treatment (Mikkelsen et al., 1981). We know of no studies in children in which plasma NE changes were measured following chronic stimulant treatment.

One possible clue to the therapeutic action of stimulants, which have multiple effects upon catecholamine systems, is the well-documented *immediate* clinical efficacy of tricyclic antidepressants in treating childhood hyperactivity. Six separate studies have shown that imipramine or amitriptyline are effective short-term treatments for hyperactive, impulsive behavioral disturbance (Winsberg et al., 1972; Rapoport et al., 1974; Waizer et al., 1974; Greenberg et al., 1975; Yepes et al., 1977; Werry et al., 1979). Tolerance to this effect has recently been documented by Linnoila et al. (1979), who demonstrated wearing off of stimulant-like effect after about four weeks of treatment, in spite of sustained plasma concentration of tricyclics. Tricyclic antidepressants have both acute and chronic effects; the demonstration of tolerance suggests that an action of tricyclics which dissipates with time may be important in mediating the therapeutic effect of stimulants in the treatment of hyperactivity. Tricyclic antidepressants reduce NE turnover (Shubert et al., 1970; Leonard and Kafoe, 1976) and re-uptake by nerve terminals acutely and chronically; there is little or no diminution with time of this effect. On the other hand, other drug effects of NE metabolism do change with time. For example, following the initial slowing of the disappearance of ^{3}H-NE in rat brain is a return to baseline levels, perhaps showing rebound, with chronic treatment (Schildkraut, 1965). Decreased presynaptic noradrenergic receptor sensitivity has been demonstrated in rat heart after three weeks of treatment with desmethylimipramine (Crews and Smith, 1978).

It is puzzling that there was no alteration in urinary MHPG or VMA following chronic mianserin treatment in the present studies. Animal studies, however, have been inconsistent in the effects of chronic mianserin treatment on brain concentration of NE and metabolites (Fludder and Leonard, 1979; Kafoe et al., 1976) and there is no comparable human data regarding this measure.

The varying degrees of sedation and orthostatic hypotension in the present study were of serious concern. One of the five subjects could not tolerate more than 40 mg/day. Another boy had an orthostatic blood pressure difference (systolic and diastolic) of 30 mmHg, which persisted for over 24 hours, following treatment with only 10 mg of mianserin. During the initial 24 hours following medication, this subject had an epileptic seizure confirmed by EEG, but this patient also had two other seizures three days following and one week following the time that mianserin was stopped and blood pressure had returned to pretreatment levels. Studies of mianserin in adults (Brogden et al., 1978) have not reported effects on blood pressure and, indeed, we also could not demonstrate a statistical difference in blood pressure or pulse with mianserin compared to placebo by preplanned group measure.

In conclusion, mianserin does not seem to be a generally effective treatment for children with attention deficit disorder with hyperactivity. Additionally, some children treated with mianserin experienced orthostatic hypotension and oversedation. While it would have been of theoretical interest to increase the number of subjects, and possibly to identify a subgroup of responders, the lack of clinical effect and the presence of significant side-effects made us reluctant to do this.

Since mianserin increases NE at the nerve terminal by an indirect method probably leading to gradual release, the results of this study suggest that the role of acute NE release, rather than absolute brain NE concentration increase, should be pursued as a possible mechanism of action of drugs used for hyperactivity.

ACKNOWLEDGMENT

The authors would like to thank Ms. Janice Grice for excellent technical advice.

REFERENCES

Arnold LE, Wender, PH, McCloskey K, Synder SH: Levoamphetamine and dextroamphetamine: Comparative efficacy in the hyperkinetic syndrome, assessment by target symptoms. *Arch Gen Psychiatry* 27:816-822, 1972

Baumann SA, Maitre L: Blockade of presynaptic alpha-receptors and of amine intake in rat brain by mianserin. *Naunyn Schmiedebergs Arch Pharmacol* 300:31-37, 1977

Brogden R, Heel R, Speight T, Avery G: Mianserin: A review of its pharmacological properties and therapeutic efficacy in depressive illness. *Drugs* 16:273-301, 1978

Brown GL, Ebert MH, Hunt RD, Rapoport JL: Urinary 3-methoxy-4-hydroxyphenylglycol and homovanillic acid response to d-amphetamine in hyperactive children. Presented at the Annual Meeting of the Society of Biological Psychiatry, Chicago, Illinois, 1979

Colburn T, Smith BM, et al: An ambulatory monitor with solid state memory. *ISA Trans* 15:149-154, 1976

Connors CK: A teacher rating scale for use in drug studies with children. *Am J Psychiatry* 126:152-156, 1969

Coppen A, Kopera H: Workshop on the clinical pharmacology and efficacy of mianserin. *Br J Clin Pharmacol* 5:91-99, 1978

Crews F, Smith C: Presynaptic alpha-receptor subsensitivity after long-term antidepressant treatment. *Science* 202:322-324, 1978

Fludder JM, Leonard BE: The action of the antidepressant drug mianserin on presynaptic alpha-andrenergic receptors in the rat brain in vivo. *Neuropharmacology* 17:1058-1060, 1978

Fludder JM, Leonard BE: Chronic effects of mianserin on noradrenaline metabolism in the rat brain: Evidence for a presynaptic alpha-adrenolytic action in vivo. *Psychopharmacology* 64:329-332, 1979

Gordon EK, Oliver J, Black K, Kopin IJ: Simultaneous assay by mass fragmentography of vanillyl mandelic acid, homovanillic acid, and 3-methoxy-4-hydroxy-phenethylene glycol in cerebrospinal fluid and urine. *Biochem Med* 11:32-40, 1974

Goyette CH, Conners CK, Ulrick RF: Normative data on revised Conners Parent and Teacher Rating Scales. *J Abnorm Child Psychol* 6:221-236, 1978

Greenberg L, Yellin A, Spring C, Metcalf M: Clinical effects of imipramine and methylphenidate in hyperactive children. *Int J Ment Health* 4:114-156, 1975

Guy W (ed): Dosage record and treatment emergent symptom scale, ECDEU, Assessment Manual for Psychopharmacology, revised. Rockville, Maryland, DHEW, ADAMHA/NIMH Psychopharmacology Research Branch, 1976 pp 223-225

Handley SL, Thomas KV: Influence of catecholamines on dextroamphetamine-induced changes in locomotor activity. *Psychopharmacology* 58:283-288, 1978a

Handley SL, Thomas KV: On the mechanism of amphetamine-induced behavioral changes in the mouse II: Effects of agents stimulating noradrenergic receptors. *Arzneimittelforsch* 28(1):834-837, 1978b

Kafoe WF, DeRidder JJ, Leonard BE: The effect of a tetracyclic antidepressant compound, Org. BG94, on the turnover of biogenic amines in rat brain. *Biochem Pharmacol* 25:2455-2460, 1976

Karoum F, Gillin JC, McCullough D, Wyatt R: Vanillyl-mandelic acid (VMA), free and conjugated 3-methoxy-4-hydroxyphenylglycol (MHPG) in human ventricular fluid. *Clin Chim Acta* 62:451-455, 1975

Kostowski W, Jerlicz, M, Bidzinski A, Hauptmann M: Evidence for existence of two opposite noradrenergic brain systems controlling behavior. *Psychopharmacology* 59:311-312, 1978

Lake CR, Ziegler MG, Kopin IJ: Use of plasma norepinephrine for evaluation of sympathetic neuronal function in man. *Life Sci* 18:1315-1326, 1976

Langer DH, Rapoport JL, Brown GL, et al.: Behavioral effects of carbidopa/ levodopa in hyperactive boys. *J Am Acad Child Psychiatry* 21(1): 10-18, 1982

Langer D, Brown GL, Lake CR, Ebert MH: Chronic d-amphetamine and norepinephrine levels in hyperactive boys, personal communication

Leonard BE: Some effects of a new tetracyclic antidepressant compound, Org. GB94, on the turnover of biogenic amines in the rat brain. *Psychopharmacologia (Berl)* 36:221-236, 1974

Leonard BE, Kafoe WF: A comparison of the acute and chronic effects of four antidepressant drugs on the turnover of serotonin, dopamine and noradrenaline in the rat brain. *Biochem Pharmacol* 25:1939-1942, 1976

Linnoila M, Gualtieri CT, Jobson K, Staye J: Characteristics of the therapeutic response to imipramine in hyperactive children. *Am J Psychiatry* 136:1201-1203, 1979

Lordern JF, Rickert EJ, Dawson R Jr, Pellymounter MA: Forebrain norepinephrine and the selective processing of information. *Brain Res,* in press

Mason ST, Fibiger HC: Noradrenaline and spatial memory. *Brain Res* 156:382-386, 1978

Mason ST, Fibiger HC: Noradrenaline and selective attention. *Life Sci* 25:1949-1956, 1979

Mikkelsen E, Lake CR, Brown GL, et al.: The hyperactive child syndrome: Peripheral sympathetic nervous system function and the effect of d-amphetamine. *Psychiatry Res* 4:157-169, 1981

Perry G, Fitzsimmons B, Shapiro L, Irwin P: Clinical study of mianserin, imipramine and placebo in depression: Blood level and MHPG correlations. *Br J Clin Pharmacol* 5:355-415, 1978

Pycock C: Noradrenergic involvement in dopamine-dependent sterotyped and cataleptic responses in the rat. *Naunyn Schmiedebergs Arch Pharmacol* 298:15-22, 1977

Rapoport JL, Buchsbaum MS, Weingartner H, et al.: Dextroamphetamine: Cognitive and behavioral effects in normal and hyperactive boys and normal adult males. *Arch Gen Psychiatry* 37:933-943, 1980

Rapoport J, Buchsbaum M, Zahn T, et al.: Dextroamphetamine: Cognitive and behavioral effects in normal prepubertal boys. *Science* 199:560-563, 1978

Rapoport J, Quinn P, Bradford G, et al.: Imipramine and methylphenidate treatment of hyperactive boys. *Arch Gen Psychiatry* 30:789-794, 1974

Rosvold H, Mirsky A, Sarason I, et al.: A continuous performance test of brain damage. *J Consult Psychology* 20:343-350, 1956

Schildkraut J: The catecholamine hypothesis of affective disorders: A review of supporting evidence. *Am J Psychiatry* 122:509-522, 1965

Schubert J, Nyback H, Sedvall G: Effect of antidepressant drugs on accumulation and disappearance of monoamine formed in vivo from labelled precursors in mouse brain. *J Pharm Pharmacol* 22:136-139, 1970

Shekim W, Dekirmenjian H, and Chapel J: Urinary catecholamine metabolites in hyperactive boys before and during treatment with dextroamphetamine. *Am J Psychiatry* 134:1276-1279, 1977

Shekim W, Dekirmenjian H, Chapel J: Urinary MHPG excretion in minimal brain dysfunction and its modification by d-amphetamine. *Am J Psychiatry* 135:667-671, 1979

Starke K: Regulation of noradrenaline release by presynaptic receptor systems. *Rev Physiol Biochem Pharmacol* 77:1-24, 1977

Svensson T, Usdin E: Feedback inhibition of brain noradrenaline neurons by tricyclic antidepressants: Alpha-receptor mediation. *Science* 202:1089-1091, 1978

Waizer J, Hoffman S, Polizos P, Engelhardt D: Outpatient treatment of hyperactive school children with imipramine. *Am J Psychiatry* 131:587-591, 1974

Werry JS, Aman M, Diamond E: Imipramine and methylphenidate in hyperactive children. *J Child Psychol Psychiatry* 20:1-21, 1979

Winsberg B, Bialer I, Kupietz S, Tobias J: Effects of imipramine and dextroamphetamine on behavior of neuropsychiatrically impaired children. *Am J Psychiatry* 128:1425-1432, 1972

Yepes L, Balka E, Winsberg B, Bialer J: Amitriptyline and methylphenidate treatment of hyperactive children. *J Child Psychol Psychiatry* 18:39-52, 1977

Zis AP, Goodwin FK: Novel antidepressants and the biogenic amine hypothesis of depression: The case for iprindole and mianserin. *Arch Gen Psychiatry* 36(10):1097-1107, 1979

Index

Acetycholine (ACh), 57
Activity Monitor, NIMH Model, 200, 203
Alpha-adrenergic receptors, presynaptic, 204
American Academy of Pediatrics Committee on Drugs, 22
Amnesic effects of postlearning electroconvulsive therapy, 130
Aromatic amino acid decarboxylase, 52, 53, 60, 65
Assent by children to research procedures, 25, 27
Attention Deficit Disorder of childhood with Hyperactivity (ADDH)
see Hyperactive Child Syndrome
conceptualization, 1-15
chronicity of ADDH: relation to clinical features, 175
CSF 5-HIAA levels, 74
dopamine deficiency as an etiology of ADDH, 179
electroencephalographic studies, 38-40
girls with ADDH, 162, 176
immediate response and later tolerance with imipramine, 206
neurophysiological studies, 39-41
stimulant related growth inhibition in ADDH children, 135-158
subclassification on basis of minor physical anomalies and plasma DBH, 159-182

[Attention Deficit Disorder of childhood with Hyperactivity (ADDH)]
methylphenidate response in ADDH compared to eneuretics, 183-195
response to Mianserin hydrochloride, 197-210
Auditory-evoked responses, 98
Autism, 98
Autoreceptors, presynaptic catecholaminergic, 75

Ballistographic chair, 187
Benefit-risk ratio of child research programs, 23-24
Benzedrine, 183
Bin theories for cortical information theories, 122-124
Biochemical studies, hyperactive children, 41-42
Biomedical model of ADDH, 14-15
Bruxism, 92

Catch-up growth, 154
Catechol-o-methyltransferase (COMT), 61
Catecholamine-sensitive adenylcyclase, 68
Cataplexy, 90
Chlorpromazine, 151
Choline acetyltransferase, 69
Chronicity of ADDH, 175
Circadian rhythms, 86

211